75 Years of
Central Government Budgets (1947-48 to 2021-22) and
Finance Commissions of India (I to XV)

Published on the Occasion of 75th Anniversary of India's Independence....

Other 75th Anniversary Special Series Titles....

75 Years of Agricultural and Rural Development in India: 1947-48 to 2021-22
by Dr. Yashvir Singh

75 Years of Industrial, Infrastructural and Logistics Development in India: 1947-48 to 2021-22
by Dr. Makarand Upadhyaya

75 Years of Central Government Budgets (1947-48 to 2021-22) and Finance Commissions of India (I to XV)

Incorporating

- A Comprehensive Description and Analysis of Budgetary Practices and Reforms in India
- Highlights of Each Central Government Budget from 1947-48 to 2021-22
- Evolution of Centre-State Financial Relations (Fiscal Federalism) in India
- Highlights and Summary of the Report of Each Finance Commission from I to XV

By

M.M. Sury

New Century Publications
New Delhi, India

New Century Publications
74, Ansari Road, Ground Floor,
Daryaganj,
New Delhi – 110 002 (India)

Tel.: 011-4101 7798; 4358 7398; 98117 88655
E-mail: info@newcenturypublications.com
www.newcenturypublications.com

Editorial office:
4800 / 24, Bharat Ram Road,
Ansari Road, Daryaganj,
New Delhi – 110 002

First Published: **2021**

ISBN: **978-81-7708-530-3**

Published by New Century Publications and printed at Milan Enterprises, New Delhi

Designs: Patch Creative Unit, New Delhi

PRINTED IN INDIA

About the Book

Finance is the life blood of a government. Arrangements for finance are more complicated in a federal set up than in a unitary form of government. A federal system creates a multiple polity based on divided functions and powers among central and state governments. Fiscal federalism, as a branch of public finance, deals with financial arrangements and their working in a federal polity.

As a financial blueprint of a government, budget is an important instrument to carry out its policies and programmes. It is through the budget that a government arranges financial resources and allocates them among competing uses. The high level of administrative, welfare and developmental activities of the Central Government make for colossal amounts of both receipts and disbursements. Such large-scale public transactions through the budget affect the economy in various ways. The level and composition of taxes influence the allocation of resources among various sectors of the economy, distribution of income among different economic classes, and macro management of the economy. Similarly, the borrowing policy of the Central Government affects the amount of national savings available to the private sector for consumption and investment. No less important are the effects of massive public expenditure on production, distribution and economic stabilization.

Budget is not merely a statement of government accounts. It reflects the government's vision and signals the policies to come in future. Budget is also the chief source of government finance statistics to facilitate research and decisions on fiscal and economic matters.

In India, the Central Government budget is designed mainly to ensure Parliamentary control and accounting scrutiny. Each year the Government has to obtain the authority of the Parliament to raise revenues to meet its expenditure. Budget of the government is perhaps the most important annual item on the agenda of the Parliament. Budget papers of the Government of India provide glimpses of the events, challenges and perceptions of the leaders. They highlight contemporary problems of the Indian economy and policy measures taken by the government to solve them, making for a fascinating study of India's march towards development.

Fiscal federalism is a subject of topical interest in India in view of some recent developments of historical importance. The Constitution (Eightieth Amendment) Act, 2000, significantly changed the manner of distribution of Central tax collections between the Central and State Governments. Prior to this Amendment, income tax and Union excise duties were the only taxes shared with the States. This Amendment altered the pattern of sharing of Central taxes between the Centre and the States by providing for the sharing of the net proceeds of all Union taxes and duties with the States.

Enactment of the Constitution (One Hundred and First Amendment) Act, 2016 and the subsequent introduction of Goods and Services Tax (GST) from July 1, 2017, marked a clear departure from the initial scheme of distribution of taxation powers between the Centre and the States envisaged in the Constitution. Prior to enactment of the said Act, taxation powers between the Centre and the States were clearly demarcated in the Constitution of India with no overlaps between their respective domains. With the introduction of GST, fiscal federalism in India has moved from mutually exclusive to concurrent powers of taxation for the Centre and the States.

Recommendations of the Finance Commission constitute the core of fiscal federalism in India. Finance Commission is a unique feature of the Indian Constitution without parallel in the existing federal constitutions of the world. Reports of the Finance Commissions provide in-depth insights into problems and their solutions in the highly complex area of federal finance. These Reports examine in detail, contemporary issues in Centre-State financial relations and recommend measures to solve them.

Spread over 29 chapters, the book is organized into 2 parts.

Part I (chapters 1 to 7) is titled Government Budgeting Procedures in India. This part provides conceptual framework for budgetary techniques, phases of budgetary cycle of the Government of India, parliamentary controls over the budget, components and structure of the budget, budgetary reforms and other topics related to the subject. It also includes highlights of each Central Budget from 1947-48 to 2021-22.

Part II (chapters 8 to 29) is titled Centre-State Financial Relations (Fiscal Federalism) in India. This part covers conceptual settings for fiscal federalism, nature and features of Indian federation, centralization of revenues and channels of transfers to states, role of the Finance Commission, vertical distribution of resources, horizontal distribution of resources, and Constitution (One Hundred and First Amendment) Act, 2016, and the changed landscape of fiscal federalism in India. It also includes highlights and summary of each Finance Commission Report from First Finance Commission to Fifteenth Finance Commission.

This work would prove useful for the students of economics, commerce, public administration and business management. An understanding of the mechanics of governmental financial transactions will also serve the needs of legislators, administrators and those in industry and trade.

About the Author

M.M. Sury received his B.A. (Hons.), M.A., and Ph.D. degrees in economics from the University of Delhi. He taught economics in the same University for 42 years. Specialising in fiscal economics, he has published extensively on the Indian fiscal system in recognised national and international journals, including *Small Industry Bulletin for Asia and the Pacific* (United Nations, Bangkok), *Bulletin for International Fiscal Documentation* (International Fiscal Association, Amsterdam), *Asian-Pacific Tax and Investment Bulletin* (Singapore), *Journal of the Indian School of Political Economy* (Pune), *Indian Economic Journal* (Bombay), and *Margin* (New Delhi). He was a Visiting Fellow at the International Bureau of Fiscal Documentation, Amsterdam (May 1989), a Fellow at the Indian Institute of Advanced Study, Shimla (1991-92) and a Visiting Fellow in the Department of Law and Management, University of Mauritius, Mauritius (September-October, 2000). He was Economic Adviser of First Delhi State Finance Commission (1996-97).

Contents

Part II: Centre-State Financial Relations (Fiscal Federalism) in India

Preface

Finance is the life blood of a government. Arrangements for finance are more complicated in a federal set up than in a unitary form of government. A federal set up creates a multiple polity based on divided functions and powers among central, state and local governments. Fiscal federalism, as a branch of public finance, deals with financial arrangements and their working in a federal polity.

Government Budgeting

Government budgets are universally accepted as a powerful tool in achieving development objectives and as an indicator of commitment to the stated policy of the government. National budgets reflect how governments mobilize and allocate public resources, and how they aim to meet the social and economic needs of their people. While presenting the budget for the year 1950-51 to the Parliament, Shri John Mathai, the then Finance Minister of India observed, "I have always held that a Government Budget in the last analysis is a human document in the sense that it involves and has reactions upon the experiences and the emotions of multitudes of men and women all over the country."

As a financial blueprint of a government, budget is an important instrument to carry out its policies and programmes. It is through the budget that a government arranges financial resources and allocates them among competing uses. Budget is also the chief source of government finance statistics to facilitate research and decisions on fiscal and economic matters. Budget is not merely a statement of government accounts. It reflects the government's vision and signals the policies to come in future.

Government budgeting is a subject of increasing importance and interest in India. The high level of administrative, welfare and developmental activities of the Central Government make for colossal amounts of both receipts and disbursements. Such large-scale public transactions through the budget affect the economy in various ways. For example, the level and composition of taxes influence the allocation of resources among various sectors of the economy, distribution of income among different economic classes, and macro management of the economy. Similarly, the borrowing policy of the Central Government affects the amount of national savings available to the private sector for consumption and investment. No less important are the effects of massive public expenditure on production, distribution and economic stabilization.

In India, the Central Government budget is designed mainly to ensure Parliamentary control and accounting scrutiny. Each year the Government has to obtain the authority of Parliament to raise revenues to meet its expenditure. Budget of the government is perhaps the most important annual item on the agenda of the Parliament. It is an instrument of financial control, economic and social development and administrative delegation. It is prepared in financial terms and the intention is to facilitate itemised financial control. Thus, budget is accountability-oriented without much emphasis on the results of proposed outlays. Recent budgetary reforms, however, have underlined the need for outcome assessment and gender mainstreaming as parts of budgetary exercise.

The budget for the year 1947-48 for undivided India, passed by the Legislature in March 1947, ceased to be operative with the partition of the country and the emergence of two independent Governments. The first budget of a free and independent India was presented to the Legislative Assembly by the then Finance Minister Shri R.K. Shanmukham on November 26, 1947. It covered a period of 7½ months from August 15, 1947 to March 31, 1948. The first full-year budget for 1948-49 was presented by the same Finance Minister on February 28, 1948.

Budget papers of the Government of India provide glimpses of the events, challenges and perceptions of the leaders. They highlight contemporary problems of the Indian economy and policy measures taken by the government to solve them, making for a fascinating study of India's march towards development. They provide an authentic and reliable source for the study of post-Independence economic history of India. The first few budgets after Independence show deep concern for the gigantic task of restoration of stability in the aftermath of Partition, rehabilitation of refugees and the country's dependence on imports of foodgrains. In his 1950-51 budget speech, the Finance Minister announced the constitution of Planning Commission under the chairmanship of Pandit Jawaharlal Nehru, ushering in the era of Five Year Plans. It was again in the 1950-51 speech that the Finance Minister announced the constitution of the First Finance Commission, an epoch-making arrangement for the evolution of sound fiscal federalism in India.

Indian economy has witnessed structural changes since Independence in 1947. From a traditional agricultural economy, India has emerged as a technologically strong, industrially diversified and militarily powerful country. This journey of the last 75 years is exemplary for other developing countries striving to achieve self-reliance and a respectable place in the world community.

Although in the context of India's federal structure, the budgetary trends and procedures should be examined at both the Central and State levels, the present exercise is confined to Central Government budgets only which form the nerve centre of financial activities of the Indian economy.

Fiscal Federalism

According to the traditional classification followed by political scientists, constitutions are either unitary or federal in nature. A federation means a union of several states brought about by the instrument of a treaty or agreement. The modern concept of federalism is associated with the establishment of American federation in 1787. Since there is no agreed definition of a federal state, the model of the US is often taken as the reference point.

India's present fiscal structure is the result of a gradual evolution, along decentralised lines, dating back to December 14, 1870 when the resolution of Lord Mayo, Viceroy of India, was issued. The Mayo resolution explained the scheme by which the Government of India envisaged enlargement of the powers and responsibilities of the Provinces.

The next landmark in the history of Centre-State financial relations was the Montague-Chelmsford Report on Constitutional Reforms which led to the passing of the Government of India Act, 1919. This Act sought to secure for the Provinces a greater degree of financial independence by abolishing the *divided heads* and effecting a complete separation between the Central and Provincial heads of revenue.

The Government of India Act, 1935 was a watershed in the evolution of Centre-State financial relations. The Act was a step towards consolidation and enhancement of Provincial autonomy in matters of resources and functions. It laid the foundations for the structure of Centre-State relations as incorporated in the present Constitution of India.

Prior to Independence in 1947, Princely States had remained outside the fiscal and financial system of the rest of the country except for certain arrangements entered into with them by the Government of India regarding such matters as maritime customs, central excises, posts and telegraph and railways. The scheme of the Government of India Act, 1935, contemplated the accession of these States to the Indian federation. Under it, the Princely States were to accede in regard to foreign relations, defence and communications, with an option to accede in regard to other Central subjects also. This followed an extensive examination of the problems connected with the assimilation of States of varying sizes and having different kinds of relationship with the Centre into a workable system of financial relations with the proposed federation. As it happened, the provisions of the Government of India Act, 1935, relating to federation never came into operation.

The partition of the country gave rise to new problems of financial adjustments, particularly in relation to the divided Provinces of Bengal and Punjab.

During the period between the achievement of Independence and the framing of the Constitution, a great step forward was taken in the unification of the country by the integration of Princely States. Within less than two years from the date of Independence (August 15, 1947), all the Princely States had been either formed into sizeable units, or merged in the neighbouring provinces or constituted into separate Centrally-administered Chief Commissioners' Provinces.

Drafting of the Constitution of independent India provided another opportunity to review the financial relations between the Centre and the States. For the purpose of incorporating financial provisions in the Draft Constitution, the President of the Constituent Assembly constituted an Expert Committee of three members under the chairmanship of Shri N.R. Sarker.

Recognizing the fact that the financial resources of the States may prove inadequate for undertaking welfare, maintenance, and development activities, the framers of India's Constitution did make elaborate, *albeit* complex, arrangements relating to flow of funds from the Centre to the States. The disequilibrium between proliferating functional responsibilities of the States and their own resources is corrected by Central transfers effected through various channels, mainly Finance Commission.

It was in the 1950-51 budget speech that the Finance Minister announced the constitution of the First Finance Commission, an epoch-making arrangement for the evolution of sound fiscal federalism in India. The First Finance Commission was set up in November 1951 and it submitted its report in December 1952 for the period 1952-57. Since then fourteen more Finance Commissions have submitted their reports, the last being the Fifteenth Commission.

Recommendations of the Finance Commission constitute the core of fiscal federalism in

India. Finance Commission is a unique feature of the Indian Constitution without parallel in the existing federal constitutions of the world. Reports of the Finance Commissions provide in-depth insights into problems and their solutions in the highly complex area of federal finance. These Reports examine in detail contemporary issues in Centre-State financial relations and recommend measures to solve them.

The Constitution of India, operative since January 26, 1950, has shown flexibility towards changing needs and aspirations of the people. The passage of the Constitution (Seventy-third Amendment) Act, 1992 marked a milestone in the history of modern India. With this amendment, a uniform structure of *panchayats* emerged throughout the country. Similarly, the passage of the Constitution (Seventy-fourth Amendment) Act, 1992 was a landmark in the history of municipal administration in India. As a result of these amendments, *panchayats* and municipalities are now constitutional bodies forming the third tier of the federal polity of India.

Furthermore, the Constitution (Eightieth Amendment) Act, 2000, significantly changed the manner of distribution of Central tax collections between the Central and State Governments. Prior to this amendment, income tax and Union excise duties were the only taxes shared with the States. This amendment altered the pattern of sharing of Central taxes between the Centre and the States significantly by providing for the sharing of the net proceeds of all Union taxes and duties with the States.

Enactment of the Constitution (One Hundred and First Amendment) Act, 2016 and the subsequent introduction of Goods and Services Tax (GST) from July 1, 2017 marked a clear departure from the initial scheme of distribution of taxation powers between the Centre and the States envisaged in the Constitution. With the introduction of GST, fiscal federalism in India has moved from mutually exclusive to concurrent powers of taxation for the Centre and the States.

Delhi **M.M. Sury**
June 17, 2021

Abbreviations/Acronyms

ADR	Alternate Dispute Resolution
AHIDF	Animal Husbandry Infrastructure Development Fund
CAG	Comptroller and Auditor General
CAS	Central Assistance to States
CBDT	Central Board of Direct Taxes
CBIC	Central Board of Indirect Taxes and Customs
CENVAT	Central Value Added Tax
CGST	Central Goods and Services Tax
CIPS	Centre for Innovation in Public Systems
CRF	Calamity Relief Fund
CSSs	Centrally-sponsored Schemes
CST	Central Sales Tax
DBT	Direct Benefit Transfers
DDG	Detailed Demand for Grants
DDMAs	District Disaster Management Authorities
DDMF	District Disaster Mitigation Funds
DIF	District Innovation Fund
DIPAM	Department of Investment and Public Asset Management
EC	Empowered Committee
FAIDF	Aquaculture Infrastructure Development Fund
FC	Finance Commission
FDI	Foreign Direct Investment
FRBM Act	Fiscal Responsibility and Budget Management Act
GCS	General Category States
GDP	Gross Domestic Product
GFR	General Finance Rules
GST	Goods and Services Tax
GST Council	Goods and Services Tax Council
HWCs	Health and Wellness Centres
IATP	Income Adjusted Total Population
IGST	Integrated Goods and Services Tax
IMR	Infant Mortality Rates
LTC	Leave Travel Concession
MAT	Minimum Alternate Tax
MFDIS	Modernisation Fund for Defence and Internal Security
MODVAT	Modified Value Added Tax
MWCD	Ministry of Women and Child Development
NCCD	National Calamity Contingent Duty
NCCF	National Calamity Contingency Fund
NDC	National Development Council

NDMF	National Disaster Mitigation Fund
NDRF	National Disaster Relief Fund
NGOs	Non-governmental Organizations
NIPFP	National Institute of Public Finance and Policy
NPDM	National Policy on Disaster Management
NPRD	Non-plan Revenue Deficit
NSDP	Net State Domestic Product
NSSF	National Small Savings Fund
OECD	Organization for Economic Co-operation and Development
OOMF	Output-Outcome Monitoring Framework
PAN	Permanent Account Number
PHCs	Primary Healthcare Centres
RBI	Reserve Bank of India
SCS	Special Category States
SDMA	State Disaster Management Authorities
SDMF	State Disaster Mitigation Funds
SDP	State Domestic Product
SDRF	State Disaster Response Fund
SFCs	State Finance Commissions
SLR	Statutory Liquidity Ratio
SOEs	Statements of Expenditure
T-bills	Treasury Bills
TCS	Tax Collection at Source
TDS	Tax Deduction at Source
TOR	Terms of Reference
UCs	Utilisation Certificates
UID	Unique Identification
UNDP	United Nations Development Programme
URN	Unique Registration Number
UTs	Union Territories
VAT	Value Added Tax
VAW	Violence against Women
WCP	Women's Component Plan
WMA	Ways and Means Advances
ZBB	Zero-base Budgeting

Unit and Currency Conversion Table

Unit Conversion

1 lakh = 0.1 million
10 lakh = 1.0 million
1 crore = 10.0 million
100 crore = 1.0 billion

Exchange Rate

The unit of currency in India is Indian Rupee, symbolized as ₹. As per reference rate of Reserve Bank of India (RBI) for June 15, 2021

US$ 1 = ₹ 73.27
UK£ 1 = ₹ 103.42
Euro (€) 1 = ₹ 88.92

Fiscal Year

Fiscal year in India runs from April 1 to March 31 of the following year.

Pre- and Post-metric Systems of Currency in India

Metric system of currency in India was introduced from April l, 1957
In the pre-metric system, one Rupee was = 16 *annas* and one *anna* was = 4 paise
In the post-metric system, one Rupee = 100 paise

Part I

Government Budgeting Procedures in India

1

Government Budgeting: Conceptual Framework

Government budgets are universally accepted as a powerful tool in achieving development objectives and as an indicator of commitment to the stated policy of the government. National budgets reflect how governments mobilize and allocate public resources, and how they aim to meet the social and economic needs of their people.

As a financial blueprint of a government, budget is an important instrument to carry out its policies and programmes. It is through the budget that a government arranges financial resources and allocates them among competing uses. Budget is also the chief source of government finance statistics to facilitate research and decisions on fiscal and economic matters.

1.1 Significance of Government Budgeting

Budgeting is the act of balancing income and expenditure. Budgeting involves the creation of a spending plan. Budgeting is important because it helps to keep spending under control. It also minimizes discretionary spending. It also ensures that money is available when needed.

Budgetary operations of the government have an important bearing on the functioning of an economy. The ideals of welfare state and economic planning have tremendously increased the magnitude of public spending, resulting in the emergence of the government as an important sector of the economy. This sector has its own money inflows and outflows. Government collects huge sums of money through taxation, borrowings, and printing of additional currency. The manner of collection of these monetary funds and the pattern of their spending influences saving and investment levels, distribution of income and wealth, allocation of resources, and the consumption behaviour of the people.

Modern economies are frequently beset with problems like inflation, excessive fluctuations in economic activities, and deficit in the balance of payments. Budget is an important instrument to carry out corrective operations. Budget is not merely an exercise in matching expenditure to income but a powerful medium to realise objectives of public policy. Budget is a description of both the fiscal policies of the government and the financial plans corresponding to them.

It is necessary for governments to have a planned appraisal of their earnings and proper means of controlling the channels of spending them. Absence of such exercises may lead to corruption, inefficiency, and even bankruptcy of the government. Hence, planned earnings and wise spending are prerequisites for the stability of a government. The medium for fulfilling these requirements is the budget. Public budgeting is desirable from government's point of view because it can answer its critics squarely and prove its honesty in financial matters. It is also important for the legislators because they can ensure that all is well with public money.

1.2 Government Budgeting versus Private Budgeting

Neither a government nor an individual can function without finance. Individuals and governments both have sources of receipts and heads of expenditure and face the problem of adjustment between the two. Both entities try to maximise welfare with limited means. In spite of these few points of similarities, public budgeting is an altogether different exercise in nature and scope as compared to private budgeting.

Individuals, unlike governments, may, at their own risk, earn and spend without planning, foresight, and proper recording of their transactions. Governments in democracies are answerable for their actions to the legislators who, in turn, enjoy the mandate of the electorate. A private individual may prefer to keep his financial transactions a secret whereas financial activities of the government get wide publicity and are subject to audit and inspection.

Financial resources at the disposal of individuals are far less than those available to a government. Like a government, a private organisation cannot impose taxes nor can it print currency. It has to cut its coat according to cloth. However, this is not a limitation with the government. Public authorities first determine the volume of expenditure and then arrange resources to meet it. In most cases, public expenditure is inelastic and has to be incurred, e.g. on defence, law and order, and general administration.

An individual regards surplus budget as a virtue and a means to accumulate capital and become rich. Contrarily, deficit budgeting is more a rule than an exception for the government.

Private budget-making is guided exclusively by profit motive while public budgeting has social welfare as the objective function. While performance of all private activities is capable of measurement with the standard of money, most public activities defy such measurement. In the absence of market mechanism, government services are determined not by profit expectations but by decisions arrived at through political and administrative procedures and based on common social objectives.

1.3 Canons of Government Budgeting

It is difficult to formulate a universally acceptable set of public budgeting principles because of the differing nature of world economies, their socio-economic objectives and political set-ups. Nevertheless, some general guidelines can be provided to government authorities in-charge of spending public funds. The list of these guidelines is as follows:

1.3.1 Annual Basis: Although a budget can be prepared for any length of time, it is a common convention to frame it on an annual basis. It is believed that one year is an optimum period for which a legislature should give financial sanction to a government and it is also a reasonable duration for the government to execute budgetary provisions.

1.3.2 Accuracy of Estimates: Budget-making involves extensive estimates of revenue and expenditure for the *ensuing* financial year. The actuals or accounts represent the figures available after the *expiry* of the financial year. Obviously, there is bound to be some divergence between the estimates and the actuals. However, the nature and the degree of this divergence are of considerable importance because it has far-reaching implications in terms of resource mobilisation, economic planning, financial stability and tax burden.

The degree of deviation between the estimates and the actuals reflects upon the skill and competence of budget makers. Excessive divergence reveals poor financial predictability of the experts. Divergence has two aspects: (a) over-estimation and (b) under-estimation. Over-estimation of revenue ends up with shortages of funds, leading to curtailment or even exclusion of certain development projects. Under inflationary conditions, it may further worsen the situation. In case public expenditure is inelastic, over-estimation of revenue will necessitate deficit financing. Also, over-estimation may slacken government efforts at additional resource mobilisation.

Conversely, under-estimation of revenues leads to unwarranted tax doses. Apart from antagonising the public, it complicates the tax structure and increases administrative costs. Unexpected resources available to public authorities generally go into unproductive projects formulated at short notice. Under-estimation also induces a government to resort to public borrowing thereby unnecessarily increasing liabilities of the public exchequer.

In countries where the process of economic planning is linked with annual budgets, the need for close relation between the budget agency and the planners is all the more important. Surplus in the revenue account of the budget is the first major source of funds available for capital expenditure. Budget-plan integration will become difficult in the face of inaccurate revenue estimates. When the emphasis is on self-reliance, i.e. dependence on internal resources, the importance of accurate revenue estimation assumes unique relevance.

1.3.3 Gross Basis: Government transactions, both on receipt and expenditure sides, should be shown on gross basis rather than net basis. It will be an unsound budgetary practice if receipts are deducted from charges and expenditure is shown on a net basis in the budget estimates. Under this faulty practice, government will approach legislature for authorisation of only that part of expenditure which cannot be met from receipts. This would render legislature's control over government expenditure meaningless. Therefore, budget estimates ought to be presented on gross basis.

1.3.4 Single Budget: It is always desirable to have one budget for a government. If different ministries/departments have their separate budgets, it would become difficult to evaluate the true financial position of a government. Furthermore, the government should try, as far as possible, to prepare a balanced budget. Surplus budgets raise doubts among people regarding the desirability of levying additional taxes. Contrarily, a deficit budget erodes government's confidence and the will to execute budgetary plans. It will be under strain all the time to look for additional funds.

1.3.5 Expiry of Appropriations: A good budgetary practice is one which makes provision for the expiry of all appropriations at the close of the financial year. This is necessary to prepare and balance the accounts and also to ascertain surpluses or deficits for each year.

1.3.6 Cash Basis: The estimates and accounts of budgetary transactions should be prepared on a cash basis. This system facilitates transactions of a year to be closed soon after their termination so that the actual trends in government finances are available to legislature and government departments for scrutiny and forecasting. The form in which budget estimates are presented should conform to that of accounts. If the scheme of classification of estimates is different from that of accounts, confusion will arise, making the task of government officials and legislators difficult.

1.4 Incremental Budgeting

Under incremental budgeting, budget for the current fiscal year becomes the base for budgetary allocations for the forthcoming year. Increase or decrease is done to expenditure incurred in the current year according to inflation. Government assumes that all ministries and departments will continue to operate at their current level of expenditure. Additional amount, where required, will be added to arrive at budget estimates for the next year. Contrarily, budgetary allocation may be reduced for departments where lesser expenditure is anticipated. Incremental budgeting method assumes that the expenditures incurred in the current year will be the starting point for estimates for the ensuing year.

Incremental budgeting ensures continuity of funding for government ministries and departments without much detailed analysis of funding requirements. With this type of budgeting, a government is likely to have stable budgets year-on-year. Thus, incremental budgeting is suitable for governments where funding requirements are usually fixed or vary little. However, incremental budgeting is not suitable for countries where major structural changes take place, warranting much more significant budget changes. Moreover, this approach may tend to make government departments spend more and unnecessarily as funds are easily available. Incremental budgeting subconsciously encourages higher spending so that the budget is maintained/enhanced next year. Incremental budgeting can cause perpetual resource allocation to certain departments even if they may not require them in subsequent years.

Thus, incremental budgeting, though very easy to compute and implement, is often associated with conservative mindset. Alternatively, zero-based budgeting (discussed below) is considered more advanced budgeting technique in the context of a dynamic economy.

1.5 Zero-base Budgeting (ZBB)

Credit for this fiscal innovation goes to Peter Pyhrr who propounded it in the early 1970s in the context of corporate industrial organisations. The idea soon caught the fancy of Jimmy Carter, the then Governor of Georgia, who became the first to adopt the ZBB approach to government budgeting in the 1973 budget of that State. When he became President, he mandated the Federal bureaucracy to prepare the United States budget for the year 1979 on the basis of ZBB. Since then a number of state governments in the United States have followed suit by adopting ZBB in varying degree depending upon their local requirements and conditions.

Under ZBB, every expenditure item is set to 0 at the beginning of each period. Every expenditure item is reviewed thoroughly every year. Only if justifiable, the expenditure is considered. In other words, each item of expenditure is challenged for its very existence in every budget cycle and no base or minimum expenditure level is presumed for any activity. Zero-base budgeting means the past is cut off, the present is regarded as a clean slate and all departments have to start from a scratch (hence zero-base). It is also called sunset budgeting meaning that the sun would set on each governmental activity after a specified period. Before the sunset date, each department would be required to present a ZBB, indicating the achievements of its activities and what would result if the activities were not renewed.

1.5.1 Essential Elements of ZBB: There are three essential elements which distinguish ZBB from conventional budgeting.

Firstly, under the conventional system, departments (called budget units) prepare and submit budgets which group many important activities under one head, making it difficult to scrutinise each activity closely. As against this aggregative approach, ZBB requires budget units which are small enough to allow close examination of their programmes. ZBB puts under magnifying glass the nature of activity of each budgetary unit. For example, in the case of health department, a separate budget needs to be prepared for controlling each disease instead of for the whole department. Once the budget unit's activity is identified, the ZBB procedure asks: what if the activity is not funded at all? Are there other ways to perform the activity and meet the unit's objectives? The onus of explanation lies squarely on the departmental heads who are responsible for the activity and for preparing its budget. For instance, the Health Department of Delhi Government may be asked what if malaria eradication programmes were not funded. A possible answer from the Department could be: 'Mosquitoes would thrive'. However, under a system of ZBB more definite and quantitative answers are sought such as the estimated increase in the incidence of malaria, likely number of man days lost, increase in public and private medical bills, and possibility of fatalities. In essence, it becomes an exercise in social cost-benefit analysis involving strenuous exercises at each departmental level.

Secondly, ZBB assumes that even if an activity needs to be financed it can be financed at a lower-than-current level. In other words, economy in public expenditure on acceptable public activities is at the heart of ZBB's second essential rule. It requires evaluation and review of all programmes and activities, current as well as new, and believes that those who are in-charge of public spending have the capacity to cut down expenditure without adversely affecting the current level of public services.

Thirdly, ZBB requires priority-ranking among competing services of a budgetary unit. This ranking is done by listing all elements of a decision package in order of decreasing benefits to the community. High-priority services are ranked at the top followed by low-priority services until all are ranked. The list so prepared is used to fund services in order of priority until available resources are exhausted. Many of the services at the fag end of the list may just be eliminated for want of funds.

In brief, the three essential principles of ZBB are the following:

1. Should a government department spend?

2. How much should it spend? and
3. Where should it spend?

1.5.2 Limitations of ZBB: Application of ZBB has various limitations. Many activities of the government may be mandatory within the existing political framework and may even lie outside the jurisdiction of the legislature. For example, in India emoluments and allowances of the President, the Speaker and Deputy Speaker of the Lok Sabha, the Chairman and Deputy Chairman of the Rajya Sabha, and the Supreme Court and High Court Judges are beyond the vote of the Parliament. Furthermore, ZBB becomes unrealistic in case of many other public services which defy application of cost-benefit analysis owing to their very nature. Defence services, law and order, and maintenance of foreign relations are cases in point. It would obviously be ridiculous to ask: What if India's membership of the UNO were not funded? And are there other ways to achieve objectives of this membership? It is clear that the application of ZBB has to be selective rather than government-wide. ZBB is an approach not a fixed procedure to be applied uniformly from one type of expenditure to another or one level of government to another. The procedure must be adapted to suit specific needs of each department.

The major threat to the ZBB approach emanates from bureaucrats because it evaluates the effectiveness of their decisions and exposes their programmes to critical public review. This new idea in public budgeting requires effective administration, communication, and training of personnel involved in the analysis. It increases paperwork considerably and one frequent complaint against ZBB is that legislators seldom find time to scrutinise the analytical exercises done by the bureaucracy. In any event, ZBB is a long-term budgetary reform and its introduction has to be done in a phased manner.

1.6 Functional, Economic and Cross-classification of the Budget

Budgetary transactions of a government can be delineated and analysed in a number of ways. A functional classification of budgetary data groups items of government expenditure in terms of broad purposes to be served, e.g. defence, health, education, agriculture and industry. Economic classification of the budget involves rearrangement of government's receipts and expenditures into meaningful economic categories. A cross-classification of the budget provides information on government's expenditure by economic categories as well as functions.

1.6.1 Functional Classification of the Budget: Functional classification of the budget groups government expenditure according to purposes to be served by such expenditure, e.g. administration, defence, education, health, economic services etc. This type of budgeting is done for administrative accountability, parliamentary control, and booking and auditing of transactions. The scheme of functional classification relates essentially to expenditure side of the budget.

A. Uses and Limitations: Functional classification is defined to include all types of expenditure which are determined by political bodies and which are related in a meaningful way to specific purposes. It ensures that receipts are collected in the manner and the form authorised by law, and expenditures are incurred by the specific authority and on specified items sanctioned by the Parliament. This classification is useful for providing general information to the public on the nature of government services and the share of public expenditure devoted to a particular service. Functional classification facilitates formulation, implementation, and review of the broad policy objectives of the government.

Although functional classification of government expenditure has its own uses, it does not furnish suitable information for analysis of government's economic policy. The purpose of such classification is primarily to ensure accountability of those spending public money to those authorising the expenditure and thus facilitating budgetary control. It does not throw light on such economic magnitudes as consumption expenditure, saving, investment, and income generation on the part of government. Pointing out the limitations of functional classification of expenditure, a document of the United Nations observed, "Under this classification, the accounts may have different classifications and not be all for the same accounting period. They may not reflect transactions at the time they take place and in some accounts appropriations may be found covering no fixed period. It is not only difficult to obtain a complete picture of government transactions from existing accounts but also difficult to put it into perspective for policy use. This is not because there is too much detail in the accounts, but because the detail is not always of the right kind nor is it summarised in suitable ways". [1]

1.6.2 Economic Classification of the Budget: To overcome the deficiencies of functional classification, the same document of the United Nations suggested an economic classification of budgetary data. To quote, "(Economic classification provides) an analysis of the transactions of government bodies according to homogenous economic categories of transactions with the other sectors of the economy directly affected by them". [2]

A. Meaning and Rationale: Economic classification splits government's total expenditure into meaningful economic aggregates, viz. how much is consumed, how much is saved, how much is invested, and how much is transferred to other sectors of the economy. Economic classification of budgetary data is necessary for the following reasons.

1. Economic classification of the budget is necessary because the activities of all government departments do not have the same economic significance. Thus, current transactions of the commercial departments of the government are on par with those of producers in the private sector while current transactions of administrative departments of the government are akin to that of private consumers. Similarly, current receipts of departmental commercial undertakings are sale proceeds of goods and services supplied to the rest of the economy whereas administrative departments have little or no income of their own and largely draw upon the incomes of other sectors to meet their expenditures. Likewise, current expenditures of the departments like Railways, Posts, and Telecommunications are intermediate expenditures reflected in the prices of goods and services supplied by them. Apparently, these are different in nature from current expenditures on goods and services purchased by the administrative departments which represent demand for goods and services for final consumption.
2. Budget distinguishes revenue receipts and revenue expenditures from capital receipts and capital expenditures. However, in reality, revenue expenditure may include

certain items which are capital expenditure from economic point of view. Revenue expenditure on education and training centres is a case in point. Contrarily, certain expenditures on capital account may, in fact, be current expenditures from a purely economic angle, e.g. capital outlay on defence.

3. Revenue expenditure, as shown in the budget, groups together direct expenditure on goods and services and expenditure of the nature of mere transfers (like pensions) intended to add to incomes of others. These have to be isolated and treated separately. Similarly, capital outlays in the budget group together capital grants, investment in shares, and direct outlays by the government on construction, machinery and equipment. These categories, however, have different significance and therefore need to be viewed separately. Thus, capital grants are outright transfers intended to add to the investible resources of the rest of the economy, investment in shares increases government's claim against enterprises falling outside the government sector, and direct outlays increase stock of physical assets in the government sector.

With the above rationale in view, the Ministry of Finance, Government of India prepared and issued for the first time an *Economic Classification of the Central Government Budget* in 1957-58. Ever since, the document *An Economic and Functional Classification of the Budget* is released by the government after a lag of 7-8 months of the presentation of the General Budget to the Parliament. To quote, "in brief, this classification involves arranging the expenditures and receipts of the Central Government including those of Railways and Post and Telegraphs by significant economic categories, distinguishing current from capital outlays, spending for goods and services from transfers to individuals and institutions, tax receipts by kind from other receipts and from borrowing and intergovernmental loans and grants etc.". [3]

B. Methodology of Economic Classification of the Budget: Economic classification of the budget is prepared by regrouping government transactions in a set of six accounts. In this system of six accounts, a distinction is drawn between transactions in goods, services, and transfers (accounts 1 to 3) and financial transactions which affect the net claims of the government on the rest of the economy (accounts 4 to 6). Transactions in goods, services, and transfers are again divided into current transactions (accounts 1 and 2) and capital transactions (account 3). Finally, a distinction is drawn between current transactions of government administration (account 1) and the current transactions of departmental commercial undertakings (account 2).

1.6.3 Cross-classification of the Budget: Cross or economic-cum-functional classification provides the break-up of Government expenditure not only by economic categories but also by functional heads. This classification is important to understand the economic significance of the government expenditure for various purposes. Thus, expenditure on medical facilities (a functional head) is split between economic categories such as current expenditure, capital expenditure, and various types of transfers and loans. Conversely, cross-classification shows how expenditure on a particular economic category, say capital formation is divided according to different purposes of public activities like education, labour welfare, family planning, sanitation etc.

Thus, under a scheme of cross classification, functional classification of expenditure can be analysed according to its economic character and economic classification of expenditure can be analysed according to the functions performed by it. Therefore, the two types of classification supplement each other and they need to be shown together for purposes of general budgeting.

Cross-classification of expenditure presents in one statement basic information on public expenditure both by economic character and by the function of the expenditure. Such a classification is particularly helpful in drawing up a programme of projected expenditure covering a period of years, and in evaluating the progress of actual expenditure.

1.7 Gender Budgeting

Government budgets are universally accepted as a powerful tool in achieving development objectives and act as an indicator of commitment to the stated policy of the Government. National budgets reflect how governments mobilize and allocate public resources, and how they aim to meet the social and economic needs of their people.

1.7.1 Meaning of Gender Budgeting: A budget, on the face of it, appears to be gender-neutral. Public expenditure and revenue are not intrinsically gendered. However, this apparent gender neutrality hides a deeper gender blindness, which tends to operate to the disadvantage of women. Budgetary policies can ignore gender-specific needs and have differential impacts on men and women because of the systemic differences between the sexes in relation to the economy.

Gender budgeting looks at government budget from a gender perspective to assess how it addresses the needs of women. In other words, gender budgeting is the application of gender mainstreaming in the budgetary process. It incorporates a gender perspective at all levels and stages of the budgetary process and paves the way for translating gender commitments to budgetary commitments and carrying out an assessment of the budget to establish its gender differential impact. It does not seek to create a separate budget but seeks to put in place affirmative action for meeting women-specific needs, thus bringing into effect gender responsive budgeting. The ultimate objective of gender budgeting is to transform traditional perceptions towards women and awaken a gender sensitive consciousness to come into the mainstream and give them their due recognition as equal citizens of the country.

1.7.2 Meaning of Gender Mainstreaming: The conventional approach to gender budgeting emphasizes isolating public expenditure—direct and indirect—for women. It is necessary to recognize that women are equal players in the economy whether they participate directly as workers or indirectly as members of the care economy. To that extent, every policy of the government—fiscal, monetary, agriculture, industry and trade—has a direct impact on the well-being of women.

Thus, it is not adequate to analyze allocation of resources for a few sectors of the economy which are traditionally considered as women-related. The exercise has to cover a gender-sensitive analysis of monetary policies, covering impact of indicators like inflation, interest rates etc and fiscal policies covering both direct and indirect taxes. Hence, gender budgeting analysis has to go hand in hand with gender mainstreaming. This is a mammoth task when there is a lot of disaggregated data which has to be gender sensitized and analyzed. Micro studies will have to be conducted to study the impact of public and fiscal policy so that they may guide macro policies. Thus, gender mainstreaming is a broader term covering a wide gamut of governmental activities.

1.7.3 Objectives of Gender Budgeting: A gender-responsive budget aims at examining budgetary resource allocations through a gender lens. It is not a separate budget for women; rather it is an analysis of the government budget in order to establish its gender-specific impact and translate gender commitments into budgetary commitments. It also examines the gendered incidence of budgetary policies for effective targeting of public spending and to offset any undesirable gender-specific consequences of previous budgetary measures).

Gender budgeting lays stress on *reprioritisation* rather than an increase in overall public expenditure and, in particular, the *reorientation* of programmes within sectors rather than changes in the overall amounts allocated to particular sectors. Moreover, one of the key thrusts of a gender-sensitive budget is to ensure a greater visibility of the unpaid *care economy.* In other words, gender responsive budgeting applies a gender lens to budgetary resource allocation, providing more visibility to women's unpaid work.

Generally, budgeting involves the following four components: (a) budgetary allocation of resources to various heads, (b) actual government outlays on various heads, (c) an accounting of how resources are utilised for a particular purpose (e.g. on administrative overheads and wages and salaries, operation and maintenance etc.) and (d) an evaluation of the effectiveness of the resources utilised in delivering the intended results.

Gender budgeting involves looking at all the four components from the point of view of women as beneficiaries. Many public goods and services, like defence and infrastructure, are not amenable to gender partitioning. However, they can have differential impact on the two sexes. For example, outlays for augmenting the supply of safe drinking water can benefit women more than men by cutting down on the time spent in fetching water from the river or ponds. The existing practice of budgeting does not pay any special attention to the impact of budgets on empowerment of women and on gender equality.

In short, the objective of gender budgeting is to enable gender mainstreaming of all sectors at all levels and stages of policies, programmes/schemes and also at the level of the implementation stage and instituting gender-friendly delivery mechanisms. Only then it can pave the way for translating gender commitments into budgetary commitments.

1.7.4 Rationale of Gender Budgeting: The rationale of gender budgeting arises from recognition of the fact that national budgets impact various sections of the society differently through the pattern of resource allocation and priority accorded to competing sectors. The budgetary policy of the government has a major role to play in achieving objectives of gender equality and growth through content and direction of fiscal and monetary policies, measures for resource mobilization, affirmative action for under privileged sections. Women stand apart as one segment of the population that warrants special attention due to their vulnerability and lack of access to state resources.

Thus, gender responsive budgetary policies can contribute to achieving the objectives of gender equality, human development and economic efficiency. The purpose of gender budgeting exercise is to assess quantum and adequacy of allocation of resources for women and establish the extent to which gender commitments are translated in to budgetary commitments. This exercise facilitates increase in accountability, transparency and participation of the community. The macro policies of the Government can have a significant impact on gender gaps in various macro indicators related to health, education, income etc. When gender equality considerations are incorporated into policy making, the concerns and needs of both women and men become integral part of the design, implementation, monitoring and evaluation of policies and programmes in all sections of society.

1.7.5 Tools of Gender Budgeting: Policies of the Government form the genesis for programmes and schemes providing the direction and describing the components of inputs that go into them. They determine the quantum of flow of the funds to different schemes, its components and also spatial spread of the programme. Unless the policies are engendered, it cannot be hoped that the programmes and the schemes that emerge from this will be gender sensitive. Therefore, it is very essential that all policies of the Government from its very inception and formulation stage be thoroughly examined from a gender perspective. The fiscal and monetary policies will need to be analyzed from a gender perspective as both have tremendous potential to have benign influence on the lives of women.

A. Gender-sensitive Indirect Taxes: Indirect taxes (i.e. taxes on commodities) impinge heavily on women as the tax incidence, by and large, affects important items of sustenance which are generally price-inelastic and even a small price rise in such items can have a negative impact on women. Conversely, withdrawal of subsidies can adversely impinge on women. For example, withdrawal of subsidy on kerosene with no other alternative fuel options will result in the woman wasting valuable productive time in gathering firewood, twigs etc and in the process also face health hazards. Thus, the ramifications of indirect taxes are quite significant as far as women's well-being is considered.

B. Gender-sensitive Taxes: The gender affirmative role of direct taxes (income tax, wealth tax etc.) can be enhanced through various incentives like reduction in stamp duties for women if assets are registered in their name, lowering of income tax slabs for women and other exemptions/concessions. As regards indirect taxes (sales tax, excise duty etc.) goods used exclusively by women (e.g. sanitary napkins) should be taxed at lower rate.

C. Gender-sensitive Monetary Policy: Monetary policy has to be viewed from a gender angle, especially in the case of credit and loan facilities and easy access of women to financial instruments and attractive saving options. In this context the spread of private micro credit lending instruments needs to be carefully regulated to ensure that women and self-help groups (SHGs) are not exploited through high interest rates.

D. Gender-sensitive National Income Accounting: Informal farm work and non-farm work where women are increasingly employed are mostly non-monetized and therefore cannot be captured in the national accounting system. Despite the sizeable value addition to the national economy, on account of home-based and other non-farm and informal activities, the contribution of women's work continues to be invisible. Women also spend considerable time in collecting fuel, fodder, and water and on care-related activities, which is not recognized as an economic activity. The statistical invisibility of such unpaid work implies that the economic system is missing out on a substantial part of the income generated and value added. It should be ensured that the national income includes these activities in their accounting system so that it forms a part of the gross domestic product (GDP).

1.7.6 Gender Budgeting in Select Countries: World-wide, there is a growing recognition of the need for a fundamental rethinking of the macro-policy framework from a gender perspective. The United Nations conferences of the 1990s affirmed a global consensus on the need for a new approach to macro policy in the sustainable human development paradigm, which is based on the cornerstones of gender equality, poverty eradication, environmental regeneration, sustainable livelihoods, employment creation and democratic governance. The United Nations Fourth World Conference on Women 1995 (the Beijing Conference) and the subsequent Beijing Platform for Action contributed to the emergence of an international consensus in integrating a gender perspective in all policies and their budgetary dimensions.

A. Australia: Australia was the first country to develop a gender-sensitive budget. In 1984, the government introduced a comprehensive assessment of the gender differential impacts of its Federal Budget. Each government agency was required to provide a *gender audit* (i.e. achievements in relation to women and girls). The audit was a comprehensive gender analysis of mainstream public expenditure, and not merely those expenditures directly allotted to females. It was found that expenditures specifically targeted to women and girls made up less than 1 per cent of the total budget.

B. South Africa: Started in 1995, the gender budget initiative in South Africa was a joint effort of parliamentarians and non-governmental organisations (NGOs). This parliamentary-NGO initiative undertook a detailed gender-sensitive analysis of expenditure portfolios like education, health, welfare, housing, labour, trade and industry, land affairs, agriculture, safety and security, transport, energy, foreign affairs well as the cross-sectoral areas of public sector employment and taxation. Later, during 1997, the Department of Finance began a parallel exercise, as a pilot for the Commonwealth initiative to integrate gender perspectives into macroeconomic policy. In a major step forward, several sections of the 1998 *Budget Review* (document tabled along with the budget) discussed gender issues in the various departments.

C. Sri Lanka: The Commonwealth initiative to integrate gender into national budgetary processes was initiated on a test basis in some countries including Sri Lanka. Sri Lanka joined the Commonwealth countries' pilot project in 1997 and the initial gender-sensitive budget exercise was co-ordinated by the Department of National Planning. It focussed on the portfolios of health, education, public sector employment, agriculture, industry and social services. The first stage of the pilot project was completed with the establishment of a gender-conscious planning mechanism in the allocation of resources coupled with greater capacity for sex-segregated data collation.

An inter-ministerial committee, comprising of representatives of the ministries of education, health, social services, industries, agriculture, women affairs and the department of census and statistics, was set up to assess the progress and performance of the gender budgeting project in Sri Lanka. The survey-based report found that there was equality of access and usage in mainstream public expenditure: 48 percent of recurrent expenditure in the education sector, 56 percent in the health sector and 57 percent in the social services sector benefited females. The report stressed that there is no need for an increase in funding for women. What was needed, instead, was an evaluation and redesign of the existing programmes, and devising appropriate benefit impact monitoring systems that would be sensitive to gender imbalances.

D. Canada: In Canada, members of Centre for Policy Alternatives, a social justice research group, have developed a gender-sensitive budget as part of the Centre's annual Alternative Federal Budget. Though there are no formal guidelines regarding gender budgeting, Human Resource Development Canada (HRDC), a government department, is committed to implementing a gender-based analysis as a part of the policy and programme development process in the country.

Following its international commitment to the Beijing Platform for Action initiative, the Government of Canada adopted the Federal Plan for Gender Equality (1995-2000). The plan was prepared through the collaboration of 24 departments and agencies, led by Status of Women Canada (SWC), another government department. The first of the Federal Plan's eight objectives made a commitment to government-wide implementation of gender-based analysis (GBA) in the development of policies, programmes and legislations GBA involves collecting reliable sex-disaggregated information about the policy area of concern, and understanding the gender trends in the economy that might have an impact on a proposed policy, programme or piece of legislation.

E. UK: Women's Budget Group, an NGO consisting of researchers and activists, is in the forefront of putting gender-sensitive budget analysis on the policy agenda. Its core recommendations to the government are the inclusion of a comparative 'gender impact statement' with every budget and public expenditure white paper.

1.7.7 Gender Budgeting in India: Gender responsive budgeting or gender analysis of budgets is a very useful tool being used in India to promote gender mainstreaming. Gender budgeting refers to presentation of budgetary data in a manner such that the gender sensitivities of budgetary allocations are clearly highlighted. Gender budgeting includes carrying out an impact analysis of government programmes and its budgetary allocations on the overall socio-economic status of women in the country. A special reference by the Union Finance Minister in his budget speech to Parliament on February 29, 2000 pertaining to the access of women to national resources, marked the dawn of gender-sensitive budgeting in India. For details, see chapter 6 of this book.

Endnotes

1. United Nations, Department of Economic Affairs, *A Manual for Economic and Functional Classification of Government Transactions* (New York, 1958), p. 4.
2. *Ibid.*, p. 33.
3. Government of India, Ministry of Finance, *An Economic and Functional Classification of the Central Government Budget,* 1979-80, p. 111.

2

Phases of Budgetary Cycle in India

Till 1857, when India was under the rule of the East India Company, there was hardly any centralized or systematic financial administration in the country. After the events of 1857, the administration of India was taken over directly by the British Government in 1858. It established a highly centralized system of financial and administrative control with the purpose of consolidating its hold on the vast territory of India. The system of centralized financial control was exercised through the establishment of Finance Department which functioned rather well till the late 1930s. A Comptroller and Auditor-General was appointed in 1860 by amalgamating audit and accounts functions. However, in the absence of a Government responsible to the legislature, he submitted his Annual Reports to the secretary of State for India in Britain.

In matters of rules, regulations, procedures, compilation of annual budgets, audit and accounts etc., the Indian system of financial administration was based on the pattern of treasury control prevalent in Britain. All revenues were required to be credited to a Public Account. Similarly, annual budgets included demands for grants and appropriation accounts as also taxation proposals. They were, however, passed with the Governor-General's approval instead of that of the legislature as was the practice in Britain.

The Government of India was also responsible for the financial administration of Provincial Governments till the introduction of Provincial Autonomy in 1937 when popularly elected Provincial governments responsible to legislatures were established. From 1921 onwards, the Central Legislative Assembly, with a non-official majority, was for the first time given the right to discuss and pass the Annual Budget of the Government of India in respect of *non-reserved* subjects, as also to pass the Finance Bill containing taxation proposals. A committee on Public Accounts, with 8 non-official members of the Central Legislative Assembly and 4 official members (including the Finance Member as chairman) was also constituted to receive and examine Annual Reports of the Auditor-General.

The system of financial control in accordance with the rules and orders in force prior to Independence was continued after August 15, 1947, pending the framing of the new constitution of India. When the new constitution was promulgated on January 26, 1950, the then prevailing system of financial control was permitted to continue, with necessary changes.

As in other democratic societies, government budgeting is a constitutional obligation in India. In the Constitution of India, procedures in respect of financial matters of the Central Government are regulated by Articles 112 to 117.

The budgetary process in India involves the following four operations:

1. Preparation of the budget.

2. Legalisation of the budget.
3. Execution of the budget.
4. Auditing of accounts.

2.1 Preparation of the Budget

Preparation of the budget involves considerable efforts on the part of the Ministry of Finance and other Ministries/Departments. It is sometime in the month of September every year that the Budget Division of the Department of Economic Affairs of the Ministry of Finance sends a circular to various Ministries/Departments, requesting them to prepare estimates of expenditure to be incurred by them in the ensuing year. Specific information is sought on the following matters:

1. Actuals of the previous year.
2. Sanctioned budget estimates for the current year.
3. Revised estimates for the current year.
4. Proposed estimates for the next financial year with explanation for any increase or decrease in estimates.

With the help of their financial advisers, individual Ministries/Departments formulate their spending plans on the basis of their previous year spending and the new schemes and projects which they intend to take up. These estimates of expenditure are furnished to the Ministry of Finance during December/January for screening and integration into the main budget.

The Ministry of Finance, after having scrutinised the estimates, embarks upon the process of compilation and co-ordination of estimates of expenditure of different Ministries/Departments. It may prune excessive demands because there are limits to financial resources available to the Government. It also ensures that the estimates conform to the various economy instructions issued from time-to-time. Before the expenditure estimates are finalised, discussions take place between the Secretary (Expenditure), Ministry of Finance, and the financial advisers of the Ministries/Departments concerned. However, the Ministry of Finance has the final say in regard to all estimates.

Estimates of revenue are prepared by the Department of Revenue, Ministry of Finance. The Department remains equipped with records of yields of various taxes for previous years and on that basis it prepares estimates for the ensuing year. It also undertakes quick estimates of non-tax revenue and non-Reserve Bank of India (RBI) funded borrowings including external aid. A view is then taken on the likely total resources including additional resource mobilisation and RBI credit to the Government. The RBI credit to the Government has to be consistent with the current state of the economy and fiscal consolidation policy (i.e. restraint on both fiscal deficit and monetised deficit).

During this period, the Finance Minister remains in close touch with the secretaries of revenue, expenditure, and economic affairs in the Ministry of Finance. The budget proposals prepared by the Ministry are examined by the Finance Minister and he may make changes in them in consultation with the Prime Minister.

Budget-making in India is a highly secretive exercise. The team of officials working on the budget go almost underground for weeks preceding the presentation of the budget to the Parliament. In line with the British tradition of parliamentary privilege, details of the budget proposals must be kept secret before they are made known to the legislators. Changes in rates of taxes and duties constitute the most sensitive part of the budgetary proposals. Any leakages of these proposals can have unsettling effect on the product as well as the capital market. Hoarders and speculators swing into action on hearing rumours of duty cuts or hikes. In case the leakage is genuine and comes to the notice of opposition party members, it can even cost the Finance Minister his job. To prevent such eventualities, elaborate security arrangements are made which, *inter alia*, include transportation of budget documents to Parliament in heavily guarded vehicles.

On the budget day (generally the first working day of February), the Finance Minister calls on the President to apprise him of the budget proposals. Similarly, the Finance Minister briefs the Cabinet about the budget shortly before it is presented to Parliament.

2.2 Legalisation of the Budget

Once the budget is prepared, it has to pass through the following review and approval stages in the Parliament.

1. Presentation of the budget by the Finance Minister in both the Houses of Parliament.
2. General discussion on revenue and expenditure proposals.
3. Presentation, discussion and voting on demands for grants.
4. Voting and passing of the Appropriation Bill.
5. Passing of the Finance Bill.

2.2.1 Presentation of the Budget: The procedure for presentation of the budget in and its passing by the Lok Sabha is as laid down in Articles 112-117 of the Constitution. The budgets of the Union Territories and States under President's rule are also presented to the Lok Sabha.

The budget is presented in the Lower House, viz. Lok Sabha (House of the People) on such a day as the President may direct. Simultaneously, a copy of the budget is laid on the table of the Upper House, viz. Rajya Sabha (House of the States).

The long-standing tradition of British Raj of presenting the budget at 5.00 P.M. was discarded in 1999. It is now presented in the morning at around 11.00 A.M.

By convention, the budget was presented on the last working day of the month of February each year till 2016-17. However, beginning 2017-18, the presentation of the Budget was advanced to first working day of February, to enable the Parliament to avoid a Vote on Account and pass a single Appropriation Bill, before the close of the current financial year.

Similarly, the colonial practice of presenting Railways Budget separately, prevalent since 1924, was discontinued beginning 2017-18. In other words, Railways Budget was merged with the General Budget. [1]

The proceedings of the day start and end with the budget speech of the Finance Minister. Conventionally, the Finance Minister will start with a review of the economic situation in the current year. He will inform the House about the document titled *Economic Survey* which is generally laid on the table of the House a couple of days before the presentation of the budget. He highlights the major points of *Economic Survey* or other economic developments such as agricultural production, price situation, balance of payments position or any other international development (say crude oil prices) which has bearing on the Indian economy. In a way he prepares the background for his budget proposals.

He then outlines the economic policy of the government in the ensuing year. What will be emphasized (infrastructure, agriculture, power etc.), what new schemes will be launched for various sections of society (generally for rural areas and poor people). In short, the presentation of the budget offers an opportunity to the Government to review and explain its financial and economic policies and programmes to the Legislature.

Then he presents the revised estimates for the current year and reasons for changes in receipts/expenditure, if any. Then he presents the budget estimates for the ensuing year. Generally, estimated expenditure is more than estimated receipts, leaving a deficit (or gap) in budget.

Then he proposes measures for additional resource mobilisation (ARM). This may include new taxes or enhancement of rates of existing taxes. He also proposes tax concession wherever required.

He then summarises the net effect of his tax proposals. By ARM he reduces the gap between expenditure and receipts. Some gap still remains (deficit financing) which he considers reasonable and believes will not have undue adverse effect on price level.

The budget papers are made available to members after the Finance Minister's speech is over, the Finance Bill has been introduced, and the House has adjourned for the day. No discussion on the budget takes place on the day it is presented to the House.

2.2.2 General Discussion: The Government has to approach the Parliament for approval of its plans to collect, keep and spend money. The budget presented to the House by the Finance Minister is discussed in two stages: the general discussion followed by a detailed discussion, and voting on the demands for grants.

The general discussion, in both the Houses of Parliament, relates to budget as a whole (or any question of principle involved therein), a review and criticism of the administration but no motion is moved at this stage nor is the budget submitted to vote. The scope of discussion is confined to an examination of the general scheme and structure of the budget, items of expenditure and tax policy as expressed in the budget and in the speech of the Finance Minister. The Finance Minister has the general right to reply at the end of the discussion. The Rajya Sabha has no further business with the budget beyond the above general discussion.

Presentation of the budget in itself does not authorise the Government to collect taxes/additional taxes or incur expenditure. For giving effect to tax proposals contained in the budget, a bill called Finance Bill (explained ahead in section 2.2.5) is introduced in the Parliament immediately after the budget speech of the Finance Minister.

2.2.3 Demands for Grants: Article 113 provides that expenditure charged upon the Consolidated Fund of India shall not be submitted to the vote of Parliament, but there is no objection to discussion thereon in either House of Parliament.

The voted portion of the estimates of expenditure shall be submitted in the form of demands for grants to the Lok Sabha, who shall have power to assent, or to refuse to assent, to any demand or to assent to any demand subject to a reduction of the amount specified therein.

Further, according to Article 113 the financial initiative is the executive's privilege. The Article reads, 'no demand for a grant shall be made except on the recommendation of the President'. The implication is that only the Government can present a demand for grant and not the private members. The purpose of this restriction is obvious because the balancing of revenue and expenditure is the job of the executive and if private members were to propose fresh items of expenditure and the Parliament were to approve of them, the Government finances will fall into disarray. Thus, limiting financial initiative to the Government protects taxpayers against improper appropriation of public funds. It is noteworthy that when a demand for a grant is presented, the Parliament can object to it, refuse it, reduce it but cannot increase it.

The estimates of expenditure for various Departments which need to be voted by the Parliament are submitted in the form of demands for grants. In case a Ministry/Department is in-charge of a number of distinct services, a separate demand for each of the major services is presented. Each demand for grant shows the total amount required for a service during the year showing revenue and capital expenditure separately. Furthermore, they are presented for gross amounts of expenditure. The demands for grants are presented to the Lok Sabha along with the budget statement. They are generally not moved in the House by the Minister concerned. The demands are assumed to have been moved and are proposed from the Chair to save the time of the House.

The Detailed Demands for Grants are laid by the respective Ministries/Departments on the table of the Lok Sabha sometime after the presentation of the Budget, but before the discussion on Demands for Grants commences. Detailed Demands for Grants further elaborate the provisions included in the Demands for Grants as also the actual expenditure during the previous year. A break-up of the estimates relating to each programme and organization is given under a number of object heads which indicate the categories and nature of expenditure incurred on that programme, such as salaries, wages, travel expenses, machinery and equipment, grants-in-aid, etc. At the end of these, detailed demands are shown the details of recoveries taken in reduction of expenditure in the accounts.

A. Charged and Voted Expenditures: Under Article 112(2), estimates of expenditure contained in the budget show separately: (i) the sums required to meet expenditure described by the Constitution as expenditure charged upon the Consolidated Fund of India and (ii) the sums required to meet other expenditure proposed to be made from the Consolidated Fund. The estimates of expenditure charged upon the Consolidated Fund are not submitted to the vote of Parliament (non-votable expenditure) but each House is competent to discuss any of these estimates. The estimates relating to other expenditure are submitted in the form of demands for grants to the Lok Sabha, and it has the power to accept, or reject any such demand, or to accept any such demand subject to a reduction of the amount specified therein.

Thus, the demands for grants indicate separately the *charged* and *voted* items of expenditure. Though normally the Government cannot spend any money without the authorisation of the Parliament, certain items of expenditure have been allowed to be incurred even without the Parliament's vote. Such items are called *charged items*. These are indispensable items of expenditure. Lest they should be subjected to changing political fortunes, they have been placed beyond the vote of the Parliament. If Parliament does not vote an item of expenditure, the Government falls immediately. But the President has to carry on, the Supreme Court has to function and liabilities of the Government have to be cleared.

Under Article 112(3) of the Constitution, the following expenditure is *charged* on the Consolidated Fund of India: (a) emoluments and allowances of the President and other expenditure relating to his office, (b) the salaries and allowances of the Chairman and the Deputy Chairman of the Council of States (Rajya Sabha), and the Speaker and the Deputy Speaker of the House of People (Lok Sabha), (c) debt charges for which the Government of India is liable, (d): (i) salaries, allowances and pensions payable to or in respect of judges of the Supreme Court, (ii) the pensions payable to or in respect of judges of the Federal Court, (iii) the pensions payable to or in respect of judges of any High Court, (e) the salary, allowances and pensions payable to or in respect of the Comptroller and Auditor-General of India, (f) any sums required to satisfy any judgement, decree or award of any court or arbitral tribunal, (g) any other expenditure declared by the Constitution or by the Parliament by law to be so charged.

B. Plan and Non-Plan Expenditures: Prior to 2017-18, out of the total expenditure of the Central Government, a significant proportion was incurred as Plan expenditure. Therefore, the demands for grants showed separately the Plan and Non-Plan expenditures of the Ministry/Department. The document *Expenditure Budget* (Volume 1) gave the total Plan provisions for each of the Ministries arranged under various heads of development and highlighted the budget provisions for the more important plan programmes and schemes. The document titled *Plan Budget* indicated the total provision for the Central Plan, Plans of Union Territories, and Central assistance for State Plans. The details of Plan outlay at both the Central and the State levels were contained in the document titled *Annual Plan* prepared separately by the Planning Commission.

A significant proportion of Plan expenditure by the Central Government was incurred on public sector undertakings through investment in shares and loans.

Non-Plan expenditure was a generic term used to cover all government expenditure not included in the Plan. It included both revenue and capital expenditure, developmental and non-developmental expenditure. A part of the expenditure was obligatory in nature as, for example, interest payments, pensions and statutory transfers to the States. A part of the expenditure was essential such as defence and internal security. Expenditure on the maintenance of assets (buildings, roads etc.) created in previous Plans was also treated as non-Plan expenditure. A large part of resources of the Government was pre-empted by various items of non-Plan expenditure.

The distinction between Plan and non-Plan expenditure ended with the completion of

Twelfth Five Year Plan on March 31, 2017. In other words, beginning 2017-18, the classification of government expenditure into Plan and non-Plan was done away with in order to take a holistic view of allocations for sectors and ministries. In fact, Planning Commission, which formulated India's Five Year Plan, itself was scrapped by the Union Cabinet on August 13, 2014.

C. Cut Motions: At the time of discussion on the demands for grants, copies of the *Annual Reports* and *Performance Budgets* of the Ministries are made available to the Members of Parliament. The presentation of demands for grants by a Ministry is an occasion to review the working of that Ministry by the Members of Parliament. The scope of discussion at this stage is confined to matters falling under the administrative purview of the Ministry. It is open to members to disapprove policies of a Ministry or to suggest measures for economy in the administration of that Ministry.

At this stage, a *cut motion* can be moved to reduce any demand for grant but no amendments to a motion seeking to reduce any demand are permissible. The motions to reduce amounts of demands for grants are called *cut motions*. The object of a cut motion is to draw the attention of the House to the matter specified therein. Cut motions can be classified into three categories.

1. **Disapproval of Policy Cut:** A cut motion which says "that the amount of the demand be reduced to ₹ 1" implies that the mover disapproves of the policy underlying the demand.
2. **Economy Cut:** Where the object of the motion is to effect economy in the expenditure, the form of the motion is "that the amount of the demand be reduced by ₹... (a specified amount)". The amount suggested for reduction may be either a lump sum reduction in the demand or omission or reduction of an item in the demand.
3. **Token Cut:** Where the object of the motion is to ventilate a specific grievance within the sphere of responsibility of the Government of India, the form of the motion is "that the amount of demand be reduced by ₹ 100". Discussion on such a cut motion is confined to the particular grievance specified in the motion and which is within the sphere of responsibility of the Government of India.

D. Principle of Guillotine: Discussion on the demands for grants in the Lok Sabha has to be completed in the budget session. These discussions take place under pressure of time and in practice only a limited number of demands are discussed in the Lok Sabha. As the budget session draws to a close, the principle of guillotine is applied, i.e. demands are passed without any detailed discussion or scrutiny.

In the Constitution of India, the real power in relation to financial matters rests with the Lok Sabha. The voting of demands takes place in this House only. Rajya Sabha can discuss the demands, if it so chooses, but it does not vote the demands.

2.2.4 Appropriation Bill: Article 114 provides for introduction of a bill to provide for the appropriation out of the Consolidated Fund of India of all moneys required to meet the grants approved by Lok Sabha and the charged expenditure. No money shall be withdrawn from the Consolidated Fund of India except under appropriation made by law passed in accordance with the provisions of this Article.

After the demands for grants are voted by the Lok Sabha, the Appropriation Bill is introduced, considered, and passed by it. The Bill incorporates all moneys required to meet: (i) charged expenditure and (ii) grants made by the Lok Sabha. This Bill is then passed as a Money Bill subject to the condition that no amendment is proposed to it in either House which has the effect of varying the amount or altering the destination of any grant or varying the amount of any expenditure charged on the Consolidated Fund of India. No money can be withdrawn from the Consolidated Fund of India, either with respect to voted grants or the non-votable *charged* items of expenditure, except under an Appropriation Act passed by the Parliament. It provides the legal authority for the withdrawal of sums from the Consolidated Fund of India. In other words, the passing of the Appropriation Bill completes the authorisation by Parliament of Government expenditure. The Parliament then goes to consider the Finance Bill.

The Appropriation Bill is first passed by the Lok Sabha and then transmitted to the Rajya Sabha. If the Rajya Sabha does not return the Bill within 14 days the Bill is deemed to be passed by both Houses. If the Rajya Sabha makes some changes and the Lok Sabha does not accept them, then also the Bill is deemed to be passed by both the Houses in the form in which the Lok Sabha had passed it.

After the Appropriation Bill is passed in the foregoing manner, the various Ministries/Departments inform the respective spending agencies and project authorities the amount allocated in the budget to each of them.

As already noted, budget of the Government was presented to Parliament on the last working day of the month of February till the year 2016-17. The Parliament had to discuss the budget, vote the demands for grants, and finally pass the Appropriation Bill. The Appropriation Bill had to be passed before March 31 so as to enable the Government to incur expenditure from the beginning of the ensuing financial year (April 1). Since the presentation, discussion, and voting of demands for grants and passing of Appropriation Bill generally went beyond the current financial year, a provision existed (and still exists) in the Constitution empowering the Lok Sabha to make any grant in advance through a *Vote on Account* to enable the Government to carry on until the voting of demands for grants and the passing of the Appropriation Bill. This enabling authorisation got enacted before March 31. However, beginning 2017-18, the presentation of the Budget was advanced to first working day of February, to enable the Parliament to avoid a Vote on Account and pass a single Appropriation Bill, before the close of the current financial year.

A. Vote on Account: Article 116 provides for vote on account, votes of credit and exceptional grants to cover expenditure for a part of any financial year pending the completion of the procedure prescribed for the voting of such grants and the passing of law in relation to that expenditure, and to make a grant for meeting unexpected demand when on account of the magnitude or the indefinite character of the service the demand cannot be stated with details ordinarily given in the *annual financial statement* (i.e. budget). The exceptional grant is intended to cover expenditure which does not form part of the current service of any financial year.

Under Article 116 of the Constitution of India, a government can present Vote on Account (popularly known as Interim Budget) to the Parliament. Literally, vote on account means vote on the accounts of the government.

The regular annual budget of the Government of India is presented to the Parliament on the first working day of February. Situations can arise when the presentation of the regular budget is not feasible or desirable. It is possible that a government is at the fag end of its term in the month of February or a government takes office just before the beginning of the financial year (running from April 1 to March 31 of the next year). Under such situations a vote on account is sought by the government. According to the Constitution, government cannot spend any money without the approval of the Parliament (Appropriation Act). Vote on account is taken so that the government is enabled to spend from the Consolidated Fund of India for 3 to 4 months after the expiry of the financial year on March 31. It cannot be for a period longer than 6 months as the Constitution stipulates that the gap between two Parliament sittings cannot be more than 6 months.

It is noteworthy that there is no constitutional restriction on presentation of a full budget by an outgoing government. It is by convention that a government at the end of its tenure opts for a vote on account. It is regarded improper that an outgoing government should impose its economic and fiscal policies on its successor. Hence, no changes are made in the rates etc. of taxes/duties and no new programmes/schemes are announced.

A vote on account is passed by the Lok Sabha after the general discussion on the budget is over and before the discussion on demands for grants is taken up. Traditionally, vote on account is treated as a formal matter and passed by the Lok Sabha without discussion.

B. Vote of Credit: Situations may arise when the Government requires huge amounts of money urgently, e.g. if the country is threatened with war. Under such extraordinary situations the Government may not be in a position to furnish details of expenditure to be incurred. To deal with such circumstances, the Parliament may grant a sum in gross to the Government on a vote called a *Vote of Credit* and leave the responsibility of distributing the money to the executive (Article 116).

C. Excess Grant: Article 115 provides for supplementary, additional or excess grants in respect of expenditure for new service not contemplated in the *annual financial statement* (i.e. budget). The procedure for withdrawal of funds in each such demand is the same as indicated earlier, namely by introduction of an appropriation bill equal to the amount of the grant approved by Parliament.

At the end of the financial year, all voted amounts lapse. If the Government incurs expenditure on any service during a financial year in excess of the grant voted by the Parliament, a demand for such excess has to be presented to the House which may vote on *excess grant* [Article 115(1)(b)]. All such cases are brought to the notice of the Parliament by the Comptroller and Auditor-General through his report on Appropriation Accounts. The excess grants are then examined by the Public Accounts Committee of the Parliament which makes recommendations regarding their regularisation in its report to the House. The demands for excess grants are made after the expenditure has actually been incurred and after the financial year to which it relates has ended.

2.2.5 Finance Bill: It is expressly laid down in the Constitution that no tax shall be levied or collected except by the authority of law (Article 265).

The regular budget contains proposals with regard to both direct and indirect taxes. These proposals regarding the levy of new taxes, modifications in the existing tax structure or continuance of existing rates of taxation for a further period are presented through the Finance Bill.

Article 117 provides for the introduction of finance bills only on the recommendation of the President and provides for compulsory introduction of such bills in the Lok Sabha and *not* in the Rajya Sabha and no such bill can be passed unless the President has recommended the consideration of the bill.

Taxation proposals take effect the moment the Finance Bill is presented, indirect taxes immediately and direct taxes on a date specified in the Bill (normally the first day of the ensuing financial year, i.e. April 1). The introduction of the Finance Bill cannot be opposed and it may be introduced without prior circulation of copies to Members. The scope of discussion on the Finance Bill is vast and the whole administration comes under review.

The procedure in respect of the Finance Bill is the same as in the case of other money bills. Only after the Finance Bill is passed and becomes the Finance Act, does the collection of revenues get legislative authority. A document titled *Memorandum Explaining the Provisions in the Finance Bill* is also presented along with the Finance Bill to facilitate easy appreciation of the taxation proposals made in the Finance Bill. As in the case of other bills, the presentation and passing of the Finance Bill involves a time lag. However, as the Finance Bill contains, *inter alia*, changes in duty rates on commodities, economic activities in the economy will get disrupted if these changes are made public but not implemented immediately. Hence, a mechanism exists under which those taxation proposals, where it will not be in public interest to defer bringing them into force forthwith, take effect immediately pending the passing of the Finance Bill. Under the Provisional Collection of Taxes Act, 1931, the Government is empowered to collect taxes for a period of 75 days or taking of decision by Parliament on the Bill, whichever is earlier. In a way, it sets out the time frame within which the budget authorisation process has to be completed in the Parliament.

A. Money Bills: Under Article 110(1), bills dealing with imposition, abolition, remission, alteration, or regulation of any tax or the regulation of the borrowing of money by the Government or the custody and payment of Government money are all money bills. [2] Money bills can be introduced only in the Lok Sabha. After a money bill has been passed by the Lok Sabha, it is sent to the Rajya Sabha for its recommendations. The Rajya Sabha cannot reject, amend or vote upon money bills. It can only offer recommendations which may or may not be accepted by the Lok Sabha. Also, the Rajya Sabha cannot take more than 14 days for considering the return of a money bill. Thus, in case a money bill is not returned to the Lok Sabha within 14 days, the bill is considered to have been passed by both the Houses. Therefore, the power of voting on money bills is limited to the directly elected Lok Sabha. Similarly, although the budget is presented before both Houses of Parliament, the demands for grants are submitted only to the Lok Sabha.

2.2.6 Supplementary Budget: It is likely that the forecasts on the basis of which the original budget was prepared go haywire due to exogenous factors (international economic crisis) and/or internal disturbances like industrial unrest, political instability etc. Government may then present to the Parliament a supplementary budget to deal with such shocks.

Furthermore, if a grant voted by the Parliament in accordance with the estimates presented in the budget for a particular service for the current financial year is found to be insufficient for the purpose of that year, the Government presents a *supplementary estimate* [Article 115(1)(a)] and the Parliament may make a *supplementary grant.* Also, the Government may approach the Parliament when a need has arisen during the current financial year for supplementary or additional expenditure on some *new service* not contemplated in the budget of that year. The supplementary demands for grants are presented to and passed by the House before the end of the financial year.

2.3 Execution of the Budget

Once the Appropriation Bill and the Finance Bill are passed, the executive departments get a green signal to collect revenue and spend money on approved schemes. Collection of revenue is the duty of the Revenue Department of the Ministry of Finance. This Department has two wings: the Central Board of Direct Taxes (CBDT) and the Central Board of Indirect Taxes and Customs (CBIC). There are detailed departmental rules governing the mode of assessment, collection and remittance of various taxes into Government treasury.

More important, however, is the executive control of public expenditure. Once the appropriations are voted and approved by the Parliament, spending authorities are authorised to draw the necessary amounts and spend them. Individual Ministries/Departments are informed by the Ministry of Finance about their respective budget allocations. All appropriated amounts lapse at the end of the financial year. Hence, they must be spent during the current financial year. Reappropriation between expenditure heads is allowed subject to prescribed rules in this regard. However, reappropriation between *voted* and *charged* items of expenditure is not allowed. Similarly, reappropriation is not permitted for meeting expenditure on a new service not provided for in the budget.

2.3.1 Maintenance of Accounts: The system of government accounts is a matter of great significance in any democratic country. The primary objective of government accounts is to facilitate the formulation, authorisation and the execution of the budget. The manner in which various items of receipt and expenditure are grouped and presented plays an important role in determining the character and quality of the decisions at various stages of the budgetary process. The adequacy and effectiveness of legislature over financial administration is chiefly determined by the form and contents of consolidated and classified financial statements.

The structure of the accounting system of the Central Government is primarily meant to satisfy the needs of Parliament and the executive including its subordinate agencies. The system ensures that the Parliament receives a full and reliable account of the funds provided to the executive.

An important feature of the accounting structure in India is its uniformity as between the transactions of the Central and the State Governments. This uniformity is intended to facilitate understanding and comparison of the variety of financial transactions both of the Centre and the States from one financial year to another.

Article 149 of the Constitution prescribes duties and powers of Comptroller and Auditor General (CAG). Under Article 150, CAG is required to prescribe the format in which the accounts of the Union and the States are to be kept. The estimates of receipts and disbursements in the budget and of expenditure in the demands for grants are shown according to this classification. The prescribed classification is intended to help the Parliament and the public to meaningfully scrutinise the allocation of resources and the purposes of Government expenditure.

Similarly, Article 151 requires the CAG to present reports relating to the accounts of the Union and the States.

CAG performs such duties and exercises such powers in relation to the accounts of the Union and of the States as may be prescribed by the Parliament. In exercise of this power, the Parliament enacted the Comptroller and Auditor-General (Duties, Powers, and Conditions of Service) Act, 1971 which after amendment in 1976, relieved him of his duty to prepare the accounts of the Union. The other important provisions relating to his duties are as follows:

1. To audit and report on all expenditure from the Consolidated Fund of India and of each State as to whether such expenditure has been in accordance with the law.
2. To audit and report on all expenditure from the Contingency Fund and the Public Account of the Union and of the States.
3. To audit and report on all trading, manufacturing, profit and loss accounts kept by any Department of the Union or a State.

Constitutional provisions have safeguarded the independence and freedom of the CAG and have placed him beyond political influences. He is an officer of the Constitution. Though appointed by the President, he may be removed on an address from both the Houses of Parliament on grounds of *proved misbehaviour* or *incapacity*. His salary and conditions of service are statutory, i.e. as laid down by the Parliament by law and are not liable to variations to his disadvantage during his term of office.

As already noted, the CAG continued to maintain accounts of the Central Government as well as of all the State Governments until 1976 when it was decided to relieve him of this responsibility in respect of Central Government accounts.

In October 1976, an organisation named Controller-General of Accounts (CGA) was set up to administer matters pertaining to the departmentalisation of accounts of the Union Government. This organisation which works as part of the Ministry of Finance performs, *inter alia*, the following main functions.

1. Prescribing the form of accounts relating to the Union and the State Governments.
2. Laying down accounting procedures.
3. Overseeing the maintenance of adequate standards of accounting by Central Accounts Offices.
4. Consolidation of the monthly and annual accounts of the Government of India.

5. Administration of rules under Article 283 of the Constitution relating to the custody of the Consolidated Fund of India, the Contingency Fund, and the Public Account.

The CGA prepares a condensed form of the Appropriation Accounts and the Finance Accounts of the Union Government.

Under a new system of *Integrated Financial Administration,* introduced with effect from October 1, 1976, the Secretary of a Ministry/Department acts as the chief accounting authority. He discharges his responsibilities through and with the assistance of the *Integrated Financial Adviser* of the Ministry/Department. It is the responsibility of the Integrated Financial Adviser to render financial advice, prepare the budget, distribute budget allocations among the various sections of the Ministry, arrange payments, compile and consolidate accounts, and also to ensure accuracy in accounts on the part of various sections of the Ministry/Department.

Under the Integrated Financial Adviser, there is a Controller of Accounts for each Ministry. The latter has under him, the Regional Pay and Accounts Officers functioning in various parts of the country. The banking business of each Ministry/Department is conducted by a designated public sector bank nominated by the RBI as its agent. The account of the Ministry/Department is operated with a branch of that public sector bank by the Pay and Accounts Officer of the Ministry/Department.

This departmentalised system of payments and accounts separates accounts from audit and provides for a separate Controller of Accounts for each Ministry. Under the old system, prevalent in the States, the primary responsibility for incurring and controlling expenditure and for maintaining accounts, rests with the departmental officers. The final accounts are compiled by the Indian Audit and Accounts Department from the initial accounts submitted by the departmental officers.

2.4 Auditing of Accounts

Preparation of accounts by CGA is not enough. It is necessary to verify the accuracy and completeness of the accounts and to ensure that the expenditure incurred has been sanctioned by the Parliament and that it has taken place in conformity with the rules sanctioned by the Parliament. Thus, the accounts prepared by CGA are audited by the CAG.

Audit of public expenditure is an ex-post check to ensure that the spending was within the budgeted amount and for the purpose intended. Audit in relation to government accounts has, at least, the following four functions:

1. **Appropriation Audit:** Its objective is to ascertain whether the amounts spent by the government have been applied to the purposes and within the limits set by the appropriations authorised by the legislature.
2. **Regulatory Audit:** It is concerned with ensuring that the various rules and regulations are fully adhered to by the spending agencies.
3. **Propriety Audit:** It includes within its scope an examination of the propriety (wisdom) of executive actions even where their legality is not in question.
4. **Efficiency Audit:** It examines the efficiency (economy) with which the agency under audit is discharging its financial responsibilities.

The appropriation audit and regulatory audit are the statutory duties of the CAG. The other two types of audit (propriety and efficiency) are discretionary in nature in the sense that it is left largely to CAG to determine whether and to what extent he should extend his audit into these areas.

The audited accounts are placed on the table of both the Houses of Parliament along with the CAG report. The CAG is responsible for auditing all expenditure of the Central and State Governments and submitting his audit reports to the President or the Governor for being placed before the appropriate legislature. The report of the CAG amounts to the issuance of a *certificate*. The *observations* of the CAG summarise objections and irregularities in relation to voted and charged expenditures in the budget.

Thus, the audit department scrutinises, independently and fearlessly, the expenditure incurred by the Central and State Governments and seeks to ensure that expenditure is not irregularly and wastefully incurred. In this manner it assists the legislature in exercising financial control over the executive.

Endnotes

1. Although Railways are a Department of the Government, traditionally the detailed railway budget was presented separately (up to 2016-17) to the Parliament about 2 to 3 days in advance of the General Budget. However, the total of the receipts and expenditure of the Railways was incorporated in the budget statement of the Government of India.
2. If any question arises whether a bill is a money bill or not, the decision of the Speaker of the Lok Sabha is final in this regard. When a bill is sent to the Rajya Sabha or is presented for the assent of the President it bears the endorsement of the Speaker that it is a money bill. This is one of the special powers of the Speaker.

3

Contents and Explanation of Budget Documents

The budget is presented in the Lok Sabha. Simultaneously, a copy of the budget is laid on the table of the Rajya Sabha. The list of Budget Documents presented to the Parliament is as under:

1. Budget Speech of the Finance Minister.
2. Annual Financial Statement.
3. Demands for Grants.
4. Finance Bill.
5. Macroeconomic Framework Statement.
6. Medium-term Fiscal Policy-cum-Fiscal Policy Strategy Statement.
7. Expenditure Budget.
8. Receipts Budget.
9. Expenditure Profile.
10. Memorandum Explaining the Provisions in the Finance Bill.
11. Budget at a Glance.
12. Output Outcome Monitoring Framework.
13. Key Features of Budget.
14. Implementation of Budget Announcements (preceding year).

The documents shown at serial numbers 2, 3 and 4 are mandated by Articles 112, 113, and 110(a) of the Constitution of India respectively.

Documents at serial numbers 5 and 6 are presented as per provisions of the Fiscal Responsibility and Budget Management Act, 2003.

Other documents are in the nature of explanatory statements supporting the mandated documents with narrative in a user-friendly format suited for quick or contextual references.

3.1 Budget Speech of the Finance Minister

Budget is presented to the Parliament by the Finance Minister on the first working day of February at around 11.00 A.M. The proceedings of the day start and end with the budget speech of the Finance Minister.

The Finance Minister will start with a review of the economic situation in the current year. He then outlines the economic policy of the government in the ensuing year. Then he presents the revised estimates for the current year and reasons for changes in receipts/expenditure, if any. Then he proposes measures for additional resource mobilisation (ARM). This may include new taxes or enhancement of rates of existing taxes. He also proposes tax concession wherever required. He then summarises the net effect of his tax proposals.

3.2 Annual Financial Statement

Article 112 of the Constitution provides for an Annual Financial Statement (popularly know as budget) of estimated receipts and expenditure of the Government of India to be laid before both the Houses of Parliament in respect of every financial year (which runs from April 1 to March 31 of the following year). Further, Article 112(2) states, "The estimates of expenditure embodied in the Annual Financial Statement shall show separately: (a) the sums required to meet expenditure described by this Constitution as expenditure charged upon the Consolidated Fund of India; and (b) the sums required to meet other expenditure proposed to be made from the Consolidated fund of India, and shall distinguish expenditure on revenue account from other expenditure".

Thus, the Annual Financial Statement distinguishes between: (i) the sums required to meet expenditure described by the Constitution as expenditure charged upon the Consolidated Fund of India and (ii) the sums required to meet other expenditure proposed to be made from the Consolidated Fund.

Similarly, the Annual Financial Statement has to distinguish expenditure on revenue account from other expenditure. In other words, the Constitution requires revenue and capital expenditures to be shown separately in the budget. The distinction between revenue and capital expenditures is not only a constitutional requirement but also an essential ingredient for policy formulation and efficient resource allocation. The revenue and capital sections put together make the Union Budget.

Hence, Union Budget can be demarcated into the part pertaining to revenue which is for ease of reference termed as Revenue Budget and the part pertaining to capital which is for ease of reference termed as Capital Budget.

In fact, Annual Financial Statement is the basic budget document. [1] It sets forth receipts and expenditures of the Government for three consecutive years. It gives details of the actual receipts and expenditures for the preceding year, revised estimates for the current year and causes for such revisions, and the budget estimates for the ensuing year. For example, Annual Financial Statement presented to the Parliament on February 1, 2020 showed actual receipts and expenditures for the year 2018-19, revised estimates for the year 2019-20 and budget estimates for the year 2020-21.

3.2.1 Accounts of the Government: The Annual Financial Statement shows the receipts and payments of the Government under the following three parts.

A. Consolidated Fund of India: It draws its existence from Article 266 of the Constitution. This is the reservoir into which all revenues received by the Government, all loans raised by the Government, and all money received by the Government in repayment of loans are paid. All expenditure of the Government is incurred from this Fund and no amount can be withdrawn from this Fund without authorisation from the Parliament. Whether the expenditure is charged on the Consolidated Fund or it is an amount voted by the Lok Sabha, no money can be issued out of this Fund unless the expenditure is authorised by an Appropriation Act.

B. Contingency Fund: Article 267 of the Constitution authorizes the existence of this Fund which is like an imprest placed at the disposal of the President of India to facilitate meeting of urgent unforeseen expenditures by the Government pending authorization from the Parliament. Parliamentary approval for such unforeseen expenditures is obtained ex-post-facto (subsequently), and an equivalent amount is drawn from the Consolidated Fund to recoup the Contingency Fund after such approval. From 1976, the corpus of the Contingency Fund authorised by the Parliament remained at the level of ₹ 50 crore. However, in the wake of Tsunami experience, the corpus of the Fund was raised from ₹ 50 crore to ₹ 500 crore as part of the budgetary exercise for the year 2005-06.

C. Public Account: Apart from the normal receipts and expenditures of the Government which relate to the Consolidated Fund, certain other transactions enter Government accounts. Moneys held by Government in trust are kept in the Public Account. For instance, transactions relating to provident funds, small saving collections, reserve/special funds etc. belong to this category where the Government acts more as a banker. These moneys, as a matter of fact, do not belong to the Government and have to be finally paid back to the persons who deposited them. Therefore, moneys thus received are kept in the Public Account and the concerned disbursements are also made therefrom. Parliamentary authorisation for payments from the Public Account is, therefore, not required.

However, approval of the Parliament is obtained when amounts are withdrawn from the Consolidated Fund and kept in the Public Account for expenditure on specific purposes such as primary education. The actual expenditure on the specific purpose is again submitted for vote of the Parliament for withdrawal from the Public Account for incurring expenditure on the specific purpose.

Estimates of receipts and disbursements in the Annual Financial Statement are shown according to the accounting classification referred to under Article 150 of the Constitution.

3.3 Demands for Grants

Article 113 provides that expenditure charged upon the Consolidated Fund of India shall not be submitted to the vote of Parliament, but there is no objection to discussion thereon in either House of Parliament.

The voted portion of the estimates of expenditure shall be submitted in the form of demands for grants to the Lok Sabha, who shall have power to assent, or to refuse to assent, to any demand or to assent to any demand subject to a reduction of the amount specified therein.

3.4 Finance Bill

It is expressly laid down in the Constitution that no tax shall be levied or collected except by the authority of law (Article 265). The regular budget contains proposals with regard to both direct and indirect taxes. These proposals regarding the levy of new taxes, modifications in the existing tax structure or continuance of existing rates of taxation for a further period are presented through the Finance Bill.

3.5 Macroeconomic Framework Statement

The Macroeconomic Framework Statement, as enjoined by the FRBM Act, 2003 contains an assessment of the growth prospects of the economy along with specific underlying assumptions. It also contains an assessment regarding the GDP growth rate, fiscal balance of the Central Government and the external sector balance of the economy.

3.6 Medium-term Fiscal Policy-cum-Fiscal Policy Strategy Statement

This statement is presented to Parliament under section 3 of the FRBM Act. It sets out the three-year rolling targets for six specific fiscal indicators in relation to GDP at market prices, namely: (a) fiscal deficit, (b) revenue deficit, (c) primary deficit, (d) tax revenue, (e) non-tax revenue and (e) Central Government debt. The statement includes underlying assumptions, an assessment of the balance between revenue receipts and revenue expenditure and the use of capital receipts including market borrowings for the creation of productive assets. It also outlines for the existing financial year, the strategic priorities of the Government relating to taxation, expenditure, lending and investments, administered pricing, borrowings and guarantees. It explains how the current fiscal policies are in conformity with sound fiscal management principles and gives the rationale for any major deviation in key fiscal measures.

3.7 Expenditure Budget

The provisions made for a scheme or a programme may be spread over a number of major heads in the revenue and capital sections in a demand for grants. In the Expenditure Budget, the estimates made for a scheme/programme are brought together and shown on a net basis on revenue and capital basis at one place. To understand the objectives underlying the expenditure proposed for various schemes and programmes in the Expenditure Budget, suitable explanatory notes are included in this volume.

3.8 Receipts Budget

Estimates of receipts included in the Annual Financial Statement are further analysed in the document Receipts Budget. The document provides details of tax and non-tax revenue receipts and capital receipts and explains the estimates. The document also provides a statement on the arrears of tax revenues and non-tax revenues, as mandated under the Fiscal Responsibility and Budget Management Rules, 2004. Trend of receipts and expenditure along with deficit indicators, statement pertaining to National Small Savings Fund (NSSF), Statement of Liabilities, Statement of Guarantees given by the Government, statements of assets and details of external assistance are also included in Receipts Budget. This also includes the Statement of Revenue Impact of Tax Incentives under the Central tax system which seeks to list the revenue impact of tax incentives that are proposed by the Central Government. [2]

This document also shows liabilities of the Government on account of securities (bonds) issued in lieu of oil and fertilizer subsidies in the past. This was earlier called 'Statement of Revenue Foregone' and brought out as a separate statement in 2015-16. This has been merged in the Receipts Budget from 2016-17 onwards.

3.9 Expenditure Profile

This document gives an aggregation of various types of expenditure and certain other items across demands.

Railways are the principal departmentally-run commercial undertaking of Government. The Budget of the Ministry of Railways and the Demands for Grants relating to Railway expenditure are presented to the Parliament together with the Union Budget from the financial year 2017-18 onwards. The Expenditure Profile has a separate section on Railways to capture all the salient aspects of the demand for grants of Railways and other details of interest regarding Railways. The total receipts and expenditure of the Railways are, incorporated in the Annual Financial Statement of the Government of India. Details of other commercially run departmental under takings are also shown in a statement. Expenditure is depicted in the Expenditure Profile and Expenditure Budget, net of receipts of the Departmental Commercial Undertakings, in order to avoid overstatement of both receipts and expenditure.

The receipts and expenditure of the Ministry of Defence Demands shown in the Annual Financial Statement, are explained in greater detail in the document Defence Services Estimates presented with the Detailed Demands for Grants of the Ministry of Defence.

The details of grants given to bodies other than State and Union Territory Governments are given in the statements of Grants-in-aid paid to non-Government bodies appended to Detailed Demands for Grants of the various Ministries.

3.10 Memorandums Explaining the Provisions in the Finance Bill

To facilitate understanding of the taxation proposals contained in the Finance Bill, the provisions and their implications are explained in the document titled Memorandum Explaining the Provisions in the Finance Bill.

3.11 Budget at a Glance

This document shows in brief, receipts and disbursements along with broad details of tax revenues and other receipts. This document provides details of resources transferred by the Central Government to State and Union Territory Governments. This document also shows the revenue deficit, the gross primary deficit and the gross fiscal deficit of the Central Government. The excess of Government's revenue expenditure over revenue receipts constitutes revenue deficit of Government. The difference between the total expenditure of Government by way of revenue, capital receipts and loans net of repayments on the one hand and revenue receipts of Government and capital receipts which are not in the nature of borrowing but which accrue to Government on the other, constitutes gross fiscal deficit. Gross primary deficit is gross fiscal deficit reduced by the gross interest payments.

In the Budget documents *gross fiscal deficit* and *gross primary deficit* have been referred to in abbreviated form *fiscal deficit* and *primary deficit*, respectively.

The document also includes a statement indicating the quantum and nature (share in Central Taxes, grants/loan) of the total Resources transferred to States and Union

Territory Governments. Details of these transfers by way of share of taxes, grants-in-aid and loans are given in Expenditure Profile. Bulk of grants and loans to States are disbursed by the Ministry of Finance and are included in the Demand 'Transfers to States' and in the Demand 'Transfer to Delhi' and 'Transfer to Puducherry'. The grants and loans released to States and Union Territories by other Ministries/Departments are reflected in their respective Demands.

3.12 Output Outcome Monitoring Framework

Prior to 2007-08, Performance Budget [3] and the Outcome Budget were presented to Parliament separately by Ministries/Departments. With effect from Financial Year 2007-08, the Performance Budget and the Outcome Budget were merged and presented as a single document titled "Outcome Budget" in respect of each Ministry/Department. From Financial Year 2017-18 onwards, the Outcome Budgets of all Ministries have been combined into one single document brought out by the Ministry of Finance in collaboration with the NITI Aayog. The Outcome Budget broadly indicates the outcomes of the financial budget of a Ministry/Department, indicating actual deliverables linked with outlays targeted during the year and in the medium-term.

Outcome Budget contains a brief introductory note on the organization and function of the Ministry/Department, list of major programmes/schemes implemented by the Ministry/Department, its mandate, goal and policy framework, budget estimates, scheme-wise analysis of physical performance and linkage between financial outlays and outcome, review covering overall trends in expenditure vis-à-vis budget estimates in recent years, review of performance of statutory and autonomous bodies under the administrative control of the Ministry/Department, reform measures, targets and achievements and plan for future refinements. As far as feasible, coverage of women and SC/ST beneficiaries under various developmental schemes and schemes for the benefit of North Eastern Region are also separately indicated.

Outcome Budget with Output-Outcome Monitoring Framework (OOMF) for Central Sector Schemes (CSs) and Centrally Sponsored Schemes(CSSs), with financial outlay of ₹ 500 crore each, is prepared by the respective Ministry/Department and the same is presented in the Parliament along with the Detailed Demand for Grants (DDG).

3.13 Key Features of Budget

The document is a snapshot summary of the economic vision of the Government and the major policy initiatives in the thrust areas of the economy for growth and welfare. Major milestones achieved in fiscal consolidation and management of the Government finances along with a bird's eye view of the key budget proposals for the ensuing fiscal year are also included in the document.

3.14 Implementation of Budget Announcements

This document summarizes the status of implementation of the announcements made by the Finance Minister in the Budget Speech of the previous year.

3.15 Budget-related Documents

3.15.1 Economic and Functional Classification of the Central Government Budget: The Budget reflects and shapes, and is, in turn, shaped by the country's economy. For a better appreciation of the impact of government receipts and expenditure on the other sectors of the economy, it is necessary to group them in terms of certain economic magnitudes, for example, how much is set aside for capital formation, how much is spent directly by the Government and how much is transferred by Government to other sectors of the economy by way of grants, loans, etc. This analysis is contained in the Economic and Functional Classification of the Central Government Budget which is brought out by the Ministry of Finance separately.

3.15.2 Economic Survey: The Economic Survey brings out the economic trends in the country which facilitates a better appreciation of the mobilisation of resources and their allocation in the Budget. The Survey analyses the trends in agricultural and industrial production, infrastructure, employment, money supply, prices, imports, exports, foreign exchange reserves and other relevant economic factors which have a bearing on the Budget, and is presented to the Parliament ahead of the Budget for the ensuing year. The Budget of the Central Government is not merely a statement of receipts and expenditure. Since Independence, it has become a significant statement of government policy.

3.15.3 Annual Report: A descriptive account of the activities of each Ministry and Department during a year is given in the document Annual Report which is brought out separately by each Ministry/Department and circulated to Members of Parliament at the time of discussion on the Demands for Grants.

3.16 Financial Emergency

The normal financial relations between the Union and the States under Articles 268 to 279 are subject to modifications in different kinds of emergencies. Thus, while an emergency (security of India) under Article 352(1) is in operation, the President may suspend, for a period not extending beyond the expiration of the financial year in which the emergency ceases to operate, all or any of the provisions relating to the division of taxes between the Union and the States and grants-in-aid (Article 354). In that event, the States will be left with their revenue under List II (State List) of the Seventh Schedule.

Under Article 360(1) of the Constitution, if the President is satisfied that a situation has arisen whereby the financial stability or credit of India or any part of the territory is threatened, he may make a proclamation of financial emergency. During the period of operation of such a proclamation:

1. The executive authority of the Union shall extend to the giving of directions to any State to observe such canons of financial propriety as may be specified in the directions.
2. Any such direction may also include:

(i) a provision requiring the reduction of salaries and allowances of all or any class of persons serving in connection with the affairs of the State,

(ii) a provision requiring all money bills or other financial bills to be reserved for the consideration of the President after they are passed by the State Legislature.

3. The President may also issue directions for the reduction of salaries and allowances of all or any class of persons serving in connection with the affairs of the Union including the judges of the Supreme Court and High Courts.

Endnotes

1. Under Article 202 of the Constitution, a similar type of financial statement for each State is presented before the legislature of that State.
2. Tax foregone on account of exemptions/concessions (also known as tax expenditures) is estimated. In the case of corporates, deduction on account of accelerated depreciation, deduction for export profits of export-oriented units and units located in software technology parks, and for profits of businesses in the power and telecom sectors are some of the major incentives.

   Tax foregone on account of exemptions under personal income tax is estimated in terms of deductions on account of certain eligible savings, investments, and expenditures under various provisions of the Income Tax Act, 1961.

   In indirect taxes, the difference between the tariff rates (i.e. the rates mentioned in the schedules of the Acts governing customs and central excise) and the effective rates that are operationalized by notifications issued from time to time constitutes the tax expenditure. Some of these exemptions are area-based or based on the category of business groups or individual items (tariff heads) under central excise or customs tariffs.

   The high levels of tax expenditure broadly indicate the plethora of exemptions and a complex tax regime. There is merit in rationalizing and minimizing them. However, these tax expenditure quantifications indicate the extent of revenue foregone under certain assumptions and simplifications. It would be inappropriate to conclude that these revenues could have actually accrued but for the exemptions and hence constitute revenue loss. One of them being that revenue is directly proportional to the rate of duty. As such, revenue foregone is to a large extent notional. Besides, lower effective rates offer the required protection for productive sectors and also facilitate the economy's competitiveness which in turn increases the tax base. Even in the case of excise on manufacture, the exemptions help achieve specific purposes and removal of exemptions would not, ipso facto, result in the same quantum of additional revenues as prices and altered demand conditions affect actual accrual.

   Tax expenditures encompass tax provisions which pertain to voluntary and involuntary activities of taxpayers. They are distinguished from 'tax incentives' which deal only with the voluntary actions of the taxpayers. Thus, while all tax incentives are tax expenditures, all tax expenditures are not tax incentives. For example, under section 88 of the Indian Income Tax Act, 1961, compulsory subscription to provident fund is eligible for tax credit in the same manner as voluntary premium paid for life insurance. The former, though tax expenditure, is not a tax incentive because it in no way influences the behaviour of individual saver. The latter, of course, is a tax incentive. See S. Surrey, *Pathways to Reforms: The Concept of Tax Expenditures* (Cambridge: Harvard University Press, 1973).
3. **Performance Budgets:** In the context of India's Five Year Plans, accountability was not merely confined to ensuring spending of funds for the various purposes and within the limits laid down in the budget. It also extended to ensuring that the expected results were achieved. The budget should help to reveal that whatever was proposed to be done during the year was actually achieved both in financial and physical terms. Performance budgeting shifts the

emphasis from the means of accomplishment to the accomplishment itself. With this intention in view, performance budgets were introduced in India as an adjunct to the Central budget in 1968-69. Initially, these were prepared and circulated to Members of Parliament in respect of a few Departments/organisations. Since 1975-76, all the Central Ministries and Departments dealing with developmental activities prepared performance budgets which were presented to the Parliament as a supplementary document to the traditional budget. Performance budgets were meant to serve as an instrument of administrative and financial control in the implementation of development programmes. They supplemented the conventional budgeting done by Ministries/Departments.

Performance budgets of the various Ministries/Departments were documents in terms of their functions, programmes, and activities/projects. For example, health is a function, malaria eradication a programme, and training of personnel for this purpose an activity. Projects generally refer to activities of capital nature, e.g. construction of a hospital building.

Performance budgets explained the scope and objectives of the schemes, their estimated cost, physical targets, achievements, reasons for shortfalls if any, cost-benefit analysis, standards of performance, and a summary of staff employed for the purpose. Moreover, performance budgets of the various Ministries/Departments also contained statements of various public sector undertakings under the charge of respective Ministries. These statements showed physical targets, achievements, details of inventory, sources of funds and their utilisation, return on capital, details of installed and utilised capacity. In short, performance budgets provided a link between financial allocations and physical achievements by the concerned spending agency.

Unfortunately, implementation of performance budgeting was not very successful in India. As a pre-requisite for success, performance budgeting requires determination of norms and standards of performance on a scientific basis so that performance could be measured without any arbitrariness. This task proved difficult with regard to many activities undertaken by the Government. There is a view that very few of governmental activities are susceptible of any physical measurement. Performance budgets can be most appropriately associated with things which government does, rather than the things which government buys. Moreover, it is difficult to evolve norms and standards for uniform application in a vast country like India with geographical variations.

As a result, performance budgets were merely an annual ritual much less a management tool for monitoring of various projects and schemes of the Government.

4

Parliamentary Control over the Budget

Parliament exercises control over both receipts and expenditure of the Central Government. By passing Appropriation Bill and the Finance Bill, the Parliament authorises the Government to collect revenues and spend money. However, the authority of the Parliament is not limited only to sanctioning appropriations. Rather, it has the means to ensure that the appropriations have been applied towards the purposes approved and within the limits imposed. For the sake of this completeness of legislative control, the Parliament constitutes its following three financial committees:

1. Public Accounts Committee.
2. Estimates Committee.
3. Committee on Public Undertakings.

A brief description of the functions of each of these committees is as follows.

4.1 Public Accounts Committee

After the report of the Comptroller and Auditor-General (CAG) is laid before the Parliament, it is examined by the Public Accounts Committee. It is a Parliamentary Committee with a non-official chairman appointed by the Speaker from amongst the members elected to the Committee. The Committee consists of 22 members: 15 members elected by the Lok Sabha from amongst its members, and 7 members of the Rajya Sabha elected by that House from amongst its members every year. To ensure that each party/group is represented on the Committee, the election is held on the basis of proportional representation system by means of single transferable vote. The term of office of the members of the Committee is one year.

Being an all-party Committee, it scrutinises the accounts and audit reports prepared by the CAG to satisfy itself that: (a) the moneys shown in the accounts as having been disbursed were legally available for, and applicable to, the service or purpose for which they have been applied or charged, (b) the expenditure conforms to the authority which governs it and (c) every re-appropriation has been made in this behalf under the rules framed by a competent authority.

The Committee also examines two reports of the CAG on revenue receipts: one relating to direct taxes, and the other pertaining to indirect taxes. While scrutinising these reports, the Committee examines cases involving under-assessments, tax evasion, and also identifies loopholes in tax laws/procedures, and makes recommendations to plug leakages of revenue.

Though normally the Committee confines itself to matters contained in audit reports, it can of its own accord inquire into irregularities which may be brought to its notice or which become of wider public interest. The Committee, however, does not examine the accounts relating to such public undertakings as are allotted to the Committee on Public Undertakings.

Since the work of the Committee is normally confined to the various matters referred to in the audit reports and appropriations accounts, its functions start only after these reports and accounts are laid on the table of the House. In view of the time constraint, the Committee selects important paragraphs from these reports for examination during its term of office. A number of working groups are constituted by the Chairman from amongst the members of the Committee for detailed examination of the subjects selected by the Committee and for considering procedural matters. A sub-committee is also constituted for scrutiny of the action taken by the Government on the recommendations contained in the previous reports of the Committee.

The Committee calls for advance information from the Ministries/Departments with regard to subjects selected by it for examination. It may also undertake on-the-spot study tours of various Departments connected with the subjects taken up for examination. For this purpose, members of the Committee are divided into study groups and each study tour is undertaken with the specific approval of the Speaker.

One of the important functions of the Committee is to find out whether any money has been spent on a service in excess of the amount granted by the House for the purpose. If so, the Committee examines the same with reference to the facts of each case, and the circumstances leading to such excess expenditure. Such excess expenditures are brought up before the House by the Government for regularisation in the manner prescribed in Article 115 of the Constitution. Similarly, the findings of the Committee on a subject are contained in its report which is presented by the Chairman to the Lok Sabha so that the irregularities noticed are discussed and remedial steps taken thereof. A copy of the report is also laid on the table of the Rajya Sabha.

After presentation to the Lok Sabha, the report is forwarded to the Ministry/Department concerned which is required to take action on the findings/recommendations contained in the report and furnish Action Taken Replies thereon within six months. Action Taken Notes received from the Ministries/Departments are examined by the Action Taken Sub-Committee. The Action Taken Reports of the Committee are presented to the House. Furthermore, replies received from the Government in respect of recommendations contained in the Action Taken Reports are also laid on the table of the House in the form of statements.

4.2 Estimates Committee

To suggest economy and efficiency in public expenditure, the Lok Sabha constitutes the Estimates Committee every year. The first such Committee was constituted in 1950. The members of the Committee are elected every year from amongst the members of the Lok Sabha according to the principle of proportional representation by means of single transferable vote. Originally, the Committee consisted of 25 members but from the year 1956-57 the membership was raised to 30 to facilitate the constitution of sub-committees and study groups for taking up intensive examination of various estimates. The Chairman of the Committee is appointed by the Speaker from amongst the members of the Lok Sabha elected to the Committee. The term of office of the members of the Committee is one year.

Though the Committee is known as Estimates Committee, it does not examine the budget estimates presented to Parliament. It is concerned with *estimates* only after they have been presented to the House. The purpose of the Estimates Committee is to ensure that public expenditure is incurred in a judicious manner and that the objectives underlying the plans and schemes are effectively achieved. In a sense, it is a mechanism to extend parliamentary control over Government expenditure beyond the granting of appropriations. Thus, the Committee examines in detail the estimates presented to the House, makes appraisals of the plans and programmes, and reviews the performance of public expenditure in various fields. In view of these objectives, it has to discharge the following responsibilities:

1. To report what economies, improvements in organisational efficiency, or administrative reforms consistent with the policy underlying the estimates, may be effected.
2. To suggest alternative policies in order to bring about efficiency and economy in administration.
3. To examine whether the money is well laid out within the limits of the policy implied in the estimates.
4. To suggest the form in which the estimates shall be presented to the Parliament.

Public undertakings allotted to the Committee on Public Undertakings are outside the purview of the Estimates Committee.

The scrutiny by the Committee of the estimates for the various Ministries/Departments is a continuing exercise throughout the financial year and the Committee reports to the House as its scrutiny proceeds. It is not incumbent on the Committee to examine the entire estimates of the Union Government in its term of one year. Therefore, it takes up only selected subjects for examination which are of current importance or which it may consider necessary to bring to the notice of the House. The subjects selected by the Committee are widely publicised in newspapers, and experts and the general public are invited to send memoranda to the Committee giving their views and suggestions on these subjects.

A number of study groups are constituted by the Chairman from amongst the members of the Committee for detailed scrutiny of the subjects selected by the Committee. The Committee calls for preliminary material from Ministries/Departments concerned in regard to the subjects selected by it for scrutiny and it also undertakes on-the-spot study tours, with the specific approval of the Speaker, of various institutions/organisations connected with the subjects taken up for examination. The findings of the Committee on a subject are contained in its report which is presented by the Chairman to the Lok Sabha.

After presentation to the Lok Sabha, the report is forwarded to the Ministry/Department concerned which is required to take action on the recommendations contained in the report and furnish Action Taken Replies within six months. The Action Taken Notes received from the Ministries/Departments are examined by the Action Taken Study Group, and Action Taken Reports of the Committee are, in turn, presented to the House. Replies received from the Government in respect of the recommendations contained in the Action Taken Reports are laid on the table of the Lok Sabha in the form of statements.

4.3 Committee on Public Undertakings

Soon after the commencement of the Constitution in 1950, there grew a demand for a separate Parliamentary Committee to review the working of public sector undertakings which were being financed from out of the Consolidated Fund of India. After a long debate, the Committee was ultimately set up in 1964. The Committee on Public Undertakings consists of 22 members: 15 elected by the Lok Sabha and 7 by the Rajya Sabha from amongst their members according to the principle of proportional representation by means of single transferable vote. The Chairman of the Committee is appointed by the Speaker from amongst the members of the Lok Sabha elected to the Committee. The term of office of the members of the Committee is one year.

The Committee is charged with the task of scrutinising the reports and accounts of public undertakings, the reports of the CAG on such undertakings, and to suggest economies, improvements in organisation/management and production that could be effected in various undertakings. Keeping in mind issues of current interest regarding public sector, the Committee selects for detailed examination such undertakings as it may deem fit. It pays particular attention to those undertakings which come under a cloud in the audit reports of the CAG. The Committee may also examine such subjects or matters which may be specifically referred to it by the House or by the Speaker. However, it is barred from examining and investigating matters of major Government policy as distinct from business or commercial functions of public undertakings.

A number of study groups are constituted by the Chairman from amongst members of the Committee for carrying out detailed examination of various subjects selected by the Committee. The Committee calls for preliminary material from the Ministries/Public Undertakings regarding the working of public undertakings selected for examination. The Committee may also call for memoranda on the subject under examination from non-official organisations and individuals who are knowledgeable in the subject under examination by the Committee. It may also undertake on-the-spot study tours of various public undertakings connected with the subjects taken up for examination.

The findings of the Committee on a subject are contained in its report which is presented by the Chairman to the Lok Sabha. A copy of the report is also laid on the table of the Rajya Sabha. After presentation to the Lok Sabha, the report is forwarded to the Ministry/Department concerned which is required to take action on the recommendations contained in the report and furnish Action Taken Replies thereon within six months. These replies are examined by the Action Taken Sub-Committee, and the Action Taken Reports of the Committee are presented to the House. Replies received from Government in respect of recommendations contained in the Action Taken Reports are also laid on the table of the house in the form of statements.

The three Committees mentioned above are instruments of Parliamentary control over government finances. However, it is noteworthy that this control is indirect in the form of influence, advice, scrutiny and criticism.

5

Components and Structure of Central Government Budget 2021-22

In India, the budget and accounts of the government are classified into revenue and capital portions. This distinction is governed by various constitutional and rule provisions on the subject. [1]

Article 112(2) of the Constitution requires that "The estimates of expenditure embodied in the annual financial statement shall show separately:

(a) The sums required to meet expenditure described by this Constitution as expenditure charged upon the Consolidated Fund of India; and

(b) The sums required to meet other expenditure proposed to be made from the Consolidated Fund of India, and shall distinguish expenditure on revenue account from other expenditure".

The same provision is repeated in Article 202 for the States.

In simple words, the Constitution requires revenue and capital expenditures to be shown separately in the budget. The distinction between revenue and capital expenditures is not only a constitutional requirement but also an essential ingredient for policy formulation and efficient resource allocation. Therefore, the budget is presented in two parts: revenue budget and capital budget.

Similarly, clause 2(e) of Fiscal Responsibility and Budget Management Act, 2003 indicates two components of expenditure in the government: (a) the revenue expenditure, and (b) those which result into increase in assets of the government. The Act aims to ensure inter-generational equity in fiscal management and long-term macroeconomic stability by achieving sufficient revenue surplus.

However, this classification has also given rise to some issues. For example, the revenue-capital classification may be dysfunctional from an economic management perspective. Over the years, essential maintenance expenditure has become a casualty of the revenue–capital distinction.

5.1 Revenue Budget

Revenue budget shows revenue receipts of the government and the expenditure met from these revenues. It thus consists of: (a) revenue receipts and (b) revenue expenditure.

Table 5.1 shows the composition of revenue budget of the Central Government for the year 2021-22.

5.1.1 Revenue Receipts: Receipts of the government which are non-redeemable are termed as revenue receipts. These receipts are divided under two heads:

1. Tax revenues.
2. Non-tax revenues.

Table 5.1: Composition of Revenue Budget of the Central Government, 2021-22

(₹ crore)

Revenue receipts		Revenue expenditure	
1. Tax revenue		Total revenue expenditure of which	29,29,000
Gross tax revenue	22,17,059	1. Interest payment	8,09,701
a. Corporation tax	5,47,000	2. Major subsidies	3,35,361
b. Taxes on income	5,61,000	a. Fertilizers	79,530
c. Customs duties	1,36,000	b. Food	2,42,836
d. Union excise duties	3,35,000	c. Petroleum	12,995
e. Service tax@	1,000	3. Grants-in-aid of creation of capital assets	2,19,112
f. GST of which	6,30,000		
i. CGST	5,30,000		
ii. IGST	---		
iii. Compensation cess	1,00,000		
g. Taxes of Union Territories	7,059		
Less: NCCD transferred to NCCF/NDRF	6,100		
Less: States' share	6,65,563		
1a. Centre's net tax revenue	15,45,397		
2. Non-tax revenue	2,43,028		
a. Interest receipts	11,541		
b. Dividends and profits	1,03,538		
c. External grants	747		
d. Other non-tax revenue	1,24,671		
e. Receipts of Union Territories	2,531		
3. Total revenue receipts (1a + 2)	17,88,424		
Revenue deficit* = 29,29,000 − 17,88,424 = 11,40,576			
Effective revenue deficit = 11,40,576 − 2,19,112 = 9,21,464**			

NCCD = National Calamity Contingent Duty.

NCCF = National Calamity Contingency Fund.

NDRF = National Disaster Relief Fund

@ Service tax was abolished by Section 17 of Constitution (One Hundred and First Amendment) Act, 2016 to pave way for the introduction of GST from July 1, 2017. Revenue represents arrears of the tax.

*Revenue deficit = Total revenue expenditure − Total revenue receipts

**Effective revenue deficit = Revenue deficit − Grants-in-aid of creation of capital assets

Source: Government of India, Ministry of Finance, Budget Papers 2021-22, *Budget at a Glance*.

A. Tax Revenues: Tax revenues comprise proceeds of taxes and duties levied by the Union. Estimates of tax revenues in the budget are based on the projected percent increase in nominal gross domestic product (GDP). Nominal growth is a measure of GDP without adjusting for inflation. If GDP growth is less than the projected, tax revenue targets will not be met which may lead to higher fiscal deficit than the budgeted one. Estimates of tax revenues also take into account the effects of taxation proposals made in the Finance Bill. Tax revenue has always occupied a dominant place in the revenue receipts of the government. From revenue angle, there are four important Central taxes, viz. income tax, goods and services tax (GST), Union excise duties and customs duties. The proceeds of these taxes are shared with the States.

The relative importance of different taxes and duties is shown in Table 5.1. Gross tax revenue was estimated at ₹ 22,17,059 crore in the budget for 2021-22. Net tax revenue of the Centre (i.e. net of States' share) was placed at ₹ 15,45,397 crore and the non-tax revenue of the Centre at ₹ 2,43,028 crore in the same budget. The two items put together composed the revenue receipts of the Central Government (₹ 17,88,424 crore), giving a ratio between tax and non-tax revenue of 86.4:13.6 (Table 5.1).

B. Non-tax Revenues: Non-tax revenues of the Government mainly consist of interest and dividends on investments made by the Government, and fee and other receipts for services rendered by it.

Receipts on account of interest on loans by the Central Government represent the most important source of non-tax revenue. These receipts comprise interest on loans to State Governments and Union Territories (UTs), interest payable by the Railways, the Department of Telecommunications, and *other interest receipts* which include interest on loans advanced to public sector enterprises, port trusts and other statutory bodies, co-operatives and Government servants.

The main items under the head *dividends and profits* include profits of the Reserve Bank of India, profits from nationalised banks, and the Life Insurance Corporation of India, dividends from the General Insurance Corporation, the Industrial Development Bank of India, and from other public sector companies and financial institutions.

The category *other non-tax revenue* includes a number of sub-heads, each comprising a large number of items. The sub-heads are: fiscal services, other general services, social services, economic services, and grants-in-aid and contributions.

Revenues from *fiscal services* include profits from circulation of coins, representing the difference between the face value of coins and their manufacturing cost, receipts relating to refining and assaying charges levied by the mints, and penalties realised against economic offences.

Receipts from *other general services* include examination fees of the Union Public Service Commission, receipts of police on account of Central Police Forces supplied to State Governments, sale of forms, gazettes, audit fees, passport and visa fees.

Then there are receipts from various social and community services, e.g. receipts from commercial services of Akashvani and Doordarshan, entry fees at museums and ancient monuments, and charges realised from patients for hospital and dispensary services.

Receipts under the head *economic services* relate to animal husbandry, dairy development, fisheries, forests, transport and communications, ports, lighthouses, tourism, roads and bridges, and import and export licence application fees. Lastly, there are cash grants-in-aid from foreign countries and international organisations.

5.1.2 Revenue Expenditure: Revenue expenditure relates to the normal running of the government departments and for rendering of various services, making interest payments on debt incurred by the government, meeting subsidies and grants given to other parties. Broadly speaking, expenditure of the government which does not result in the creation of physical or financial assets is treated as revenue expenditure. All grants given to State Governments/Union Territories and all other parties are treated as revenue expenditure even though some of the grants may be used for creation of assets. Revenue expenditure which results in the creation of capital assets is reduced from revenue deficit to arrive at the *effective revenue deficit*.

Effective revenue deficit = Revenue deficit – Grants for creation of capital assets.

A. Functional Categories of Revenue Expenditure: Revenue expenditure is classified under the following four categories:

(a) General Services: This category includes both civil and defence services. Civil services include: (a) *Organs of State* like the Parliament, the President, the Vice-President, and the Council of Ministers, administration of justice, elections, and audit, (b) *Fiscal Services* like collection of customs duties, Union excise levies, income tax, wealth tax and other taxes levied by the Government, currency, coinage and mint, (c) *Interest Payments* on market loans, external loans, and loans from various reserve funds, (d) *Administrative Services* like Union Public Service Commission, police, jails, public works, external affairs, pensions and secretariats and attached offices of the Ministries of Finance, Home Affairs, Law, Justice and Company Affairs, Defence and External Affairs. In short, expenditure on general services relates to the maintenance of law and order, defence of the country, and upkeep of the general organs of the Government.

(b) Social and Community Services: This category includes expenditure incurred on basic social amenities to benefit citizens as consumers. It relates to expenditure on education, art and culture, scientific services and research, medical services, family planning, public health, sanitation, water supply, housing, urban development, information and publicity, broadcasting, labour and employment, and social security and welfare. Expenditure on the secretariat and attached offices of the various Ministries dealing with these services are also included under this head.

(c) Economic Services: This category includes all such expenditures which promote productive activity within the economy. In other words, benefits of expenditure under this category accrue to citizens as producers. The major heads of expenditure of this sector are: (a) *General Economic Services* like foreign trade and export promotion, co-operation and secretariats and attached offices of the various Ministries dealing with programmes of economic development, (b) *Agriculture and Allied Services* like irrigation schemes, soil and water conservation programmes, animal husbandry, dairy development, fisheries, forestry, community development, food subsidy to Food

Corporation of India and other services related to agriculture, (c) *Industry and Minerals* which include large-scale industries, village and small industries, and development of mines and minerals, (d) *Water and Power Development* including navigation, drainage, flood control, power houses, (e) *Transport and Communications* such as ports, light houses, shipping, civil aviation, roads and bridges, tourism and other transport and communication services.

(d) Unallocable: Expenditures which cannot be related to specific purposes are included under this head. The main items are: statutory grants-in-aid, ways and means advances, ad hoc loans, grants to Nepal and Bhutan, technical and other loans to foreign countries.

The rationale underlying the categorisation of Government expenditure into the above-mentioned four categories is that while general services relate to the defence of the country and the general upkeep of the Government, social services provide basic amenities to citizens as consumers, economic services extend benefits to citizens as producers, and unallocable expenditures signify lack of specific purpose.

B. Major Items of Revenue Expenditure: The three main items of revenue expenditure are: (a) interest payments, (b) defence services and (c) subsidies. Interest payments constitute the single largest component of revenue expenditure. The high level of interest payments is directly linked to high reliance on borrowings. The allocation for defence also represents a significant component of revenue expenditure. Defence expenditure started increasing steadily after the Chinese aggression in 1962 and the Indo-Pak conflicts in 1965 and 1971. Fertilizers, food and petroleum are the three main items subsidised by the Government through budgetary support.

5.2 Capital Budget

Capital budget comprises capital receipts and capital expenditure of the government. It shows capital requirements of the government and their financing patterns. Capital account signifies that the economic role of the government extends far beyond collecting and spending tax revenue. It reflects government's influence over the economy through its acquisition and disposition of a significant portion of the annual savings of the people. The amount of savings available to the private sector for investment is reduced by the amount of capital raised by public authorities.

Table 5.2 shows the composition of capital budget of the Central Government for the year 2021-22.

5.2.1 Capital Receipts: Those receipts of the Government which create liability or reduce financial assets may be called capital receipts.

Capital receipts are divided into two parts: (a) non-debt receipts and (b) debt receipts. This distinction is important to understand the meaning and financing of fiscal deficit.

A. Non-debt Receipts: Non-debt receipts have two main components:

(a) Recoveries of Loans and Advances: The receipts under this head pertain to the recoveries of loans and advances made by the Central Government to State and Union Territory Governments, foreign governments, industrial and commercial undertakings and financial institutions in the public sector, municipalities, port trusts, companies and institutions in the private sector, co-operative societies, and government employees.

(b) Disinvestment Receipts: Disinvestment means the sale of shares of public sector undertakings by the government. These shares are earning assets at the disposal of the government. If these shares are sold to get cash, then earning assets are converted into cash. So it is referred to as disinvestment.

Table 5.2: Composition of Capital Budget of the Central Government, 2021-22

(₹ crore)

Capital receipts		Capital expenditure	
A. Non-debt receipts, of which	1,88,000	Total capital expenditure (i.e. gross budgetary support for capital expenditure	5,54,236
(i) Recoveries of loans and Advances	13,000		
(ii) Disinvestment receipts	1,75,000		
B. Debt receipts (net of payment) of which	14,35,428		
(i) Market borrowings (Government securities + treasury bills)	9,67,708		
(ii) State provident funds (net)	20,000		
(iii) External debt (net)	1,514		
Total capital receipts	16,94,812		

Source: Government of India, Ministry of Finance, Budget Papers 2021-22, *Budget at a Glance.*

B. Debt Receipts: The main components of debt receipts are as under:

(a) Market Borrowings: These include the regular market floatations by the Government. In other words, these are borrowings by the Government from Reserve Bank of India (RBI) and other parties through the sale of Government securities and treasury bills. [2]

(b) Provident Funds: Receipts under this head relate to State Provident Funds and Public Provident Funds. Credit assumed is net of the deposits into the fund including interest on balances and withdrawals including temporary advances therefrom.

(c) Small Savings: These comprise post office savings accounts, post office time deposits, recurring deposits, national saving certificates, social security certificates, *kisan vikas patra,* national saving scheme, and post office monthly income scheme.

(d) External Debt: Self-explanatory as it is, this category shows loans received from friendly foreign countries and international organisations.

5.2.2 Capital Expenditure: Expenditure of the government which lead to the creation of physical or financial assets or reduction in recurring financial liabilities falls under the category of capital expenditure. Such expenditure pertains to payments on acquisition of assets like land, buildings, machinery, equipment, as also investments in shares, and loans and advances given to State Governments, public sector enterprises and other parties. Capital disbursements are of two kinds: those spent directly (capital outlays) and those spent indirectly by extending loans and advances.

A. **Functional Categories of Capital Expenditure:** Capital non-Plan expenditure covers various general, social, and economic services provided by the Government. The four broad categories of this expenditure are the following.

(a) General Services: This sector includes capital expenditure on civil and defence services. It accommodates capital outlay on all non-residential buildings, e.g. office and administrative buildings, other than those for functional purposes like hospitals, schools and godowns. Regarding defence services, provision for capital expenditure on acquisition of land and construction works, machinery and equipment, military farms etc. is included under this sector of expenditure.

(b) Social and Community Services: This sector includes capital expenditure on buildings for schools, technical institutions (mainly in Union Territories), scientific research organisations, hospitals, dispensaries, medical stores and research laboratories. Also included under this sector are capital outlays on studios, transmitters, machinery and equipment, and buildings for All India Radio and Doordarshan. Still further, this sector also accommodates capital outlays and loans granted under various schemes for the resettlement of displaced persons as well as other social security and welfare programmes.

(c) Economic Services: This sector includes capital outlays and loans granted for various schemes of economic development in the field of agriculture and allied services, industry and minerals, petroleum, chemical and fertiliser industries, aircraft and ship building industries, telecommunication and electronics industries, mining and metallurgical industries, water and power development, roads and bridges and other economic services.

(d) Loans and Advances: Loans and advances are given to State Governments, Union Territories, foreign governments (like Nepal, and Bhutan), and Central Government employees for various purposes.

Various components and measures of budget deficit of the Central Government Budget for 2021-22 are presented in Table 5.3.

5.3 Various Measures of Budget Deficit and Their Significance

Budget deficit is a multi-dimensional concept. It may refer to overall deficit, fiscal deficit, revenue deficit, primary deficit, monetised deficit or some other mismatch between receipts and expenditures of the Government. The various measures of budget deficit have their own relevance for different purposes. In general, budget deficit is used as an indicator of the financial health of the Central Government.

5.3.1 Overall Deficit (or Budgetary Deficit): This conventional measure of budget deficit represents the excess of aggregate disbursements over aggregate receipts, both revenue and capital. In other words, it shows the gap in the total receipts and total disbursements of the Government. This deficit determines the growth of liquidity and inflationary pressure in the economy.

Table 5.3: Components and Measures of Budget Deficit of the Central Government Budget for 2021-22

(₹ crore)

1. Revenue receipts	**17,88,424**
2. Tax revenue (net to Centre)	15,45,397
3. Non-tax revenue	2,43,028
4. Capital receipts	**16,94,812**
5. Recovery of loans	13,000
6. Other receipts (disinvestment receipts)	1,75,000
7. Total receipts (1+4)	**34,83,236**
8. Total expenditure (9+12)	**34,83,236**
9. On revenue account, of which	29,29,000
10. Interest payments	8,09,701
11. Grants-in-aid for creation of capital assets	2,19,112
12. On capital account	5,54,236
13. Revenue deficit (9–1)	**11,40,576 (5.1)**
14. Effective revenue deficit (13–11)	**9,21,464 (4.1)**
15. Fiscal deficit [8–(1+5+6)]	**15,06,812 (6.8)**
16. Primary deficit (15–10)	**6,97,111 (3.1)**

Note: Figures in parentheses are as a percentage of GDP.
Source: Government of India, Ministry of Finance, Budget Papers 2021-22, *Budget at a Glance.*

Overall budget deficit = Aggregate disbursements – Aggregate receipts

The overall deficit does not fully capture the structural imbalances in the fiscal operations of the Government. Thus, beginning with the 1997-98 budget, the practice of showing overall deficit was discontinued.

5.3.2 Revenue Deficit: Revenue deficit refers to the excess of revenue expenditure over revenue receipts.

Clause 2(e) of Fiscal Responsibility and Budget Management Act, 2003 defines revenue deficit as "the difference between revenue expenditure and revenue receipts which indicates increase in liabilities of the Central Government without corresponding increase in assets of that Government". The Act, therefore, seems to conform to the classical view about use of borrowed funds and implicitly aims at balancing the current and capital sides of the budget in its application to the Union Government as a distinct budgeting and accounting entity.

Revenue deficit = Revenue expenditure – Revenue receipts.

In the 2021-22 budget, revenue deficit of the Central Government was shown at ₹ 11,40,576 crore, which was 5.1 percent of GDP (Table 5.3).

Revenue deficit signifies dis-savings on the part of the Government. In other words, it shows the use of the savings of other sectors of the economy to finance a part of the consumption expenditure of the Government. Ideally, Government should ensure surplus in the revenue budget to show that it also contributes to savings in the economy. [3]

A. Effective Revenue Deficit: It is the difference between revenue deficit and grants for creations of capital assets.

In the 2021-22 budget, effective revenue deficit of the Central Government was shown at ₹ 9,21,464 crore, which was 4.1 percent of GDP (Table 5.3).

5.3.3 Fiscal Deficit: Fiscal deficit, an internationally used concept, shows the excess of all expenditure, both revenue and capital, *over* revenue receipts plus non-debt capital receipts.

Fiscal deficit = Total expenditure – (Revenue receipts + Non-debt capital receipts).

In the 2021-22 budget, fiscal deficit was shown at a figure of ₹ 15,06,812 crore, which was 6.8 percent of the GDP (Table 5.3).

Fiscal deficit is reflective of the total borrowing requirements of the Government. It measures the entire shortfall in the non-debt resources for financing the Central Government expenditure and fully reflects the impact of fiscal operations on the indebtedness of the Government by quantifying the total borrowings by the Government.

A. Financing of Fiscal Deficit: Total borrowing requirements of the Government are financed through various sources which mainly include: (a) subscriptions of individuals and households to small saving schemes of the government, (b) commercial banks, and other financial institutions, through statutory liquidity ratio (SLR) instrument, and (c) the Reserve Bank of India (RBI). Fiscal deficit makes no distinction between different types of borrowings although the implication of borrowings from the RBI is different compared to borrowings from other sources. Thus, borrowings from individuals and commercial banks and other institutions does not involve expansion of money supply. It simply reflects reallocation of available funds between government and non-government sectors. However, borrowing from RBI leads to printing of more currency and hence increase in the money supply in the economy. In fact, the amount of unsubscribed public debt is purchased by the RBI.

Since fiscal deficit is met by borrowings, it leads to accumulation of internal debt of the Government. The servicing of this debt has become a serious problem in India. Interest payments on the part of government constitute a sizeable part of the revenue expenditure of the government (Table 5.1). A judicious macro-management of the economy requires progressive reduction in the fiscal deficit and revenue deficit of the Government. With the discontinuance of the concept of overall deficit, fiscal deficit is now the key indicator of deficit. Any abnormal growth in fiscal deficit is potentially inflationary.

Table 5.4 shows the financing of fiscal deficit in the Budget of the Central Government for the year 2021-22.

B. Is Fiscal Deficit Always Worrisome? Higher fiscal deficits may not be a matter of concern always. Taking clue from Keynesian economics, it is argued that fiscal deficits would be inflationary only if the economy is at full employment level or characterised by supply constraints in certain crucial sectors. If the economy is buoyant, marked by excessive industrial capacity, large food stocks, enormous foreign exchange reserves, and low/moderate inflation, a high dose of fiscal deficit is not only noninflationary, but virtuous for sustaining high growth rate. Create work/jobs, generate incomes and boost demand, even if it means, as Lord Keynes said, "digging the holes and filling the holes". To quote, "Indian kings used to build palaces during famines and droughts to provide employment and improve the economic fortunes of the private sector. Economic theory, in effect, makes the same recommendation: in a recessionary year, government must spend more than during expansionary times. Such counter-cyclical fiscal policy stabilizes the business cycle by being contractionary (reduce spending/increase taxes) in good times and expansionary (increase spending/reduce taxes) in bad times. On the other hand, a pro-cyclical fiscal policy is the one wherein fiscal policy reinforces the business cycle by being expansionary during good times and contractionary during recessions". [4]

Table 5.4: Sources of Financing Fiscal Deficit: Budget Estimates 2021-22

(₹ crore)

A. Debt receipts (net) of which:	14,35,428
(a) Market borrowings (Government securities plus treasury bills)	9,67,708
(b) State provident funds	20,000
(c) External debt	1,514
B. Draw down of cash balances	71,383
Total (A + B)	15,06,812

Source: Government of India, Ministry of Finance, Budget Papers 2021-22, *Budget at a Glance.*

5.3.4 Primary Deficit: The fiscal deficit, as already explained, does not necessarily reflect the extent to which current discretionary fiscal actions improve or worsen the Government's net indebtedness. In particular, interest payments in the current period are obligatory but reflect the impact of debt increased by past budgets. Hence, the concept of primary deficit, indicating the precise extent to which current fiscal action affects the indebtedness of the Central Government. It is measured by deducting interest payments from fiscal deficit.

Primary deficit = Fiscal deficit – Interest payments.

In the 2021-22 budget, primary deficit was shown at a figure of ₹ 6,97,111 crore which was 3.1 percent of GDP (Table 5.3).

5.3.5 Monetised Deficit: Besides ways and means advances (WMA), [5] the RBI also supports the Government's borrowing programme. In India, the management of public debt and the floatation of market loans are entrusted to the RBI. Net increase in the borrowings of the Central Government from the RBI is termed as monetised deficit (or debt monetisation). In other words, it indicates the level of support extended by the RBI to the government's borrowing programme. Hence, it captures the monetary impact of fiscal operations of the government. With the issue of more money to the government, the money supply in the economy increases, as a result of which the inflationary pressure can prevail.

In the case of State Governments, monetised deficit refers to ways and means advances given to them by the RBI net of their deposits with the RBI.

A. Magnitude and Timing of Monetised Deficit: The net effect of monetised deficit is an increase in the money supply in the economy. When money supply in the economy increases, it puts pressure on the supply of goods and services. Since supply cannot be increased easily, prices have a tendency to rise. Rise in prices is accompanied by its own adverse effects which are very disorderly because the burden of price rise falls inequitably on different classes. Monetised deficit is a kind of *inflation tax* which compels people to save involuntarily.

Magnitude, timing, and consequences of monetised deficit are subjects of controversy among economists. In developing countries, governments are always looking for more and more resources to finance development schemes. Taxes are by far the most important source of public revenue but a great part of revenue from taxes goes to meet the administrative expenditure of the governments. Next in importance are borrowings, internal as well as external. When this source is also exhausted, then a government resorts to monetised deficit in order to claim a part of the real resources in the economy.

Monetised financing is generally resorted to during war or for development purposes. Apparently, if it is for development purposes, its ill-effects will be short-lived because when the development schemes mature, the improved production level will reduce inflationary pressure in the economy. Contrarily, if it is for war purposes, the adverse consequences are long-drawn, causing widespread dislocation in the economy.

In the initial stages of development, a modest dose of monetised financing may be justified on grounds of monetisation of the economy. When developmental activities pick up, the demand for money also increases because of increasing transactions. A controlled and gradual increase in money supply plays an important role by boosting investment in the economy. However, a reckless monetary expansion may prove dangerous by aggravating inflationary tendencies. In a supply-constrained economy, the Keynesian investment multiplier operates more in money terms than in real terms. During inflation, fixed income groups are adversely affected and the poor suffer the most. Producers, distributors, speculators, and hoarders are the gainers. In the extreme case, if inflation becomes uncontrolled, people may lose faith in the currency itself. Thus, no society can afford a continuous and significant rise in the general price level. It is rightly said that monetised deficit, like fire, is a good servant but a bad master.

B. Crowding Out Effect: The phenomenon of crowding out of private investment is based on the notion that supply of savings in the economy is fixed. Therefore, higher fiscal spending may increase the demand for loanable funds and hence exert an upward pressure on interest rates, thereby discouraging private investment.

However, for emerging economies such as India, an increase in public expenditure in areas that boost private sector's propensities to save and invest, may enable private investment rather than crowding it out. In other words, in an economy that has unemployed resources, an increase in government spending increases the aggregate demand in the economy, which may induce the private sector to increase their investment in new machinery to cater to the increased demand, and hence put the unused resources to productive uses. This may have multiplier effects on aggregate demand, resulting in higher growth rates. In fact, if the public expenditure is directed to sectors where the fiscal multipliers are large (e.g. infrastructure development), such spending may significantly crowd in private investment as well.

Moreover, in a rapidly growing economy, the supply of savings is not fixed but expands with income growth.

The foregoing account of the various kinds of deficit in the budget indicates different aspects of budgetary imbalance. Overall deficit determines the growth of liquidity and inflationary pressure in the economy. Revenue deficit measures Government's negative contribution to domestic savings. In other words, it indicates the extent of borrowing required to finance current expenditure. The large interest payments are the main cause of revenue deficit. This deficit highlights the need to bring down expenditure and augment tax revenue, preferably through better compliance.

Fiscal deficit indicates the extent of Government borrowings from all sources necessary to balance the budget.

Thus, various measures of budget deficit help to identify areas of weaknesses in the budget of the government.

5.4 Budget and the External Sector

Budgetary operations of the Government get linked up with the external sector through the imposition of import duties, tax concessions and/or subsidies on exports, and through foreign aid.

If the import duties are too high (i.e. high tariff wall), domestic industries get undue protection, resulting in general inefficiency, high production cost and inferior production. Low level of import duties exposes the domestic industries to international competition which may prove beneficial in the long-run. Similarly, if import duties on raw materials and machinery are reduced, the production cost of domestic industries will be lowered. However, lowering of import duties can adversely affect domestic industry if it leads to dumping by the foreigners.

Endnotes

1. In theory, the rationale for revenue-capital separation is supported on several considerations. Separation provides greater control over public debt and its utilization. It facilitates implementation of the Golden Rule followed by many countries which requires that current account is balanced over an economic cycle and Governments borrow only to invest and not to pay for current spending. Debt financing of capital expenditures is justified to ensure inter-generational equity. The separation facilitates strategic allocation of borrowed funds for capital expenditure. It, thus, provides a framework for the best use of borrowed resources. It enables better determination of responsibility within Government. Capital expenditures need greater care in selection and execution of capital projects. Separate disclosure facilitates economic analysis of the budget and spending, besides generating information on capital formation.

   Critics, however, put forth several arguments against the separation. The criteria for economic returns should be applied to all expenditures and not just to capital expenditures. From the stabilization point of view, it is the size of the overall deficit and the pattern of its financing that is far more important. Capital budgets may contribute to a shift in emphasis toward 'brick-and mortar' projects. This may systematically bias allocation of resources towards capital expenditures without adequate provisioning for essential maintenance and operating costs. Investment proposals, however, need to consider both capital and operating costs together for a holistic view of the costs involved and the benefits. Budget policy and planning requires a unified consideration of all budgetary proposals. Borrowing spending can be more expansionary than taxation spending. Further, information on capital formation can be presented in supplementary tables to the main budget rather than resorting to separation of revenue and capital.

On balance, it can be said that the need for separation of revenue and capital budgets should be seen not merely as a rationalization of borrowing but in the wider context of the formulation of fiscal policy, in terms of overall expenditures and the appropriate mix of taxation and borrowing.

2. **Treasury Bills (T-bills):** When the Central Government wants to borrow internally, it goes to the financial market. It can borrow by issuing two types of debt instruments: treasury bills and government bonds. Treasury bills are issued when the Government needs money for short period while bonds are issued when it needs money for long period.

   Bill market is a sub-market of the money market in India. There are two types of bills, viz. treasury bills and commercial bills. While treasury bills are issued by the Central Government, commercial bills are issued by financial institutions.

   T-bills are short-term (up to one year) money market instruments, issued by the Reserve Bank of India (RBI) on behalf of the Central Government to meet temporary liquidity shortfalls. T-bills enable investors to park their short-term surplus funds while reducing the market risk. T-bills have a maximum maturity of a 364 days. Hence, they are categorized as money market instruments (money market deals with funds with a maturity of less than one year).

   T-bills are auctioned by RBI at regular intervals and issued at a discount to face value. Presently, the active T-bills are 91-days T-bills and 364-days T-bills. The 91-days and 364-days T-bills are issued on weekly auction (Wednesday) basis.

   T-bills are issued on discount to face value. The holder gets the face value on maturity. The return on T-bills is the difference between the issue price and face value. Thus, return on T-bills depends upon auctions. When the liquidity position in the economy is tight, returns are higher and vice versa. For example, a 91- days T-bill of Rs.100 (face value) may be issued at say ₹ 98.30, i.e. at a discount of ₹ 1.70 and would be redeemed at the face value of ₹ 100.

   T-bills are issued only by the Central Government. State Governments do not issue any treasury bills. Treasury bills are available for a minimum amount of ₹ 25,000 and in multiples of ₹ 25,000.

   Since T-bills are issued by the Government (sovereign papers), they carry zero risk. Similarly, due to their short-term maturity, they are highly liquid assets. The secondary market for T-bills is very active so they have a higher degree of tradability. There is no tax deduction at source.

   Individuals, firms, trusts, institutions and banks can purchase T-bills. The commercial and co-operative banks use T-bills for fulfilling their statutory liquidity ratio (SLR) requirements. T-bills are usually held by financial institutions including banks. They have a very important role in the financial market beyond investment instruments. Banks meet their SLR requirement by investing in T-bills also. Banks give T-bills to the RBI to get money under repurchase option (repo).

While inter-bank money markets and central bank lending via repo operations or discounting, provide liquidity for banks, private non-bank money market instruments, such as commercial bills and commercial paper provide liquidity to the commercial sector. Unlike in developed economies where money markets are promoted by financial intermediaries out of efficiency considerations, in India, as in many other developing countries, the evolution of the money market and its structure has been integrated into the overall deregulation process of the financial sector.

3. **Revenue Surplus Turned into Revenue Deficit:** Till the year 1978-79, it was almost customary that Central budgets recorded a surplus on revenue account, representing a measure of savings on the part of the Government. The surplus on revenue account used to offset, though partially, deficit on capital account and, therefore, the overall deficit. The deficit on capital account indicated the excess of capital expenditure over various types of capital receipts. Since capital expenditure is mainly developmental in nature, leading to creation of physical and financial assets, the budgetary trend was generally welcome except for the magnitude of the overall deficit.

However, beginning with the year 1979-80, revenue account assumed a reversal of role by registering regular and in some years growing deficits. As already noted, the revenue deficit was placed at ₹ 11,40,576 crore in the 2021-2022 budget (Table 5.3). Revenue deficit is met by using a part of the borrowed resources to finance a portion of the consumption expenditure of the Government. Increased borrowings lead to increased interest payments which, in turn, necessitate still larger borrowings, landing the economy in a vicious circle of deficit and debt.

It is interesting to note the reasons responsible for the change from surplus to deficit in the revenue account. The main contributory factor for this change may be traced back to the recommendations of the Seventh Finance Commission which doubled the States' share in Union excise duties from 20 percent to 40 percent, and increased their share in income tax from 80 percent to 85 percent for the period of its award (1979-84). The Eighth Finance Commission further enhanced the share of States in excise revenue from 40 percent to 45 percent, and the Tenth Finance Commission from 45 percent to 47.5 percent. However, the Tenth Finance Commission decreased the share of States in income tax from 85 percent to 77.5 percent. The Eleventh Finance Commission fixed the share of States at 28 percent of the net proceeds of all Central taxes/duties. The recommendations of the recent Finance Commissions have considerably eroded the current revenues of the Central Government.

The non-tax revenue of the Government has also suffered on account of shortfalls in surplus generation by public sector undertakings. Emergence of revenue deficits in the government's budgets has resulted, to a considerable extent, from the manner of plan budgeting and financing. At the time when planning was initiated, the expectation was that the finances for the plan would come out of surpluses to be generated by the public sector, although some draft on the private sector savings was not ruled out. This expectation did not materialise as the public sector savings turned out to be inadequate and the bulk of the requirements for the plans were made out of borrowings.

While the Centre's share in divisible taxes has shrunk, several factors have contributed to the faster growth of its revenue expenditure, particularly interest payments, staff salaries and pension payments. It may be recalled that Government gave 25 percent more to its employees than what was recommended by the Fifth Central Pay Commission. This *magnanimity* of the Government was rightly termed as fiscal suicide by no less a person than Professor Suresh

Tendulkar who himself was a member of the Commission. His prophecy has come true if one looks at the unmanageable levels of fiscal and revenue deficits in the recent budget. It is noteworthy that consequent upon the implementation of the recommendations of the Fifth Pay Commission, the salary bill and pension outgo of the Central Government increased sharply, straining its fiscal position. In 1996-97, salaries accounted for 13.5 percent and pensions 4.0 percent of revenue receipts (net of States' share) of the Central Government. In 1997-98, the figures stood at 16.4 percent and 5.0 percent respectively [Government of India, *Economic Survey*, 1998-99, p. 23].

4. Government of India, Ministry of Finance, *Economic Survey, 2020-21*, Volume I, p. 45.

5. **WMA and Overdraft:** As a banker to the Central Government, Reserve Bank of India (RBI) gives temporary loan facilities to it. This temporary loan facility is called Ways and Means Advances (WMA). WMA scheme for the Central Government was introduced on April 1, 1997, after putting an end to the four-decade old system of Ad hoc Treasury Bills to finance the Central Government deficit. The WMA scheme is designed to meet temporary mismatches in the receipts and payments of the government. This facility can be availed by the government if it needs immediate cash from the RBI. The WMA is to be vacated after 90 days. The size and cost of WMA are mutually decided by the RBI and the Government of India. Interest rate for WMA is currently charged at the repo rate.

   WMA is outside the RBI's support to the Government borrowing programme during the year. WMA is not a permanent source of financing the Government's deficit. WMA is intended to strengthen fiscal discipline and provide greater autonomy to the RBI in its conduct of monetary policy. It also strengthens the fiscal-monetary co-ordination and debt management. WMA scheme is also available to State Governments.

   When WMA limit is crossed the Government takes recourse to overdrafts, which are not allowed beyond 10 consecutive working days. The interest rate on overdrafts is 2 percent more than the repo rate. The minimum balance required to be maintained by the Government of India with the Reserve Bank of India will not be less than ₹ 100 crore on Fridays, on the date of closure of Government of India's financial year and on June 30, the date of closure of the annual accounts of the RBI, and not less than ₹ 10 crore on other days.

6

Budgetary Reforms in India

It may be recalled that the external payments crisis of 1991, which led to the initiation of economic reforms in India, was the result of deteriorating fiscal situation during the latter half of 1980s. Fiscal imbalance was identified as the underlying cause of the twin problems of inflation and the difficult balance of payments position. Budgetary reforms were needed in this context.

6.1 Fiscal Responsibility and Budget Management (FRBM) Act, 2003

6.1.1 Background: To promote the conduct of prudent and accountable fiscal policy, the Government introduced in the Lok Sabha in December 2000 the Fiscal Responsibility and Budget Management Bill, 2000. The Bill provided for a legal and institutional framework to: (a) eliminate revenue deficit, (b) bring down fiscal deficit, (c) contain the growth of public debt and (d) stabilise debt as a proportion of GDP within a timeframe. The Bill, covering only the finances of the Central Government, defined the principles of fiscal responsibility in terms of budgetary deficit, government borrowings and public debt.

Two indicators of budgetary deficit, namely revenue deficit and fiscal deficit were the focus of the Bill. Thus, the Bill proposed elimination of revenue deficit and progressive reduction of the fiscal deficit to not more than 2 percent of GDP within a period of 5 financial years following the promulgation of the law. However, the proposed legislation contained provisions to ensure flexibility in fiscal management under emergency situations like war and natural calamities.

Under borrowing-related norms, the Bill proposed to prohibit certain types of borrowing from the Reserve Bank of India (RBI). Similarly, under debt-related norms, it proposed to prescribe a limit on the debt stock. Thus, the Bill envisaged that within a period of 10 financial years, the total liabilities (including external debt at current exchange rate) would not exceed 50 percent of the estimated GDP.

Emphasising the importance of the Bill, the *Economic Survey*, 2000-01 observed, "The introduction of Fiscal Responsibility and Budget Management Bill, 2000 in Lok Sabha in December, 2000 is a historic step in our fiscal history. It shifts the emphasis of fiscal management from a purely short term perspective to a longer time horizon for conduct of prudent and accountable fiscal policy. Introduction of rule-based budget management practices will also enable the economic agents and the community at large to take informed decisions. Besides, its enactment is likely to be seen as a demonstration of our country's resolve to maintaining macroeconomic stability. Placing limits on the Central Government borrowings, debt and deficits and emphasising greater transparency in fiscal operations would also greatly facilitate effective conduct of monetary policy". [1]

In an unexpected move, the Central Government decided on February 4, 2003 to dilute the Bill, dispensing with the proposed reduction in fiscal deficit by 0.5 percent annually. The diluted Bill did not have a provision on reducing revenue and fiscal deficits. It emphasised the need to uphold the spirit of sound fiscal management rather than achieve it through legislative measures. The Bill was passed by the Lok Sabha on May 7, 2003. The Act was enacted on August 26, 2003.

The Fiscal Responsibility and Budget Management Act, 2003 and the Fiscal Responsibility and Budget Management Rules, 2004 made under Section 8 of the Act came into force on July 5, 2004.

Highlighting the importance of FRBMA, the *Economic Survey*, 2006-07 noted, "FRBMA is an important institutional expression to ensure fiscal prudence and support for macroeconomic balance. With the enactment of the FRBMA, the traditional annual budgeting moved to a more meaningful medium-term fiscal planning framework. According to the Rules, revenue deficit is to be reduced by an amount equivalent to half percent or more of the estimated GDP at the end of each financial year and eliminated by March 31, 2009. Fiscal deficit is to be reduced by an amount equivalent to 0.3 percent or more of the estimated GDP at the end of each financial year and reduced to no more than three percent of the estimated GDP by the financial year ending on March 31, 2009". [2]

6.1.2 Main Provisions of the FRBM Act, 2003: These are as under:

Section 1 of the Act pertains to short title, extent and commencement of the Act. Section 2 deals with definitions of the terms used in the Act.

According to Section 3 of the Act, the Central Government shall lay in each financial year before both Houses of Parliament the following statements:

1. Macroeconomic Framework Statement.
2. Fiscal Policy Strategy Statement.
3. Medium Term Fiscal Policy Statement.

Section 4 of the Act prescribes principles of fiscal management. It states,

"(1) The Central Government shall: (a) take appropriate measures to limit the fiscal deficit up to three percent of gross domestic product by the 31st March 2021; (b) endeavour to ensure that: (i) the general government debt (Centre and States) does not exceed sixty percent, (ii) the Central Government debt does not exceed forty percent of the gross domestic product by the end of financial year 2024-2025; (c) not give additional guarantees with respect to any loans on the security of the Consolidated Fund of India in excess of one-half percent of gross domestic product, in any financial year; (d) endeavour to ensure that the fiscal targets specified in clauses (a) and (b) are not exceeded after stipulated target dates.

(2) The Central Government shall prescribe the annual targets for reduction of fiscal deficit for the period beginning from the date of commencement of....the Finance Act, 2018 and ending on 31st March 2021:

Provided that exceeding annual fiscal deficit target due to ground or grounds of national security, act of war, national calamity, collapse of agriculture severely affecting farm output and incomes, structural reforms in the economy with unanticipated fiscal implications, decline in real output growth of a quarter by at least three percent points below its average of the previous four quarters, may be allowed for the purpose of this section.

(3) Any deviation from fiscal deficit target under sub-section (2) shall not exceed one-half percent of the gross domestic product in a year.

(4) The Central Government shall, in case of increase in real output growth of a quarter by at least three percent points above its average of the previous four quarters, reduce the fiscal deficit by at least one-quarter percent of the gross domestic product in a year".

Section 5 of the Act relates to borrowing from Reserve Bank of India (RBI). It states,

"(1) The Central Government shall not borrow from the Reserve Bank.

(2) Notwithstanding anything contained in sub-section (1), the Central Government may borrow from the Reserve Bank by way of advances to meet temporary excess of cash disbursement over cash receipts during any financial year in accordance with the agreements which may be entered into by that Government with the Reserve Bank.

(3) Notwithstanding anything contained in sub-section (1), the Reserve Bank may subscribe to the primary issues of Central Government securities due to ground or grounds specified in the proviso to sub-section (2) of Section 4.

(4) Notwithstanding anything contained in sub-section (1), the Reserve Bank may buy and sell the Central Government securities in the secondary market or convert Central Government securities held by it with other securities of the Central Government as mutually agreed between the Reserve Bank and the Central Government".

Other provisions of the Act are as follows: Measures for fiscal transparency (Section 6); measures to enforce compliance (Section 7); laying of review reports (Section 7A); power to make rules (Section 8); rules to be laid before each House of Parliament (Section 9); protection of action taken in good faith (Section 10); jurisdiction of civil courts barred (Section 11); application of other laws not barred (Section 12); and power to remove difficulties (Section 13).

6.1.3 Deviation from Fiscal Deficit Target in the Budget for 2020-21: When Finance Minister Nirmala Sitharaman presented the budget for 2020-21 to the Parliament on February 1, 2020, she showed a fiscal deficit of ₹ 7,96,337 crore which was 3.5 percent of gross domestic product (GDP). This 3.5 percent was composed of two components: 3 percent as mandated by the Fiscal Responsibility and Budget Management (FRBM) Act, 2003 and the 0.5 percent as allowed under Sections 4(2) and 4(3) of the same Act during emergencies.

6.2 Fiscal Responsibility Legislations by States

Twelfth Finance Commission (XII-FC) award (for the period 2005-06 to 2009-10) contained incentives to promote fiscal reforms. Consequently, many States undertook fiscal measures to reform their tax systems and expenditure management practices. XII-FC recommended that each State should enact fiscal responsibility legislation as a precondition for debt relief on loans owed to the Centre. Although there were variations across States in the choice of target and the time-frame for achieving the target, most stipulated an elimination of the current deficit (revenue deficit) by March 31, 2009 and reduction in the gross fiscal deficit as a percent of gross State domestic product (GSDP) to 3 percent by March 31, 2010 in line with the targets prescribed by XII-FC. In addition, several States imposed limits on guarantees and targeted a reduction in their total explicit liabilities.

Almost all State Governments have enacted fiscal responsibility legislations (Table 6.1). State Governments have adopted a rule-based framework for fiscal correction and consolidation by enacting fiscal responsibility legislations. Karnataka was the first to enact one in September 2002 followed by Kerala and Tamil Nadu in 2003, and Punjab in 2004. Subsequently, other States enacted such legislations.

Table 6.1: Enactment of Fiscal Responsibility Legislation by the States

S. No.	State	Month and Year of Enactment	S. No.	State	Month and Year of Enactment
1.	Karnataka	September 2002	14.	Manipur	August 2005
2.	Kerala	August 2003	15.	Nagaland	August 2005
3.	Tamil Nadu	May 2003	16.	Madhya Pradesh	August 2005
4.	Punjab	May 2003	17.	Chattisgarh	September 2005
5.	Uttar Pradesh	February 2004	18.	Andhra Pradesh	October 2005
6.	Gujarat	March 2005	19.	Uttarakhand	October 2005
7.	Himachal Pradesh	April 2005	20.	Arunachal Pradesh	March 2006
8.	Maharashtra	April 2005	21.	Meghalaya	March 2006
9.	Odisha	June 2005	22.	Bihar	April 2006
10.	Rajasthan	May 2005	23.	Goa	May 2006
11.	Assam	May 2005	24.	Jammu & Kashmir	August 2006
12.	Tripura	June 2005	25.	Mizoram	October 2006
13.	Haryana	July 2005	26.	Jharkhand	May 2007

Source: Reserve Bank of India, *India's Financial Sector: An Assessment*, March 2009, Volume VI, p. 144.

The process of fiscal consolidation under FRBMA has been continuous. It has yielded rich dividends in terms of creating fiscal space for increased spending on infrastructure and social sectors. The traditional annual budgeting has moved to a more meaningful medium-term fiscal planning framework. FRBMA provides the basic structure around which many fiscal measures have been implemented. Some of the important amongst these include: (a) reducing peak rates of customs duties, (b) rectifying anomalies like inverted duty structure, (c) rationalizing excise duties, (d) relying on voluntary tax compliance, (e) introduction of State level value added tax (VAT), (f) increasing productivity of expenditure through an outcome budget framework and (g) innovative financing mechanisms like creation of special purpose vehicles for infrastructure projects.

6.3 Budgetary Reforms Suggested by Eleventh Finance Commission (XI-FC)

FC-XI (period of award 2000-01 to 2004-05) dealt at length with the current budgetary practices and made valuable suggestions to improve the situation. It observed,

"A major weakness of the budgetary process of governments in the States and also at the Centre is the practice of spreading resources over too many projects. Often only a token amount is provided in the year in which the project is announced but this commits the future budgets also for which no detailed estimates are provided in the current year's budget and the projects remain incomplete for years for lack of adequate funds. For government expenditure to be brought under the discipline of resource availability and efficiency in resource use, proper budgeting and strict discipline in matters of launching new projects is required. Also there should be a commitment to completion of projects within the stipulated period and to provide necessary funds.

Another necessary reform in budgeting is to do a way with the dichotomy between 'plan' and 'non-plan' in expenditure. With the introduction of planning, budget heads have come to be divided under 'plan' and 'non-plan' and the distinction runs through all items of expenditure on revenue as well as capital accounts. Apart from creating problems in keeping the revenue deficits and thereby fiscal deficit in control, as pointed out earlier, the distinction has had a deleterious effect on the quality of public services. Essential maintenance has been neglected as they do not come under the plan and existing assets including schools and hospitals are starved of much needed support for their running". [3] It is noteworthy that beginning 2017-18, the classification of government expenditure into Plan and non-Plan was done away with in order to take a holistic view of allocations for sectors and ministries. In fact, the Planning Commission, which formulated India's Five Year Plan, itself was scrapped by the Union Cabinet on August 13, 2014.

6.4 Budgetary Reforms Suggested by Twelfth Finance Commission (XII-FC)

In the context of the current budgetary practices in India, XII-FC (period of award 2005-06 to 2009-10) observed, "The conventional budget exercises have focused on allocation of resources to different heads, without taking into account how these government expenditures get translated into outputs and outcomes. Outputs are the direct result of government expenditure and outcomes are the final results. Thus, in the context of education, opening a new school or appointing a new teacher is an output and reduction in the rate of illiteracy is an outcome. Issues of efficiency require consideration whether the same outcome can be achieved at lower costs and whether the same costs can produce better outcomes. A critical part of budgetary reforms must include information on the relationship between expenditures and the corresponding performance in producing real results as in determining the size of the budget and its allocation among different heads. Although in the past there have been attempts at introducing performance budgeting, such endeavours have receded in importance. There is need to bring back performance budgeting as an integral part of the preparation and evaluation of budgets, both for the centre and the states. Thus, the management of public expenditures should be guided by economy, efficiency, and effectiveness. [4] It is noteworthy that presently a document titled *Output Outcome Monitoring Framework* is presented to the Parliament along with other budget documents.

6.5 Budgetary Reforms Suggested by the Committee on Capital Account Convertibility

It may be recalled that in August 1994, by accepting obligations under Article VIII of the articles of agreement of the IMF, India made the Rupee convertible for current account transactions. As regards capital account convertibility, a committee (Chairman: S.S. Tarapore) was constituted in 1997 which chalked out a phased road map for making the capital account convertible. The East Asian crisis intervened soon thereafter, leading to lack of popular enthusiasm for capital account convertibility.

In view of external sector remaining robust and gaining strength every year and the relative macro economic stability, the government set up another committee (Chairman: S.S. Tarapore) on March 20, 2006 for setting out a roadmap towards fuller capital account convertibility. The Committee submitted its Report on July 31, 2006.

After reviewing the existing capital controls, it detailed a broad five-year time frame for movement towards fuller convertibility in three phases:

Phase I (2006-07)

Phase II (2007-08 to 2008-09)

Phase III (2009-10 to 2010-11)

The Committee recommended the meeting of various indicators/targets as a concomitant to the movement towards fuller capital account convertibility. Some of these recommendations, which pertained to current budgetary practices, were the following.

1. Meeting targets under the Fiscal Responsibility and Budget Management Act (FRMBA), 2003.
2. Shifting from the present measure of fiscal deficit to a measure of the Public Sector Borrowing Requirement (PSBR).
3. Segregating Government debt management and monetary policy operations through the setting up of the Office of Public Debt independent of the RBI.
4. Imparting greater autonomy and transparency in the conduct of monetary policy.

6.6 Gender Budgeting in India

Gender responsive budgeting or gender analysis of budgets is a very useful tool being used in India to promote gender mainstreaming. Gender budgeting refers to presentation of budgetary data in a manner such that the gender sensitivities of budgetary allocations are clearly highlighted. Gender budgeting includes carrying out an impact analysis of government programmes and its budgetary allocations on the overall socio-economic status of women in the country. A special reference by the Union Finance Minister in his budget speech to Parliament on February 29, 2000 pertaining to the access of women to national resources, marked the dawn of gender-sensitive budgeting in India.

It is noteworthy that the National Policy for Empowerment of Women, 2001 had envisaged introduction of a gender perspective in the budgeting process as an operational strategy. A task force was set up at the national level in 2001 to examine this issue. On its recommendation, a sub-group was set up to suggest a framework for introduction of gender budgeting in the Government. The sub-group recommended that Gender Budgeting Units be set up in identified Departments, as well as an Inter-departmental

Steering Committee to identify issues for gender budgeting that cut across departments.

6.6.1 Ministry of Women and Child Development (MWCD): In 2004-05, MWCD adopted the mission statement of Budgeting for Gender Equity. Since then, several initiatives have been taken by MWCD to operationalize gender budgeting. A strategic framework of activities to implement Budgeting for Gender Equity was disseminated to all relevant agencies. It identified the following areas for gender mainstreaming:

1. Quantification of allocation of resources for women in Union/State/Local Budgets.
2. Gender audit of policies of governments.
3. Impact assessment of various schemes.
4. Analyzing programmes and strategies.
5. Institutionalizing generation and collection of gender disaggregated data.
6. Consultations and capacity building.

Further, guidelines for gender-sensitive review of public expenditure and policy were framed in the form of checklists both for beneficiary-oriented sectors (such as health, rural development, human resource development, labour, drinking water, textiles, agriculture etc) and for mainstream sectors that may appear *gender neutral* like defence, power, telecom, transport etc.

MWCD has conducted several workshops and training programmes to disseminate the tools of gender budgeting and has advocated that a review may be undertaken with respect to the following:

1. Gender-based profile of public expenditure.
2. Beneficiary needs assessment.
3. Impact analysis.
4. Participative budgeting.
5. Spatial mapping.

MWCD has also requested various Ministries of the Government of India to set up Gender Budgeting Cells for the following purposes:

1. To undertake review of the public expenditure and policy.
2. To collect gender disaggregated data.
3. To conduct gender-based impact analysis, beneficiary needs assessment and beneficiary incidence analysis.

As a result of these efforts 43 Ministries/Departments have set up Gender Budget Cells as a nodal agency for all gender responsive budgeting initiatives.

Through a consensus approach the Department has also advocated broad framework within the ambit of which the gender budgeting initiatives could be undertaken by all stake-holders including Government Departments (Centre and States), voluntary organizations, researchers and international bodies like United Nations Development Programme (UNDP). The intention is to synergise the activities taking place in realm of gender budgeting and help collage the information base on the subject.

6.6.2 Women's Component Plan (WCP) in Five Year Plans [5]**:** WCP was the first major initiative taken by the Government to address women-related issues and requirements on a systematic basis involving the inputs from major Ministries/Departments. WCP involved efforts to ensure that not less than 30 percent of funds/benefits were earmarked for women under the various schemes.

Plan documents reflected the evolving trends in gender matters. Seventh Five Year Plan (1985-90) introduced the concept of monitoring of 27 beneficiary-oriented schemes for women.

Eighth Five Year Plan (1992-97) highlighted, for the first time, a gender perspective and the need to ensure a definite flow of funds from the general developmental sectors to women. The Plan document made an express statement that the benefits of development from different sectors should not bypass women and special programmes on women should complement the general development programmes.

On February 19, 1999, the National Development Council (NDC), one of the highest policy making bodies in the country, adopted the empowerment of women and socially disadvantaged groups as a specific objective of the Ninth Five Year Plan (1997-02). One of the strategies adopted for achieving this objective was to identify a *women's component plan* to ensure that not less than 30 percent of funds and benefits from developmental sectors flow to women. Hence, Ninth Plan adopted Women Component Plan as one of the major strategies and directed both the Central and State Governments to ensure "not less than 30 percent" of the funds/benefits are earmarked in all the women related sectors. Special vigil advocated on the flow of the earmarked funds/benefits through an effective mechanism to ensure that the proposed strategy brings forth a holistic approach towards empowering women.

Tenth Five Year Plan (2002-07) reinforced commitment to gender budgeting to establish its gender-differential impact and to translate gender commitments into budgetary commitments. It continued the process of dissecting the Government budget to establish its gender-differential impact and to translate gender commitments into budgetary commitments.

In the Eleventh Five Year Plan (2007-12), for the first time, women were recognized not just as equal citizens but as agents of economic and social growth. The Plan Document observed, "The approach to gender equity is based on the recognition that interventions in favour of women must be multi-pronged and they must: (i) provide women with basic entitlements, (ii) address the reality of globalization and its impact on women by prioritizing economic empowerment, (iii) ensure an environment free from all forms of violence against women (VAW)—physical, economic, social, psychological etc., (iv) ensure the participation and adequate representation of women at the highest policy levels, particularly in Parliament and State assemblies, and (v) strengthen existing institutional mechanisms and create new ones for gender main-streaming and effective policy implementation". [6]

6.6.3 Gender Budgeting in Union Budgets: The Finance Minister in his budget speech to Parliament on February 29, 2004 highlighted the perceived need for budgetary data to be presented in a manner that highlight the gender sensitiveness of the budgetary allocations. He observed, "Women's groups have met me and urged me to consider gender budgeting. This means that the budget data should be presented in a manner that the gender sensitivities of the budgetary allocations are clearly highlighted. An expert group on Classification System of Government Transactions has submitted its report on July 6, 2004. It has recommended appropriate systems for data collection and representation in the budget. The group has also recommended introduction of periodic benefit-incidence analysis. Government will examine the recommendations, and I hope it will be possible for me to implement some of them in the Budget for 2005-06". [7]

This was followed by a more emphatic commitment in the budget speech of the Finance Minister to Parliament on February 28, 2005, wherein the budgetary allocations under 10 demands for grants estimated at ₹ 14,379 crore were highlighted in a separate statement as a part of the Gender Budgeting exercise. The budget speech on February 28, 2006 revealed an estimated allocation of ₹ 28,737 crore for the benefit of women under 24 demands for grants in 18 Ministries and Departments. [8]

Gender outcome assessment and evaluation is of utmost importance for ensuring the success of gender budgeting. For this it is necessary that the gender funds flowing into schemes are properly and correctly assessed. The Finance Ministry has made it mandatory that gender outcomes form a part of the Outcome Budget prepared by every Ministry/Department as part of the Budget Documents.

6.6.4 Gender Budgeting at the Level of States: In the meeting of the National Development Council held on June 27-28, 2005, the Prime Minister emphasized upon the need for State Governments to join hands in the area of gender budgeting. He observed, "The issue of gender bias is another area which needs focused attention. In the Union Budget for 2005-06, we have made a beginning in gender budgeting by incorporating a separate statement highlighting gender sensitivities of budgetary allocations under 10 demands for grants, to be extended to all Central Ministries. But this task will remain incomplete unless all the States join hands in ensuring development justice to women. This is one of the important instruments to tackle the growing violence against women, which begins even before their birth and continues through their entire life span. It cuts across caste, class community and prevails in all parts, rural and urban. This is the right forum to pledge our wholehearted and unequivocal support for ensuring a violence-free world for our women and girl children".

The above position only reinforces the importance of extending gender budgeting initiatives to the State Governments. Further, implementation of almost all important schemes of the Government of India is with State Governments. Thus, any exercise in gender budgeting is incomplete without State Government initiatives. States should consider setting up Gender Budget Cells in key departments.

It is noteworthy that State Governments collectively reflect a higher amount of women-related expenditure than Government of India.

In spite of these promises and commitments and focus on women development and empowerment, the present status of women continues to be quite dismal in terms of important human development parameters like health, nutrition, literacy, educational attainments, skill levels, occupational status etc. There are various gender-specific barriers which prevent women from gaining access to their rightful share in the flow of public goods and services. Unless the felt needs of women are incorporated and mainstreamed in the development process, the fruits of economic growth are likely to bypass a significant section of the country's population.

This calls for a focused priority for strengthening and expanding gender budgeting in all its aspects.

6.7 Recent Budgetary Reforms

The Budget for 2017-18 contained three major reforms.

First, the presentation of the Budget was advanced to February 1, to enable the Parliament to avoid a Vote on Account and pass a single Appropriation Bill for 2017-18, before the close of the current financial year. This would enable the Ministries and Departments to operationalize all schemes and projects, including the new schemes, right from the commencement of the next financial year. They would be able to fully utilise the available working season before the onset of the monsoon.

Second, the merger of the Railways Budget with the General Budget was a historic step. The colonial practice of presenting Railways Budget separately, prevalent since 1924, was discontinued. This decision brought the Railways to the centre stage of Government's fiscal policy and facilitated multi-modal transport planning between railways, highways and inland waterways. The functional autonomy of Railways will, however, continue.

Third, the classification of government expenditure into plan and non-plan was done away with. This will help take a holistic view of allocations for sectors and ministries. This would also facilitate optimal allocation of resources.

6.8 Digitisation of the Budget

Beginning 2021-22, the Union Budget went paperless in the wake of ongoing coronavirus pandemic. For the first time since Independence in 1947, the budget papers presented on February 1, 2021 were not printed. The government had received permission for the same from both Houses of Parliament. Previously, around a staff of 100 people was required to stay at the printing press for about a fortnight. They were needed to stay on till the budget documents were printed, sealed and delivered on the day of the budget presentation (February 1). Now, soft copies of the budget are made available to all members of the Parliament and the general public.

The *Economic Survey*, presented to the Parliament 2-3 days ahead of the budget, also went digital with the budget documents. To enhance the e-readability, the aligning of the text in the Survey was changed from double column to single column. However, the tradition of presenting the Survey in two volumes continues. Volume I provides evidence-based economic analyses of the challenges of policy-making and tools to make it more effective. Volume II reviews recent developments in the major sectors of the economy. A statistical appendix is also part of the Survey.

Endnotes

1. Government of India, *Economic Survey*, 2000-01, p. 52.

2. Government of India, *Economic Survey*, 2006-07, p. 18.
3. *Report of the Eleventh Finance Commission*, June 2000, p. 33.
4. *Report of the Twelfth Finance Commission*, November 2004, p. 79.
5. The cycle of Five Year Plans in India was abolished after the completion of Twelfth Five Year Plan on March 31, 2017. In fact, Planning Commission, which formulated India's Five Year Plan, itself was scrapped by the Union Cabinet on August 13, 2014.
6. Government of India, Planning Commission, *Eleventh Five Year Plan* (2007-12), Volume II, pp. 184-185.
7. Government of India, Ministry of Finance, Budget Papers 2004-05, *Speech of the Finance Minister*, pp. 17-18.
8. Government of India, Ministry of Finance, Budget Papers 2006-07, *Speech of the Finance Minister*, p. 6.

7

Highlights of Central Government Budgets in India: 1947-48 to 2021-22

Note: The budget for the year 1947-48 for undivided India, passed by the Legislature in March 1947, ceased to be operative with the partition of the country and the emergence of two independent governments. The first budget of a free and independent India was presented to the Legislative Assembly by the then Finance Minister Shri R.K. Shanmukham Chetty on November 26, 1947. This interim budget covered a period of 7½ months from August 15, 1947 to March 31, 1948. The first full-year budget for 1948-49 was presented by the same Finance Minister on February 28, 1948.

The highlights presented below pertain to regular budgets. Interim budgets presented from time-to-time have been ignored with the exception of interim budget for the year 1947-48 presented on November 26, 1947.

Year	Budget Presented by
1947-48	Shri R.K. Shanmukham Chetty, Minister of Finance, Interim Budget (November 26, 1947)
1. First budget of independent India. 2. Focus on adjustments necessitated by the economic consequences of partition. 3. Rehabilitation of refugees from Pakistan imposes a heavy burden on the Central exchequer. 4. Expert Committee under the Chairmanship of Sir Purushottamdas Thakurdas submits interim report on food position in the country. 5. Reliance on the import of foodgrains imposes a heavy strain on the finances of the Government. 6. Prices show an unchecked upward tendency. 7. Agreement reached between the Central Government and the Provincial Governments concerned regarding the setting up of the Damodar Valley Authority.	
1948-49	Shri R.K. Shanmukham Chetty, Minister of Finance (February 28, 1948)
1. First regular budget of independent India. 2. Budget overshadowed by Mahatma Gandhi's death. 3. Food problem continues to cause anxiety and conditions turn for the worse in large parts of the Madras Presidency following the failure of the monsoon. 4. Deterioration in industrial relations, leading to strikes and disruption of work. 5. Substantial adverse balance in India's external payments. 6. Problems in financial settlements with Pakistan.	

7. Payment of municipal taxes on house property exempted from income tax.
8. Estate Duty Bill reintroduced.

1949-50	**Shri John Mathai, Minister of Finance (February 28, 1949)**

1. Food situation worsens due to floods in Bihar and the United Provinces, the damage caused by the cyclone in Bombay and the outbreak of famine in parts of Gujarat, Saurashtra, Rajasthan and Kutch.
2. Keeping the inflationary trends under control is a major problem.
3. State of the capital market a concern for the Government.
4. Sharp decline in the sterling balances held by the Reserve Bank of India.
5. Progress made in the work of the Income Tax Investigation Commission reviewed.
6. Capital gains tax abolished.

1950-51	**Shri John Mathai, Minister of Finance (February 28, 1950)**

1. First budget of the Republic of India.
2. First budget under the new Constitution.
3. Parliament asked to set up an Estimates Committee to scrutinise the expenditures of various Departments of the Government.
4. Planning Commission set up under the Chairmanship of Pandit Jawaharlal Nehru.
5. Recommendations of the Committee (under the Chairmanship of Shri V.T. Krishnamachari) which examined the financial arrangements necessary on account of the integration of the States accepted.
6. Business profits tax abolished.
7. Committee to inquire into the whole question of national income estimation set up.

1951-52	**Shri C.D. Deshmukh, Minister of Finance (February 28, 1951)**

1. Inflationary situation aggravated due to severe natural calamities like the earthquake in Assam, the floods in certain parts of Bihar and Uttar Pradesh, the failure, for the fifth year in succession, of the North-East monsoon over a large area of Madras.
2. Grow More Food plan re-oriented to concentrate on selected areas with assured water supply.
3. Bill to implement recommendations of the Income Tax Investigation Commission introduced.
4. Provision made for capital outlay on Sindri Fertiliser Factory and Bangalore Machine Tool Factory.

1952-53	**Shri C.D. Deshmukh, Minister of Finance (May 23, 1952)** **Note: An interim budget for the same year was presented on February 29, 1952 by the same Minister of Finance**

1. First budget presented to the Parliament elected under the new Constitution.
2. Steady drop in prices.

3. Licensing restrictions on the export of jute goods withdrawn.
4. Committee (under the Chairmanship of Shri V.T. Krishnamachari) examines the achievements of the Grow More Food Campaign.
5. Demands for grants to be presented for the gross amount of the expenditure.
6. Rise in the rate of deficit in the balance of payments.

1953-54	Shri C.D. Deshmukh, Minister of Finance (February 27, 1953)

1. Prices on the whole remain steady at lower levels.
2. Industrial and agricultural production shows increase.
3. Balance of payments position slightly favourable.
4. Report of the First Finance Commission placed before the Parliament.
5. Taxation Enquiry Commission under the Chairmanship of Dr. John Mathai set up.
6. Exemption limit for income tax increased from ₹ 3,600 to ₹ 4,200.

1954-55	Shri C.D. Deshmukh, Minister of Finance (February 27, 1954)

1. Improvement in the general food situation.
2. Satisfactory balance of payments position.
3. Revenue from estate duty included in the budget for the first time.
4. Compensation to displaced persons for the loss of immovable properties in West Pakistan.
5. Central Advisory Committee set up to guide and organise the campaign to mobilise savings.

1955-56	Shri C.D. Deshmukh, Minister of Finance (February 28, 1955)

1. Hindi version of the budget speech presented for the first time.
2. Women's Savings Campaign launched.
3. 10-year National Plan Certificates issued.
4. 15-year Annuity Certificates launched.
5. Report of Taxation Enquiry Commission (Chairman: Dr. John Mathai) submitted, many recommendations implemented.
6. Last Budget of the First Five Year Plan.
7. Report of the Rural Credit Survey submitted.

1956-57	Shri C.D. Deshmukh, Minister of Finance (February 29, 1956)

1. Budget for the first year of the Second Five Year Plan.
2. National Small Industrial Corporation along with four regional Small Industries Services Institutes set up.
3. More recommendations of the Taxation Enquiry Commission (1953-54) implemented.
4. Rate of income tax on highest slab of income, i.e. above ₹ 1,50,000 increased from 88.6 percent to 91.9 percent.
5. Excise duty extended to vegetable non-essential oils and all kinds of diesel.

1957-58	Shri T.T. Krishnamachari, Minister of Finance (May 15, 1957) Note: An interim budget for the same year was presented on March 19, 1957 by the same Minister of Finance

1. A White Paper reviewing the major economic developments in the economy during 1956 circulated along with Budget Papers.
2. Economic classification of the budget presented.
3. Continuing strain on foreign exchange resources.
4. Establishment of Refinance Corporation announced.
5. National Plan Savings Certificates launched.
6. Tobacco Expert Committee appointed under the Chairmanship of Shri Raghuramaiah.
7. Expenditure tax introduced for the first time in the world.
8. Tax on railway passenger fares levied.

1958-59	Shri Jawaharlal Nehru, Prime Minister and Minister of Finance (February 28, 1958)

1. Objective of socialist pattern of society reiterated.
2. Stability in prices.
3. Continuous strain on balance of payments since the beginning of the Second Five Year Plan.
4. Gift tax introduced.
5. Major changes in Excise Duty Act.

1959-60	Shri Moraji R. Desai, Minister of Finance (February 28, 1959)

1. Drop in agricultural production.
2. Growth of industrial production also declines.
3. Upward trend in prices.
4. Continuous pressure on the balance of payments.
5. Demands for grants to be presented by individual Ministries to Parliament.
6. Rates of wealth tax increased.
7. Wealth tax on companies abolished.
8. Excess dividends tax abolished.

1960-61	Shri Moraji R. Desai, Minister of Finance (February 29, 1960)

1. Stock markets buoyant.
2. Reserve Bank's sterling assets relatively stable.
3. Central Pay Commission submits report.
4. Central Economy Board to keep watch on growth in Government expenditure.

1961-62	Shri Moraji R. Desai, Minister of Finance (February 28, 1961)

1. A decade of planned development completed.
2. Balance of payments situation takes a turn for the worse.

3. Third Finance Commission constituted.
4. 5-year tax holiday for newly started hotels.

1962-63	**Shri Moraji R. Desai, Minister of Finance (April 23, 1962)** **Note: An interim budget for the same year was presented on March 14, 1962 by the same Minister of Finance**

1. Increase in the rate of income tax on Indian companies from 45 percent to 50 percent.
2. Expenditure tax abolished.
3. Rates of wealth tax increased.
4. Rate of import duty on cars increased from 100 to 150 percent.

1963-64	**Shri Moraji R. Desai, Minister of Finance (February 28, 1963)**

1. External payments position causes concern.
2. General surcharge of 10 percent levied on all import duties.
3. Export duty on tea abolished.
4. A comprehensive scheme of compulsory savings introduced.

1964-65	**Shri T.T. Krishnamachari, Minister of Finance (February 29, 1964)**

1. Rise in price level causes concern.
2. Amendments in Banking Companies Act and Companies Act to have strategic control over the private sector.
3. Rate of super tax in the case of non-resident companies increased from 38 percent to 40 percent.
4. Annuity Deposit Scheme comes into force.

1965-66	**Shri T.T. Krishnamachari, Minister of Finance (February 27, 1965)**

1. First budget after Pandit Jawaharlal Nehru's death.
2. Small Savings Certificates introduced.
3. Foreign exchange reserves deplete to critical level.
4. Compounded levy scheme for small power-looms further simplified.
5. Recommendations of the Tea Finance Committee accepted.
6. New Gold Bond Scheme launched.

1966-67	**Shri Sachindra Chaudhuri, Minister of Finance (February 28, 1966)**

1. Unprecedented failure of monsoons.
2. Duty on cigars and cigarettes raised.
3. Expenditure tax abolished due to administrative reasons.
4. Rate of surtax provided under the Companies (Profits) Surtax Act, 1964, reduced.
5. Exemption limit of income tax for individuals raised from ₹ 3,000 to ₹ 35,000.
6. Excise duty on crystal sugar raised from ₹ 28.65 to ₹ 37 per quintal.

1967-68	**Shri Moraji R. Desai, Deputy Prime Minister and Minister of Finance (May 25, 1967)** **Note: An interim budget for the same year was presented on March 20, 1967 by the same Minister of Finance**

1. Serious food situation created by the drought.
2. Sharp increase in prices due to drought.
3. Slow down in industrial output.
4. Export duty on jute manufactures reduced.
5. Priority industry treatment extended to approved hotels run by Indian companies.
6. Interim report of S. Bhoothalingam Committee on Tax Reforms submitted.

1968-69	**Shri Moraji R. Desai, Deputy Prime Minister and Minister of Finance (February 29, 1968)**

1. Agreement signed to import 3.5 million tonnes of foodgrain from the USA under PL 480.
2. Second session of UNCTAD held in New Delhi.
3. Dividend tax on excess distributions discontinued.
4. Surtax on company profits reduced from 35 percent to 25 percent.
5. Export Markets Development Allowance introduced.
6. Annuity Deposit Scheme discontinued.

1969-70	**Shri Moraji R. Desai, Deputy Prime Minister and Minister of Finance (February 28, 1969)**

1. First Budget of the Fourth Five Year Plan.
2. Economy shows signs of revival.
3. Export duty on jute manufactures reduced.
4. Tax holiday concession for new industrial undertakings and ships extended.
5. Agricultural wealth also brought under Wealth Tax Act.

1970-71	**Shrimati Indira Gandhi, Prime Minister and Minister of Finance (February 28, 1970)**

1. Special schemes for small farmers.
2. Urban Development Corporation set up.
3. Exemption limit in respect of gifts made lowered from ₹ 10,000 to ₹ 5,000.
4. Export duty on jute manufactures reduced.
5. Duty on cigarettes enhanced.

1971-72	**Shri Y.B. Chavan, Minister of Finance (May 28, 1971)** **Note: An interim budget for the same year was presented on March 24, 1971 by the same Minister of Finance**

1. Millions of refugees from Bangladesh cross over to India.
2. Surcharge on personal income tax increased from 10 percent to 15 percent.

3. Wealth tax rates drastically raised.
4. Excise duty on cigarettes increased.
5. Tax imposed on foreign travel.

1972-73	Shri Y.B. Chavan, Minister of Finance (March 16, 1972)

1. Establishment of Sixth Finance Commission announced.
2. Report of Direct Taxes Enquiry Committee (Chairman: Justice K.N. Wanchoo) submitted.
3. Exemption in respect of casual and non-recurring income in excess of ₹ 1,000 in a year withdrawn.
4. Deduction of tax at source in respect of payments made to contractors by the Government introduced.
5. Capital gains arising from the transfer of jewellery held for personal use also made chargeable to capital gains tax.

1973-74	Shri Y.B. Chavan, Minister of Finance (February 28, 1973)

1. Refugees from Bangladesh return to their homeland.
2. Failure of monsoon creates severe drought and scarcity conditions.
3. Abnormal increase in prices.
4. Refugees relief levies withdrawn.
5. Report of the Committee on Taxation of Agricultural Wealth and Income (Chairman: Dr. K.N. Raj) submitted.
6. Excise duties on luxury articles like refrigerators and air-conditioners increased.

1974-75	Shri Y.B. Chavan, Minister of Finance (February 28, 1974)

1. First year of the Fifth Five Year Plan.
2. Steep rise in crude oil prices turn terms of trade against India.
3. Acute inflationary pressure prevails in the economy.
4. New accounting classification prescribed by the Comptroller and Auditor General comes into force.
5. Recommendations of the Third Pay Commission accepted.
6. Maximum marginal rate of income tax reduced from 97.75 percent to 75 percent.

1975-76	Shri C. Subramaniam, Minister of Finance (February 28, 1975)

1. Tax holiday concession in respect of new industrial undertakings extended for a further period of five years.
2. Investment in equity shares of new companies engaged in priority industries exempted from wealth tax for a period of five years.
3. Tobacco Excise Tariff Committee's recommendation of a uniform tariff rate for all forms of non-flue-cured unmanufactured tobacco implemented.
4. Rate of Central sales tax on inter-State sale of goods raised from 3 percent to 4 percent.

1976-77	Shri C. Subramaniam, Minister of Finance (March 15, 1976)

1. 20-Point Economic Programme launched.
2. Maximum marginal rate of income tax reduced from 77 percent to 66 percent.
3. Compulsory deposit scheme for income-taxpayers extended for one more year.
4. Rate of stamp duty levied on instruments such as receipts and bills of exchange raised.

1977-78	Shri H.M. Patel, Minister of Finance (June 17, 1977) Note: An interim budget for the same year was presented on March 28, 1977 by the same Minister of Finance

1. First regular budget of Janata Party Government.
2. Inadequate rate of growth identified as fundamental problem of the Indian economy.
3. Primacy of agriculture emphasised.
4. Development of small scale industries underscored.
5. Policy of reduction in rates of direct taxes reversed.
6. Compulsory Deposit Scheme for income-taxpayers extended for another two years.

1978-79	Shri H .M. Patel, Minister of Finance (February 28, 1978)

1. Budget based on economic policy resolution of the Janata Party.
2. Relative price stability achieved.
3. Satisfactory balance of payments position.
4. Small industries and rural industries emphasised in the New Industrial Policy statement.
5. Chokshi Committee Report on Direct Tax Laws submitted.
6. Final Report of the Jha Committee on Indirect Taxes submitted.
7. Exemption limit for estate duty increased from ₹ 50,000 to ₹ 1 lakh.
8. Rate of excise duty on residuary tariff Item 68 increased from 2 percent *ad valorem* to 5 percent *ad valorem*.

1979-80	Shri Charan Singh, Deputy Prime Minister and Minister of Finance (February 28, 1979)

1. Agricultural production at a record level for the second year in succession.
2. Recommendation of the Seventh Finance Commission accepted by the Government.
3. Rate of surcharge on income tax on non-corporate taxpayers increased from 15 percent to 20 percent.
4. Compulsory Deposit Scheme for income-taxpayers extended for a further period of two years.
5. Rates of wealth tax increased.
6. Rate of surcharge on income tax in the case of companies increased from 5 percent to 7.5 percent.

1980-81	**Shri R. Venkataraman, Minister of Finance (June 18, 1980)** **Note: An interim budget for the same year was presented on March 11, 1980 by the same Minister of Finance**
1. Decline in Gross National Product in 1979-80 by about 3 percent. 2. Policy of reduction in rates of direct taxes reintroduced. 3. Maximum marginal rate of income tax reduced from 72 percent to 62 percent. 4. Exemption limit for wealth tax increased from ₹ 1 lakh to ₹ 1.5 lakh. 5. Special Excise Duty at the rate of 1/20th of the effective basic excise extended to all commodities.	
1981-82	**Shri R. Venkataraman, Minister of Finance (February 28, 1981)**
1. Sixth Five Year Plan approved by the National Development Council. 2. The budget reflects the objectives, priorities and programmes of the Sixth Plan. 3. Budget makes provision for 1982 Asian Games. 4. Compulsory Deposit Scheme for income-taxpayers extended for another two years. 5. Surcharge on income tax payable by all classes of companies reduced from 7.5 percent to 2.5 percent. 6. Exemption limit of ₹ 50,000 for estate duty raised to ₹ 1.5 lakh, the same as under the Wealth Tax Act.	
1982-83	**Shri Pranab Mukherjee, Minister of Finance (February 27, 1982)**
1. Fight against inflation a high priority of the Government. 2. Emphasis on domestic production of petroleum and petroleum products, fertilisers, steel, edible oils, and non-ferrous metals. 3. Two new savings instruments issued, namely Social Security Certificates and Capital Investment Bonds. 4. Encashment benefit in lieu of unavailed earned leave exempted from income tax. 5. Hotel Receipts Tax Act, 1980 repealed. 6. 1982 designated as the Productivity Year.	
1983-84	**Shri Pranab Mukherjee, Minister of Finance (February 28, 1983)**
1. Increase in industrial production by 8.6 percent in 1981-82. 2. Fourth Central Pay Commission appointed. 3. Income tax surcharge on non-corporate taxpayers increased from 10 percent to 12.5 percent. 4. Compulsory Deposit Scheme (Income Tax Payers) Act, 1974, extended for two years. 5. Surcharge on income tax payable by companies increased from 2.5 percent to 5 percent. 6. Levy of wealth tax in the case of closely-held companies revived.	
1984-85	**Shri Pranab Mukherjee, Minister of Finance (February 29, 1984)**
1. Industrial performance shows an improvement over the previous year. 2. Higher allocations provided for steel, non-ferrous metals, paper and cement.	

3. Rate structure relating to personal income tax substantially revised.
4. Exemptions available under Sections 33B, 35C, 80CC, 80D and 80E of the Income Tax Act withdrawn.
5. Additional Excise Duty in respect of cigarettes increased.

1985-86	Shri Vishwanath Pratap Singh, Minister of Finance (March 16, 1985)

1. First year of the Seventh Five Year Plan.
2. Surcharge on income tax in the case of all the categories of non-corporate taxpayers discontinued.
3. Compulsory Deposit Scheme for income taxpayers abolished w.e.f. April 1, 1985
4. Wealth tax exemption limit raised to ₹ 2,50,000.
5. Estate duty abolished w.e.f. March 16, 1985.
6. Interest tax withdrawn w.e.f. March 31, 1985.
7. Export duty abolished on all items except coffee, unmanufactured tobacco, mica and hides and skins.
8. Rate of excise duty in respect of Item 68 of the excise tariff raised from 10 percent to 12 percent.

1986-87	Shri Vishwanath Pratap Singh, Minister of Finance (February 28, 1986)

1. Budget based on Long Term Fiscal Policy announced in December 1985.
2. Improvement in the functioning of the infrastructure sector a top priority of the Government.
3. Indira Awaas Yojna for scheduled castes and scheduled tribes launched.
4. Date of determining the cost of asset in regard to capital gains tax advanced from January 1, 1964 to April 1, 1974.
5. Government empowered with pre-emptive right to purchase properties offered for sale in the market at the prices agreed to by the transferor.
6. Modified Value Added Tax (MODVAT) introduced.

1987-88	Shri Rajiv Gandhi, Prime Minister and Minister of Finance (February 28, 1987)

1. Government's intention to appoint a National Commission on Rural Labour announced.
2. New Education Policy adopted.
3. A new saving scheme based on the net saving principle introduced.
4. Tax on expenditure in expensive hotels levied at the rate of 10 percent of the expenditure.
5. MODVAT scheme extended to most of the remaining items.

1988-89	Shri Narayan Datt Tiwari, Minister of Finance (February 29, 1988)

1. Buffer stock policy leads to large build up of food stocks.
2. Industrial production increases by more than 8 percent during four successive years since 1984-85.

3. Kisan Vikas Patra introduced.
4. Standard deduction for income taxpayers increased from 30 percent to 33.33 percent.

1989-90	Shri S.B. Chavan, Minister of Finance (February 28, 1989)

1. Indian economy shows features of strength.
2. Last year of the Seventh Five Year Plan.
3. Drought surcharge on wealth tax and income tax withdrawn.
4. Rate of expenditure tax under the Expenditure Tax Act, 1987 enhanced.
5. Rate of foreign travel tax increased.
6. Raw wool imported by Khaki and Village Industries Commission exempted from the whole of duty.

1990-91	Prof. Madhu Dandavate, Minister of Finance (March 19, 1990)

1. Budget for the first year of the Eighth Five Year Plan.
2. Cabinet Committee on Prices formed to take effective steps to increase the supply of essential commodities.
3. Strain on balance of payments position.
4. Rampant tax evasion causes concern.
5. Employment Guarantee Scheme for the drought prone areas and areas with acute problem of rural unemployment launched.
6. A system of tax rebate on the gross amount of savings introduced.

1991-92	Dr. Manmohan Singh, Minister of Finance (July, 24 1991) Note: An interim budget for the same year was presented on March 4, 1991 by Shri Yashwant Sinha, Minister of Finance.

1. Economy in deep crisis.
2. Balance of payments situation precarious.
3. Economy faces double digit inflation.
4. Process of economic reforms starts.
5. Corporate tax rate for widely-held companies increased from 40 percent to 45 percent.
6. Corporate tax rate for closely-held companies increased from 45 percent to 50 percent.
7. Import tariff peaks above 150 percent eliminated.
8. Rajiv Gandhi Foundation established.

1992-93	Dr. Manmohan Singh, Minister of Finance (February 29, 1992)

1. Budget for the first year of the Eighth Five Year Plan.
2. Budget based on Industrial Policy Statement of July 1991.
3. Phased reduction in the statutory liquidity ratio (SLR) starts following the recommendation of the Narasimham Committee.
4. Interim report of Tax Reforms Committee (Chairman: Dr. Raja Chelliah) submitted.

5. Indexation of capital gains for inflation introduced.
6. Cut-off date for valuation of assets in relation to capital gains shifted from April 1 1974 to April 1, 1981.
7. Wealth tax only in respect of non-productive assets.
8. Basic exemption for wealth tax increased to ₹ 15 lakh.
9. Wealth tax to be imposed at the flat rate of 1 percent.
10. Peak import tariff reduced from 150 percent to 110 percent.

1993-94	**Dr. Manmohan Singh, Minister of Finance (February 27, 1993)**

1. 5-year tax holiday for new industrial undertakings located in all the North-Eastern States.
2. Separate auxiliary duty merged with basic customs duty.
3. Special excise duty merged with basic excise duty.

1994-95	**Dr. Manmohan Singh, Minister of Finance (February 28, 1994)**

1. Foreign currency reserves increase from US$ 1 billion in June 1991 to US$ 13 billion, restoring international confidence in India.
2. Further reduction in the peak rate of customs duty.
3. Extension of MODVAT to capital goods and petroleum products.
4. Reduction in the total number of *ad valorem* excise rates to about half the existing number.
5. Removal of complicated price list procedures.

1995-96	**Dr. Manmohan Singh, Minister of Finance (March 15, 1995)**

1. Signs of a strong revival in domestic industrial investment.
2. Foodgrains production at an all time record of 185 million tonnes.
3. Public stock of foodgrains at record level of 31 million tonnes.
4. Report of the Tenth Finance Commission submitted.
5. Peak rate of import duty reduced from 65 percent to 50 percent.
6. Uniform excise duty of 15 percent on parts of capital goods as against existing rates varying from 10 percent to 25 percent.

1996-97	**Shri P. Chidambaram, Minister of Finance (July 22, 1996)** **Note: An interim budget for the same year was presented on February 28, 1996 by Dr. Manmohan Singh, Minister of Finance**

1. Budget based on Common Minimum Programme of the United Front Government.
2. Stress on growth with social justice.
3. Special tax rebate for senior citizens raised.
4. Rate of surcharge on corporation tax reduced from 15 percent to 7.5 percent.
5. Minimum Alternate Tax (MAT) introduced.
6. Standard deduction for salaried employees having an income up to ₹ 60,000 increased from ₹ 15,000 to ₹ 18,000.

1997-98	Shri P. Chidambaram, Minister of Finance (February 28, 1997)
1. Foodgrains production at 191 million tonnes. 2. Drop in domestic crude oil production. 3. Sluggish performance of the power sector. 4. Income tax net widened by the introduction of one-by-four economic criteria scheme.	
1998-99	**Shri Yashwant Sinha, Minister of Finance (June 1, 1998) Note: An interim budget for the same year was presented on March 25, 1998 by the same Minister of Finance.**
1. Budget based on the National Agenda for Governance. 2. Development of infrastructure a top priority. 3. Emphasis on social sector development. 4. Saral–a simple one page taxpayer friendly form for income tax return introduced. 5. Gift tax abolished w.e.f. September 30, 1998. 6. Service tax extended to more services.	
1999-00	**Shri Yashwant Sinha, Minister of Finance (February 27, 1999)**
1. East Asian financial crisis leads to unprecedented global turmoil. 2. Major reforms in indirect taxes to promote productivity. 3. Expenditure Reforms Commission set up. 4. Zero-based budgeting to be initiated. 5. Guarantee Redemption Fund established. 6. ₹ 10,000 crore proposed to be raised through disinvestment programme. 7. Basic rates of customs duty reduced from 7 to 5. 8. One-by-six scheme of income tax extended to 19 more cities 9. Across-the-board surcharge of 10 percent on all categories of taxpayers.	
2000-01	**Shri Yashwant Sinha, Minister of Finance (February 29, 2000)**
1. 50-day Kargil conflict and super cyclone in Orissa create economic uncertainty. 2. 16 percent single rate Central Value Added Tax (CENVAT) introduced. 3. Many essential items exempted from excise duty. 4. Expert Group set up to examine all aspects of service tax. 5. Surcharge increased from 10 percent to 15 percent on non-corporate tax payers. 6. One-by-six scheme extended to another 79 cities in the country.	
2001-02	**Shri Yashwant Sinha, Minister of Finance (February 28, 2001)**
1. Intensification of infrastructure investment part of budget strategy. 2. Service tax extended to many more services. 3. Peak level of import duty reduced from 38.5 percent to 35.5 percent. 4. All surcharges payable by corporates and non-corporate assessees withdrawn except the surcharge of 2 percent for relief to quake hit areas of Gujarat.	

2002-03	Shri Yashwant Sinha, Minister of Finance (February 28, 2002)
1. VRS for surplus Government employees announced. 2. Service tax extended to many more services. 3. Peak rate of import duty reduced from 35 percent to 30 percent. 4. Exemption available to employees receiving amounts up to ₹ 5 lakh as VRS compensation extended to various other categories of employees. 5. New surcharge of 5 percent across-the-board on all categories of taxpayers levied. 6. 2 percent Gujarat earthquake surcharge abolished.	
2003-04	**Shri Jaswant Singh, Minister of Finance (February 28, 2003)**
1. Tenth Five Year Plan approved by the National Development Council. 2. Standard deduction raised to 40 percent of salary or ₹ 30,000 whichever is less. 3. VRS payments up to ₹ 5 lakh exempted even when taken in instalments. 4. Leave Travel Concession (LTC) facility restored. 5. Dividends made tax free in the hands of shareholders. 6. 12.5 percent dividend distribution tax levied on domestic companies. 7. Central Government agrees to compensate 100 percent of the loss in the first year, 75 percent of the loss in second year and 50 percent of the loss in third year, resulting from the introduction of VAT by State Governments. 8. Constitutional amendment proposed to enable the Government to levy tax on services. 9. Central sales tax on inter-State sales reduced to 2 percent. 10. Task Forces on Direct and Indirect Taxes (Chairman: Dr. Vijay Kelkar) submit reports. 11. Task Force on Corporate Governance (Chairman: Shri Naresh Chandra) submits report.	
2004-05	**Shri P. Chidambaram, Minister of Finance (July 8, 2004)** **Note: An interim budget for the same year was presented on February 3, 2004 by Shri Jaswant Singh, Minister of Finance.**
1. *Antyodaya Anna Yojana* to be continued and expanded. 2. Agricultural credit to be doubled in three years. 3. Cess of 2 percent on all Central taxes. Whole of the amount collected as cess to be earmarked for education. 4. An Investment Commission to be set up. 5. Sectoral cap for foreign direct investment (FDI) in telecommunications to be raised from 49 percent to 74 percent; in civil aviation from 40 percent to 49 percent; and in insurance from 26 percent to 49 percent. 6. ₹ 4,000 crore disinvestment target for the year 2004-05. 7. States to implement VAT from April 1, 2005. 8. Tax exemption withdrawn in respect of interest earned from a Non-Resident (External) Account and interest paid by banks to a non-resident or to a not-ordinarily resident on deposits in foreign currency. 9. A *defined contribution* pension scheme introduced from January 1, 2004 for Central Government employees.	

2005-06	Shri P. Chidambaram, Minister of Finance (February 28, 2005)
1. The basic exemption limit for personal income tax increased: in general to ₹ 1 lakh; for women to ₹ 1.35 lakh; and for senior citizens to ₹ 1.85 lakh. 2. The personal income tax rates modified: to 10 percent for income between ₹ 1 lakh to ₹ 1.5 lakh; 20 percent for income between ₹ 1.5 lakh to ₹ 2.5 lakh; 30 percent for income above ₹ 2.5 lakh. 3. Surcharge at 2.5 percent applicable in the case of individuals, HUFs, association of persons and body of individuals on taxable income above ₹ 10 lakh. 4. Standard deduction withdrawn. All prevailing sectoral caps/rebate under Sections 88, 88B and 88C removed.	

2006-07	Shri P. Chidambaram, Minister of Finance (February 28, 2006)
1. Income Tax Act amended to provide for compulsory obtaining of the permanent account number (PAN) before entering into prescribed transactions, and also to allot PAN suo moto in certain cases. 2. In order to tax unaccounted money being contributed to charitable and religious organizations by way of anonymous donations, such donations brought to tax at the rate of 30 percent in the hands of certain charitable and religious organizations in certain cases. 3. The peak rate of duty on non-agricultural products reduced from 15 percent to 12.5 percent. Ad valorem component of duty on textiles fabrics and garments also reduced to 12.5 percent. 4. Duty on ores and concentrates reduced from 5 percent to 2 percent. 5. Duty on mineral products, except for marble, granite, asbestos and cement reduced from 15 percent to 5 percent.	

2007-08	Shri P. Chidambaram, Minister of Finance (February 28, 2007)
1. Peak rate of customs duty on non-agricultural products reduced from 12.5 percent to 10 percent. 2. Customs duty on most chemicals and plastics reduced from 12.5 percent to 7.5 percent. 3. Excise duty exemption limit for small scale industry (SSI) raised from ₹ 1 crore to ₹ 1.5 crore. 4. Surcharge on income tax on all firms and companies with a taxable income of ₹ 1 crore or less removed. 5. In order to facilitate the creation of urban infrastructure, issue of tax-free bonds through State Pooled Finance Entities allowed.	

2008-09	Shri P. Chidambaram, Minister of Finance (February 29, 2008)
1. Eleventh Plan records first year growth rate of 8.7 percent. 2. R. Radhakrishna Committee on agricultural indebtedness submits its report. 3. A comprehensive debt waiver and debt relief scheme for farmers announced. 4. Three schemes designed to provide social security to workers in the unorganized	

	sector announced: Aam Admi Bima Yojana; Rashtriya Swasthya Bima Yojana; and Indira Gandhi National Old Age Pension Scheme. 5. Threshold limit of exemption from income tax increased from ₹ 1,10,000 to ₹ 1,50,000 in the case of all assesses. 6. General CENVAT rate on all goods reduced from 16 percent to 14 percent. 7. Service tax extended to 4 more services. 8. Import duty on steel melting scrap and aluminium scrap reduced from 5 percent to nil.
2009-10	**Shri Pranab Mukherjee, Minister of Finance (July 6, 2009)** **Note: An interim budget for the same year was presented on February 16, 2009 by the same Minister of Finance.**
	1. ₹ 25 crore each allocated for two campuses of Aligarh Muslim University at Murshidabad in West Bengal and Malappuram in Kerala. 2. Income tax exemption limit increased from ₹ 2.25 lakh to ₹ 2.40 lakh for senior citizens; from ₹ 1.80 lakh to ₹ 1.90 lakh for women tax payers; and from ₹ 1.50 lakh to ₹ 1.60 lakh for all other categories of individual taxpayers. 3. Basic customs duty on LCD panels reduced from 10 percent to 5 percent to support indigenous production of LCD televisions. 4. Basic customs duty on permanent magnets (a critical component for wind-operated electricity generators) reduced from 7.5 percent to 5 percent. 5. Branded jewellery fully exempted from excise duty.
2010-11	**Shri Pranab Mukherjee, Minister of Finance (February 26, 2010)**
	1. Symbol (₹) for the Indian rupee formalised, giving it a clear distinguishing identity like US Dollar ($), British Pound Sterling (£), Euro (€) and Japanese Yen (¥). 2. Surcharge of 10 percent on domestic companies reduced to 7.5 percent. 3. Rate of minimum alternate tax (MAT) increased from 15 percent to 18 percent of book profits. 4. Full exemption from excise duty to trailers and semi-trailers used in agriculture. 5. To encourage the use of bio-degradable materials, import of compostable polymer exempted from basic customs duty.
2011-12	**Shri Pranab Mukherjee, Minister of Finance (February 28, 2011)**
	1. Exemption limit for the general category of individual taxpayers increased from ₹ 1,60,000 to ₹ 1,80,000. 2. For senior citizens: (a) qualifying age reduced from 65 years to 60 years, (b) exemption limit increased from ₹ 2,40,000 to ₹ 2,50,000 and (c) a new category of very senior citizens (80 years and above) created, with exemption limit of ₹ 5,00,000. 3. Surcharge of 7.5 percent on domestic companies reduced to 5 percent. 4. Full exemption from excise duty to air-conditioning equipment and refrigeration panels for cold chain infrastructure.

5. Basic customs duty of 5 percent on specified agricultural machinery reduced to 2.5 percent. 6. Stainless steel scrap fully exempted from basic customs duty.	
2012-13	**Shri Pranab Mukherjee, Minister of Finance (March 16, 2012)**
1. Exemption limit for the general category of individual taxpayers enhanced from ₹ 1,80,000 to ₹ 2,00,000. 2. Upper limit of the 20 percent tax slab increased from ₹ 8 lakh to ₹ 10 lakh. 3. Deduction of up to ₹ 10,000 for interest from savings bank accounts allowed to individual taxpayers. 4. Basic customs duty on wool waste and wool tops reduced from 15 percent to 5 percent. 5. Excise duty on matches manufactured by semi-mechanised units reduced from 10 percent to 6 percent.	
2013-14	**Shri P. Chidambaram, Minister of Finance (February 28, 2013)**
1. National Livestock Mission launched with an allocation of ₹ 307 crore. 2. Cabinet Committee on Investment (CCI) set up to monitor investment proposals as well as projects under implementation, including stalled projects. 3. Tax credit of ₹ 2,000 provided to every person having total income up to ₹ 5 lakh. 4. Surcharge on domestic companies, whose taxable income exceeds ₹ 10 crore per year, increased from 5 percent to 10 percent. 5. Handmade carpets and textile floor coverings of coir or jute totally exempted from excise duty.	
2014-15	**Shri Arun Jaitley, Minister of Finance (July 10, 2014)** **Note: An interim budget for the same year was presented on February 17, 2014 by Shri P. Chidambaram, Minister of Finance**
1. *Sab ka Saath Sab ka Vikas* to reflect development strategy of the government. 2. A national multi-skill programme called Skill India launched for the youth with emphasis on employability and entrepreneurial skills. 3. *Pradhan Mantri Krishi Sinchayee Yojana* launched with an initial allocation of ₹ 1,000 crore. 4. Income tax exemption limit increased from ₹ 2.5 lakh to ₹ 3.0 lakh for senior citizens (above 60 years of age) and from ₹ 2.0 lakh to ₹ 2.5 for other categories of individual taxpayers. 5. Basic customs duty on battery waste and battery scrap reduced from 10 percent to 5 percent. 6. Basic customs duty at 10 percent imposed on specified telecommunication products. 7. Free baggage allowance increased from ₹ 35,000 to ₹ 45,000.	

2015-16	Shri Arun Jaitley, Minister of Finance (February 28, 2015)
1. Micro Units Development Refinance Agency (MUDRA) Bank, with a corpus of ₹20,000 crore, and credit guarantee corpus of ₹ 3,000 crore, created. 2. Pradhan Mantri Suraksha Bima Yojna, covering accidental death risk of ₹ 2 lakh for a premium of just ₹ 12 per year launched. 3. Transport allowance exemption under income tax increased from ₹ 800 to ₹ 1,600 per month. 4. Yoga included within the ambit of charitable purpose under Section 2 (15) of the Income Tax Act. 5. Education cess and the secondary and higher education cess subsumed under Central excise duty. 6. Clean energy cess increased from ₹ 100 to ₹ 200 per metric tonne of coal etc. to finance clean environment initiatives.	
2016-17	**Shri Arun Jaitley, Minister of Finance (February 29, 2016)**
1. Department of Disinvestment re-named as Department of Investment and Public Asset Management (DIPAM). 2. 100 percent deduction of profits for 3 out of 5 years for start-ups set up during April 2016 to March 2019. 3. Surcharge raised from 12 percent to 15 percent on persons, other than companies, firms and cooperative societies, having income above ₹ 1 crore. 4. Tax collection at source at the rate of 1 percent on purchase of luxury cars exceeding value of ₹ 10 lakh and purchase of goods and services in cash exceeding ₹ 2 lakh. 5. To discourage consumption of tobacco and tobacco products, excise duty increased on various tobacco products, other than beedi, from 10 to 15 percent.	
2017-18	**Shri Arun Jaitley, Minister of Finance (February 1, 2017)**
1. The presentation of the budget was advanced to February 1 to enable the Parliament to avoid a vote on account and pass a single Appropriation Bill before the close of the financial year. 2. Railways budget was merged with the general budget. 3. Plan and non-plan classification of expenditure discontinued. 4. Skill Acquisition and Knowledge Awareness for Livelihood Promotion Programme (SANKALP) launched with an allocation of ₹ 4,000 crore. 5. Threshold limit for audit of business entities who opt for presumptive income scheme increased from ₹ 1 crore to ₹ 2 crore. 6. Rate of tax for individual assesses with income between ₹ 2.5 lakh and ₹ 5 lakh reduced from 10 percent to 5 percent.	
2018-19	**Shri Arun Jaitley, Minister of Finance (February 1, 2018)**
1. Two new Funds with a corpus of ₹ 10,000 crore set up: (a) Fisheries and Aquaculture Infrastructure Development Fund (FAIDF) for fisheries sector and (b)	

	Animal Husbandry Infrastructure Development Fund (AHIDF) for financing infrastructure requirement of animal husbandry sector. 2. Target to provide free LPG connections under Ujjwala Scheme increased from 5 crore to 8 crore poor women. 3. Standard deduction of ₹ 40,000 allowed to salaried taxpayers in lieu of the existing exemption in respect of transport allowance and reimbursement of miscellaneous medical expenses. 4. Exemption of interest income on deposits with banks and post offices increased from ₹ 10,000 to ₹ 50,000 for senior citizens. TDS not required to be deducted on such income. 5. New scheme for assessment of income tax through electronic mode to eliminate person-to-person contact, leading to greater efficiency and transparency. 6. With the roll out of GST from July 1, 2017, the name of Central Board of Excise and Customs (CBEC) was changed to Central Board of Indirect Taxes and Customs (CBIC).
2019-20	**Shrimati Nirmala Sitharaman, Minister of Finance (July 5, 2019)** **Note: An interim budget for the same year was presented on February 1, 2019 by Shri Piyush Goyal, Minister of Finance.**
	1. Target of disinvestment receipts for the financial year 2019-20 set at ₹ 1,05,000 crore. 2. 25 percent rate of tax applicable to companies having annual turnover up to ₹ 250 crore widened to include all companies having annual turnover up to ₹ 400 crore. 3. PAN and Aadhaar made interchangeable, allowing those who do not have PAN to file income tax returns by simply quoting their Aadhaar number. 4. Tax deduction at source (TDS) of 2 percent levied on cash withdrawal exceeding ₹ 1 crore in a year from a bank account. 5. Custom duty on gold and other precious metals increased from 10 percent to 12.5 percent.
2020-21	**Shrimati Nirmala Sitharaman, Minister of Finance (February 1, 2020)**
	1. Investment Clearance Cell set up to provide end-to-end facilitation and support, including pre-investment advisory, information related to land banks and facilitate clearances at Centre and State levels. 2. 70 out of around 100exemptions and deductions in the income tax law removed to simply tax regime. 3. Businesses having turnover of more than ₹ 1 crore were required to get their books of account audited by an accountant. This threshold was increased to ₹ 5 crore in order to reduce compliance burden on small enterprises. 4. The process of registration of all new and existing charity institutions was made completely electronic by issuing a unique registration number (URN). 5. *Vivad Se Vishwas* (Trust instead of Dispute) Scheme launched under which a taxpayer was required to pay only the amount of the disputed taxes and was given complete

	waiver of interest and penalty provided he paid the taxes by March 31, 2020. 6. Central Board of Direct Taxes (CBDT) mandated to adopt a Taxpayers' Charter.
2021-22	**Shrimati Nirmala Sitharaman, Minister of Finance (February 1, 2021)**
	1. Budget presented in the midst of Covid-19 pandemic. 2. Six pillars of budget proposals: (a) health and wellbeing, (b) physical and financial capital, and infrastructure, (c) inclusive development for aspirational India, (d) reinvigorating human capital, (e) innovation and R&D, and (f) minimum government and maximum governance. 3. A new centrally-sponsored scheme, PM AtmaNirbhar Swasth Bharat Yojana launched with an outlay of about ₹ 64,180 crore over 6 years. 4. Jal Jeevan Mission (Urban) launched to provide universal water supply in all 4,378 Urban Local Bodies with 2.86 crore household tap connections. It would be implemented over 5 years, with an outlay of ₹ 2,87,000 crore. 5. Senior citizens (75 years of age and above), and having only pension and interest income, exempted from filing their income tax return. 6. Insurance Act, 1938 to be amended to increase the permissible foreign direct investment (FDI) limit from 49 percent to 74 percent in insurance companies and allow foreign ownership and control with safeguards.

Part II
Centre-State Financial Relations (Fiscal Federalism) in India

8

Federation and Fiscal Federalism: Conceptual Settings

8.1 Meaning and Features of a Federation

According to the traditional classification followed by political scientists, constitutions are either unitary or federal in nature. A federation means a union of several states brought about by the instrument of a treaty or agreement. The modern concept of federalism is associated with the establishment of American federation in 1787. Since there is no agreed definition of a federal state, the model of U.S.A. is often taken as the reference point.

Federalism is a dynamic and not a static concept. It can best be understood in terms of its essential features. The consensus of opinion is that a federal system involves the following essential features.

8.1.1 Dual Government: In a unitary state, there is only one Government, namely the national government. However, in a federal state, there are two layers of government: the union government and the state governments. A component state has no right to secede from the federation. This distinguishes a federation from a confederation.

8.1.2 Distribution of Powers: A federal state involves a division of authority between the federal government and the states. The method of distribution may not be alike in different federal constitutions.

8.1.3 Supremacy of the Constitution: A federal state derives it existence from the constitution. Every power (executive, legislative, or judicial) whether it belongs to the Union or to the State is subordinate to and controlled by the constitution.

8.1.4 Authority of Courts: As already noted, the legal supremacy of the constitution is essential to the existence of a federal system. There should be no violation of the provisions of the constitution by any tier of government. This is secured by vesting in the courts a final power to interpret the constitution.

8.1.5 Doctrine of Harmonious Construction: Harmonious construction means that different entries in different lists are so interpreted that a conflict between them is avoided. It must be accepted that the constitution does not want to create conflict and make any entry nugatory. Hence, whenever there appears to be a conflict between two entries in the two different lists, the two entries should be so interpreted that each of them is given effect. For this purpose, the scope and meaning of one may be restricted so as to give meaning to the other.

8.1.6 Doctrine of Pith and Substance: In a federal set up, the central and the state governments should keep themselves within the respective domain assigned to them. In other words, no government should trespass into the legislative powers reserved for the other. A law made by a government which encroaches upon the field assigned to the other government is invalid. However, before a law is declared invalid, the courts should apply the rule of pith and substance.

The rule of pith and substance means that a law enacted by a legislature which is competent to enact it shall not become invalid merely because it incidentally touches a matter outside the competence of that legislature. It often happens that a legislation intending to deal with a subject in one list touches also upon a subject in another list. Blind adherence to a strict interpretation would result in a large number of statutes being declared invalid. Thus, where such overlapping occurs, it is asked what in 'pith and substance' is the effect of the enactment in question and in which list is the true character to be found.

8.1.7 Rule of Repugnancy: Repugnancy or inconsistency between two pieces of legislation means that conflicting results are produced when both the laws are applied to the same facts. Repugnancy between two legal provisions can arise in a number of ways.

A. Tests of Repugnancy

1. An obvious case of repugnancy arises when one statute says 'do it' and the other statute says 'do not do it'. In such a case there is clear and direct inconsistency between the two Acts and the situation is absolutely irreconcilable.
2. Even if there is no apparent conflict between the two statutes, yet there may be repugnancy because both cover the same field. For example, when a statute describes an offence already created by another statute, and imposes a different punishment, repugnancy arises between the two.
3. When two statutes pertain to the same subject mater, but when Parliament intends to make its enactment a complete code and cover the whole field. In such a case, the State law whether passed before or after would be overruled on the ground of repugnancy.

8.2 Economic Basis of Decentralisation

Devolution of funds follows devolution of functions. The financing pattern of a government can be examined and decided only in the light of functions assigned to it. In fact, two factors determine the level of expenditure of a government: (a) its functional jurisdiction and (b) the standard at which its different functions are to be performed.

How should the responsibilities for providing public goods and services be shared between the central, state and local governments? According to the theory of fiscal federalism, functions which involve national interest, economies of scale, lumpy investments, and substantial spatial externalities (spill overs) should be left to the national government. Defence services are a case in point. Functions the benefits of which largely confine to regional jurisdictions and which are subject to heterogeneous preferences should be assigned to the state governments. Sanitation, street lightning, fire safety are services the benefits of which are localised and hence should be assigned to and performed by local governments (e.g. municipalities). In short, expenditure and service responsibilities should be assigned according to the benefit area of each service.

8.3 Advantages of Decentralised Decision-making

Decentralised decision-making meets the politico-economic aspirations of the people at the sub-national level.

Decentralisation of political and administrative powers is a virtue because it institutionalises the participation of those affected by local decisions. Following are the main advantages of decentralisation in a democratic set up.

1. Decentralisation of governmental functions allows better matching of public goods supply to local needs, tastes and preferences and hence increases social welfare.
2. State/local governments are more responsive and accountable to people than national government. Linkages between the decision to spend and that to raise resources improve fiscal discipline.
3. Mobilisation of resources at the state/local level reduces dependence and strain on the finances of national government.

8.3.1 Tiebout Hypothesis: According to Charles Tiebout, competition among local governments ensures efficiency in the supply of public goods, just as competition among firms ensures efficiency in the supply of private goods. He has argued that competition among local governments will result in these governments supplying goods and services individuals want the most, and producing these goods in an efficient manner. [1]

Federal system of government is a mixed blessing. It has the advantage of economic integration which promotes industrial and defence capabilities of a nation. However, a country cannot reap fully the economies of scale if provision for public goods is decentralised.

8.4 What is Fiscal Federalism?

A federal set up creates a multiple polity based on divided functions and powers among central, state and local governments.

Fiscal federalism deals with the division of governmental functions and financial relations among various levels of government within a federal structure. As a sub-field of public finance, fiscal federalism is concerned with understanding which functions and instruments are best centralised and which are best placed in the sphere of decentralised levels of government. From an operational perspective, it consists of the division of responsibilities in respect of taxation and public expenditure between the Centre and State Governments. In short, fiscal federalism deals with financial arrangements and their working in a federation.

8.5 Problems of Multi-level Finance: Vertical and Horizontal Imbalances

Although a federal system provides for divided governmental functions and powers, imbalances often (rather invariably) arise between functional responsibilities and financial resources at different layers of the government. This is so because revenue-raising capacities and revenue needs of various federating units are different. This is a characteristic feature of all federations, particularly of those whose economies are more dynamic. Even in older federations (like the United States, and Canada) financial conflicts persist between the national and sub-national governments and their once-for-all solution is unachievable.

The mismatch between functions and financial powers occurs partly because of changing responsibilities of different tiers of government and partly due to the dominant position of the national government in regard to taxation powers, which is often by design. Therefore, vertical imbalances of resources and expenditure responsibilities emerge between different levels of the government, calling for transfer of resources from the centre to the states. This is the familiar problem of federal finance. Financial imbalances at the vertical level (centre versus states), and at the horizontal level (among the states) are sought to be removed/reduced through constitutional arrangements, and in some countries through political bargaining as well.

8.6 Financing of Public Expenditure

8.6.1 Taxes: Tax revenue is generally the main source of financing public expenditure at different levels of the government. In most democratic countries, taxation powers of central, state and local governments are mentioned in the constitution itself. Taxation powers of the government at different levels may be mutually exclusive or overlapping. For example, most tax fields in Canada are jointly occupied by the federal and provincial governments. Personal income tax, corporation income tax, general sales tax, and consumption taxes (excise duties) are levied by the federal as well as provincial governments in that country. Customs duties which belong exclusively to the federal government are the only notable exception. The joint occupancy of tax fields has often caused friction not only between the federal and provincial governments but also among the provinces themselves. Mark Krasnick, a Canadian fiscal expert, observed, "The fact that both the federal government and the provinces occupy the lucrative income and commodity tax fields implies that in addition to any competition or conflict that may exist among the provinces, competition also exists between the federal government and the provinces. This conflict concerns the manner in which the tax capacity of a particular tax base is shared between the two levels; or, to use the common jargon, the way in which tax room is apportioned". [2]

In India, the centre and the states have no concurrent powers of taxation. Taxes with inter-state base and those in the case of which all-India uniformity in rates is desirable, to facilitate industry and trade, are vested in the central government. Taxes which are location-specific and relate to subjects of local consumption are with the states. Broadly speaking, taxes on production are levied by the centre and taxes on sale and purchase by the state governments. The absence of joint occupancy of tax fields has successfully minimised double taxation, tax rivalry between the centre and the states, and duplicate tax administration.

A. Assignment of Taxes: Assignment of a tax means transfer of taxation power from a higher level to a lower level of government. Taxation power includes the following: the right to levy the tax, collect the tax, and appropriate the proceeds from the tax. Thus, there can be three interpretations of assignment of a tax.

In the first case, the higher level government may levy a tax but allow the lower level government to collect it and retain fully the proceeds therefrom. Taxes levied by the Government of India under Article 268 of the Constitution fall under this category. [3]

Secondly, the higher level government may levy and collect a tax but handover the entire proceeds to a lower level government. Taxes levied by the Government of India under Article 269 of the Constitution are a case in point. [4]

Finally, the higher level government may transfer a tax to a lower level government lock, stock and barrel, a situation which defines assignment of a tax in its strictest sense.

Assignment of taxes should not be unconditional. Along with the determination of tax domain for a state, the central government ought to prescribe conditions so that the underlying purpose of assignment is adequately served. Thus, it should be obligatory on the part of a state to levy the tax assigned to it. Not only this, the state should not have powers to alter the basic structure of the assigned tax. The state may enjoy flexibility in fixing the tax rates within a minimum and maximum range prescribed by the central government. Tax exemptions/concessions should be minimum because a state is not expected to serve national objectives through its tax policy. As at other levels, tax default through disputes should be discouraged by requiring full payments prior to disputing an assessment.

8.6.2 Transfers: Transfers (tax sharing and grants) are used to correct vertical fiscal imbalances. However, before such transfers are effected, it should be ensured that taxes, duties, and levies assigned to the lower level government are being optimally tapped. Thus, tax effort, if not a pre-condition, should at least form part of the formula for transfers.

A. Need for Transfers: The need for transfers arises because the own revenues of a lower level government are generally insufficient to meet the expenditure required for providing services allotted to it. Very often central government retains with it elastic revenue sources such as income tax, excise levies, and customs duties. Contrarily, inelastic sources of revenue (such as sales tax, excise on liquor, and motor vehicle tax) are allotted to state governments. The gap between 'own resources' and expenditure needs indicates the degree of dependence of state governments on the central government. The theory of fiscal federalism justifies intergovernmental transfers on the following grounds.

(a) Fiscal Gap Correction: Fiscal gap occurs when there is a mismatch between the expenditure needs and revenue means of a state. Fiscal capacity and fiscal needs differ because geographical and climatic conditions are more favourable in some areas as compared to others. Hence, the access to revenue base varies from region to region. Similarly, per unit cost of services (e.g. supply of drinking water) varies depending upon the nature of terrain, and density of population. Sometimes fiscal gap may occur due to inappropriate assignment of revenue sources and functional responsibilities.

(b) Minimum Standard of Services: Transfers from the centre to the states may be needed to upgrade the existing level of services to ensure a common minimum standard across regions. For example, the central government may provide grants to states to ensure a national standard in the provision of some public services (say 70 litres of drinking water per person per day).

(c) Inter-jurisdictional Spill Overs: Spill overs (or spatial externalities) occur where the benefits of a locally provided service spread to persons who are not legally required to contribute to costs of the service. Services the benefits of which generally spill over to neighbouring jurisdictions include public transport, subsidised educational and medical facilities, anti-pollution measures, parks and recreational facilities. Inter-governmental grants are a major and often the most practical way of correcting for spill over effects.

(d) Performance of Agency Functions: Central government may use the services of state governments to implement certain schemes of national importance, e.g. disease control, preserving ecological balance, propagation of research and improved technology. Funds (often in the form of grants) are provided to state governments to perform such agency functions.

B. Forms of Transfers: Transfers from the higher level to a lower level of government are made in the form of: (a) tax sharing, (b) grants and (c) loans. The first two items generally account for the bulk of transfers on the revenue account.

(a) Tax Sharing: Formula-based tax sharing is a predictable source of revenue and the state governments automatically gain from the buoyancy of the shared central taxes. There are two types of tax sharing mechanism. Under the first method (called global sharing), the whole of the central tax revenue forms a pool for sharing with the state governments. A certain percentage of the total tax revenue of the centre is allocated to the state governments. The second method (called scheduler or itemised sharing) involves sharing of revenue from individual central taxes. Tax sharing may take the form of a fixed amount or a fixed proportion of tax revenue. Central government should share at least one buoyant tax (e.g. income tax) with state governments.

(b) Grants: Grants have the advantage of being targeted towards fiscally disadvantaged states to reduce horizontal fiscal imbalances. They can also be made conditional regarding their utilisation. Grants are given mainly for the purpose of equalisation, though they are often given to promote the objectives and priorities of the central government. It is noteworthy that while a state cannot be denied a part of a shared central tax even if it has no demonstrated financial need, grants are given upon genuine financial needs of a state. It is possible that even before tax devolution from the centre, some high-income states have surplus in their revenue account.

Keeping in mind the criteria of fiscal equity and efficiency, three types of grants may be given by the central government to states.

1. **General Purpose (or Unconditional) Grants:** These are given to offset fiscal disadvantages arising from lower taxable capacity and/or higher unit cost of the services provided (due to bad terrain etc.). Such equalising grants have to be general and their basic purpose is to enable different states to come up to a minimum standard of services provided.
2. **Specific Purpose (or Conditional) Grants:** These are tied to the achievement of specific objectives. They may be with or without matching requirements. They are used to ensure minimum levels of specified public services to be provided by state governments. Such grants are justified also where services have spill over effects. Thus, afforestation, slum improvement and literacy drives create benefits not only to local residents but also to community as a whole. Such schemes should preferably be financed through grants from the centre to the states.

3. **Incentive Grants:** These are given for the purpose of encouraging states to streamline their operations. These grants should depend on the measures taken by the states to strengthen their financial position.

(c) Loans: Financial resources from the higher level of government to lower level of government also flow in the form of loans. These loans are generally given for capital projects

C. Principles of Transfers: The designing of a sound system of transfers is of vital importance in the context of financial discipline and promotion of local initiatives. Central government may keep in mind the following broad principles so that amount transferred is equitably distributed among the states.

1. The scheme of transfers should be based on well-defined objective criteria so that financially weak states are adequately assisted. These may include size of population, level of economic development, availability of infrastructure, and minimum service standards.
2. The system of transfers should be so designed that states are not discouraged to mobilise resources on their own. Contrarily, the system should contain in-built mechanism to promote internal mobilisation of resources and their judicious management. For this purpose, the following additional criteria may be adopted and given due weightage: tax effort, adoption of sound financial management, innovations in the provision of public services, and economy in expenditure.
3. The amount and frequency of transfers should be reasonably predictable. They should be pre-determined rather than being open-ended. Transparency, through explicit and identifiable budget entries, should also be ensured.

8.6.3 Borrowings: Long-term borrowings by a government are justified when the benefits of a capital project undertaken by it are likely to be reaped over a long period of time, i.e. by more than one generation of taxpayers. The financing of such projects should place the repayment burden on the present as well as future generations. If long-term capital projects are financed out of current revenues and/or short-term borrowings, the future generations would enjoy free riding. Thus, it is both fair and efficient that projects with long-term benefits are financed through long-term borrowings.

Access to long-term borrowings by a lower level government though desirable is hindered by a variety of factors. Generally, central government imposes restrictions on the borrowing powers of the state governments which, in turn, impose restrictions on the borrowing powers of the local bodies under them. Since borrowings by the lower level government are guaranteed, in most case, by the higher level government, the latter has a right to impose such restrictions. These restrictions apply to:

1. Purpose of debt (productive or unproductive).
2. Amount of debt.
3. Duration of debt (long-term, medium-term or short-term).
4. Interest rate on debt.
5. Any other restriction (generally lower-level governments are not allowed to borrow outside the country.

Approval of the higher level government, often cumbersome, is needed before the debt is floated.

Moreover, capital markets in underdeveloped countries are not fully developed. As in the developed West, bond markets cannot be successfully introduced in the absence of institutional set up in place. Besides, the track record of state/local governments as borrowers is rather poor. Till they establish their credit worthiness, and financial intermediaries come of age, borrowings by lower level governments in developing countries are unlikely to be important.

8.7 Earmarking of Revenue

Earmarking is a fiscal practice under which revenue from one or more sources is pooled into a separate independent fund which is used to finance a pre-determined public service.

The purpose of earmarking is to ensure stable funding for important public activities. Another objective of earmarking is to introduce market prices into the budgetary process. In this context, earmarked taxes represent market prices charged indirectly for rendering public services.

8.7.1 Conditions for Successful Earmarking: For successful earmarking, the following conditions need to be satisfied.

A. Expenditure Specificity: Expenditure to be financed through earmarked revenue should be well-defined and specific, i.e. the taxpayers should be able to identify its obvious benefits.

B. Tight Linkage: The linkage between earmarked revenue (e.g. motor vehicle tax) and pre-determined expenditure (e.g. construction of a flyover) should be tight. If the amount earmarked is substantially less than the amount spent on the designated function, earmarking will be less effective.

C. Strong Benefit Linkage: There should be a close correspondence between the tax levied and the benefit received. Preferably, the tax should take the form of a direct user charge, e.g. a toll.

Traditionally, financing of expenditure on construction and maintenance of municipal roads and bridges from out of tolls, motor vehicle taxes, and fuel taxes has been considered an activity with strong economic rationale for earmarking. Similarly, airport tax is levied to meet expenditure on airport maintenance. The principle of earmarking could be applied to such municipal services as water supply and sewage disposal through water and sewer charges, using the base for property tax. However, earmarking should not be applied indiscriminately because too many funds created under it would be difficult to manage.

Endnotes

1. For more on Tiebout hypothesis, see: 1. Harvey S. Rosen and Ted Gayer, *Public Finance* (New York: McGraw Hill), International Eighth Edition (2008), pp. 511-514. 2. Joseph E. Stiglitz, *Economics of the Public Sector* (New York: W.W. Norton and Company) Third Edition, 2000, pp. 735-737.
2. Mark Krasnick (1986), *Fiscal Federalism,* University of Toronto Press, Toronto, p. 6.

3. Article 268 of the Constitution refers to such stamp duties as are mentioned in Entry 91 of List I (Union List) of the Seventh Schedule of the Constitution, namely rates of stamp duty in respect of bills of exchange, cheques, promissory notes, bills of lading, letters of credit, policies of insurance, transfer of shares, debentures, proxies, and receipts.
4. Article 269 of the Constitution refers to taxes on the sale or purchase of goods and taxes on the consignment of goods, except as provided in Article 269A. These taxes correspond to Entries 92A and 92B of List I (Union List) in the Seventh Schedule of the Constitution.

Taxation arrangements under Articles 268 and 269 of the Constitution are of special importance. They place under the charge of the Union the taxes and duties which have inter-State character and require uniformity in rate structure for the smooth conduct of business and trade activities throughout the country. These two Articles mention taxes/duties which shall be levied by the Centre but assigned completely to the States within which they are leviable.

9

Nature and Features of Indian Federation

Prior to Independence in 1947, India was a dependency of the United Kingdom and consisted of British India, and the Princely States. It encompassed the entire area which now forms the four countries of India, Pakistan, Myanmar, and Bangladesh.

9.1 Constitution and India's Federal Structure

The Constitution of India which was adopted by the Constituent Assembly on November 26, 1949, became operative on January 26, 1950. It provides for two layers of Government, one at the Central level, and the other at the level of the States.

The very first Article of the Constitution defines India, also known as Bharat, as a Union of States. It is a *Sovereign, Socialist, Secular, Democratic Republic* with a parliamentary system of government. Though the word federation has been deliberately avoided in the Indian Constitution, the political system introduced by it possesses all the essentials of a federal polity. Other important countries of the world with federal set up of government are: US, Canada, Australia, Brazil, and Nigeria.

India's constitution, the longest and the most exhaustive constitution of any independent nation in the world, is the supreme organic law of the land. Both the Centre and State Governments derive their authority from the constitution. The States are not allowed to secede from the union.

India is the largest democratic federal republic in the world, inhabited by 121 crore people (Census 2011) and covering an area of 3.29 million square kilometres.

Politically, the country is divided into 28 States and 8 Union Territories (UTs), collectively called the Republic of India. Out of the 8 UTs, 3 have their own legislatures: (i) Delhi, (ii) Pondicherry and (iii) Jammu and Kashmir). The remaining 5 are without legislature: (i) Andaman and Nicobar Islands, (ii) Lakshadweep, (iii) Chandigarh, (iv) Ladakh, and (v) Dadra and Nagar Haveli and Daman and Diu.

There are wide variations in the size and economic structure among the States. According to 2011 Census, Uttar Pradesh, with 20 crore people, was the largest State, and Sikkim, with 6 lakh people, was the smallest. The country has a three-tier federal structure with governments at Union, States and Local levels.

Below the State Governments, in urban areas there are 96 municipal corporations, 1,494 municipalities, and 2,092 smaller municipalities (called *Nagar Panchayats*). There are 2,47,033 rural local bodies or *panchayats*, of which 515 are at the district level, 5,930 at the block level, and 2,40,588 at the village level. However, the devolution of powers to the third level is uneven among States and their participation in public service delivery is negligible.

Why did the framers of the Constitution opt for a federal set up? Answering this question, the Commission on Centre-State Relations, 1988, observed, "In a country too large and diverse for a unitary form of Government, they envisaged a system which would be worked in co-operation by the two levels of government—national and regional—as a common endeavour to serve the people. Such a system, it was conceived, would be most suited to Indian conditions as it would at once have the advantages of a strong unified central power, and the essential values of federalism". [1]

9.2 Division of Powers

A federal polity like India requires division of powers and responsibilities between the Centre and the States and generally brings in its wake problems and conflicts in Centre-State relations. Hence, the Constitution describes in detail the legislative powers and functions of the two tiers of Government.

There is a division of legislative, administrative and financial powers and functions between the Union and the State Governments. Under Article 246 read with Seventh Schedule of the Constitution, these powers and functions have been defined through precise entries in the three lists in the Schedule. Thus, the Centre has exclusive powers to legislate in respect of matters contained in List I (Union List) such as defence, foreign affairs, citizenship, railways, posts and telegraph, telephones, broadcasting, airways, banking, coinage and currency. Entries 82 to 91 and 92A and 92B of this list pertain to taxation powers.

Similarly, the States enjoy the power to legislate on matters mentioned in List II (State List) such as public order, police, public health, local government, agriculture and fisheries. Entries 45 to 63 (excluding 52 and 55) of this list relate to taxation powers of the States.

The Parliament and the State Legislatures have concurrent powers to make laws on any matters in List III (Concurrent List). The framers of the Constitution recognised that there was a category of subjects of common interest which could not be allocated exclusively either to the Union or the States. Some of the items included in the Concurrent List are marriage and divorce, forests, economic and social planning, population control and family planning, legal, medical, and other professions. This list does not contain any head of taxation. [2] Residuary powers of legislation including taxation belong to the Centre as per Entry 97 of List I.

The foregoing three-fold division of subjects of legislation rests on the ground that matters of national concern are placed in List I and those of purely State or local significance in List II. Matters of common Centre-State interest are included in List III.

The Supreme Court stands at the head of India's judiciary to guard this distribution of powers and to invalidate any action which violates the limitations imposed by the Constitution.

According to Article 254 of the Constitution of India, if any provision of a State law is repugnant to any provision of a Central law, then the Central law shall prevail and the law made by the State shall be void to the extent of repugnancy. The most common application of Article 254 arises when both the Central and State Governments enact legislation on the same matter contained in List III of the Seventh Schedule of the Constitution. In such a situation, if there is repugnancy then Central law prevails over the State law.

Indian constitution has a strong Central bias. The financial powers of the Central Government are overwhelming. According to some scholars, the constitution of India is neither purely federal nor purely unitary but is a combination of both. India's constitution is sometimes described as federal in times of peace and unitary in times of war.

9.3 Centrally Biased Constitution and its Justification

From its very inception, the Constitution is loaded in favour of the Centre. Constitutional amendments effected subsequently have tilted the balance further in favour of the Centre. The concept of a strong Centre has been incorporated in the anatomy of the Constitution through a variety of devices, among which the following are noteworthy.

9.3.1 Supremacy of Union Legislative Power: Article 246(2) and (3), and Article 254 (1) establish the supremacy of Union legislative power. Thus, where with respect to a matter, there is irreconcilable conflict or overlapping as between the three lists of the Seventh Schedule, the legislative power of the States must yield to that of the Union. This is how the non-obstante provisions of clauses (1) and (2) of Article 246 is interpreted. Similarly, Article 254(1) states that a law made by a State legislature, repugnant to a law made by the Parliament or an existing law applicable in that State, in regard to any matter enumerated in the Concurrent List, shall be void to the extent of repugnancy.

9.3.2 Union Control over State Legislation: Articles 200 and 201 establish control of the Union executive over State legislation. Article 200 provides that a Bill passed by a State Legislature shall be presented to the Governor who may give his assent, withhold his assent or return the same for reconsideration by the legislature. However, if it is again passed by the State legislature, with or without amendment, he shall not withhold his assent. The Governor may also reserve the Bill for consideration of the President (in effect the Union Council of Ministers) who may in turn signify his assent, withhold the same or return it for reconsideration. However, in contrast to the position of the Governor, the President need not give his assent when such a Bill is returned with or without amendment after reconsideration by the legislature of the State (Article 201).

9.3.3 Emergency Provisions: Articles 352 and 360 provide for certain emergency provisions. Article 352 provides for proclamation by the President of a grave emergency whereby the security of India is threatened by war or external aggression or armed rebellion. When such a proclamation is in operation, the Union may assume for its organs all the legislative and executive powers of the States. A proclamation of emergency has the effect of converting the State List into Concurrent List and, therefore, if the Parliament legislates on any subject in the State List, the State laws, to the extent of repugnancy, shall be null and void and the law made by the Parliament shall prevail.

Article 360 envisages yet another type of emergency, i.e. financial emergency. If the President is satisfied that a situation has arisen whereby the financial stability or credit of India or of any part of its territory is threatened, he may proclaim a financial emergency. When such an emergency is in operation, the executive authority of the Union extends to directing any State for the purpose of securing observance of canons of financial propriety.

9.3.4 Restrictions on Taxation Powers of the States: Constitution also imposes certain restrictions on the taxation powers of the States. Although a State legislature enjoys the power to levy any of the taxes mentioned in List II, in the case of certain taxes, this power is subject to restrictions imposed by substantive provisions of the Constitution. For example, a State legislature is empowered to levy a tax on professions, trade, calling or employment vide Entry 60 of List II. However, the total amount payable in respect of any one person to the State by way of such tax is not to exceed ₹ 2,500 per annum [Article 276(2)].

9.3.5 Restrictions on Borrowing Powers of the States: Under Article 292 the executive power of the Centre extends to borrowing, either within or outside India, upon the security of the Consolidated Fund of India, within such limits, if any, as may from time-to-time be fixed by Parliament. However, the borrowing power of a State (Article 293) is subject to a number of restrictions: (i) it cannot borrow outside India; (ii) it can borrow within the territory of India subject to the following conditions (a) limitations as may be imposed by the State Legislature, (b) consent of the Union Government to raise fresh loan if the Union has guaranteed an outstanding loan of the State, (c) consent of the Union to raise fresh loan if a Union loan to the State remains outstanding. Since all the States are in debt to the Centre, they have to obtain Centre's permission for raising loans. These restrictions are meant to avoid uncontrolled borrowings by the States and thus to prevent the possibility of any State becoming defaulter or insolvent. In short, the Centre enjoys almost unlimited powers to borrow from internal and external sources while the borrowing powers of the States are subject to various restrictions

9.3.6 President's Rule: Lastly, there is the controversial Article 356. According to it, if the President on receipt of a report from the Governor of a State, or otherwise, is satisfied that a situation has arisen in which the Government of the State cannot be carried on in accordance with the provisions of the Constitution, he may by proclamation assume to himself all or any of the functions of the State Government. He may also declare that the powers of the Legislature of the State shall be exercised by or under the authority of the Parliament.

In view of the above provisions of the Constitution, some experts call it unitary in extraordinary situations, such as war (or emergency), and federal in normal times. It is also called as a quasi-federal Constitution.

Similarly, a scrutiny of the taxation powers contained in the Union List and the State List reveals that major and elastic sources of tax revenue belong to the Centre while relatively inelastic sources of revenue come under the purview of State Governments.

Why is there a need for a strong Centre? According to the Commission on Centre-State Relations, 1988, "The primary lesson of India's history is that, in this vast country, only that polity or system can ensure and protect its unity, integrity and sovereignty against external aggression and internal disruption, which ensures a strong Centre with paramount powers, accommodating, at the same time, its traditional diversities. This lesson of history did not go unnoticed by the framers of the Constitution. Being aware that, notwithstanding the common cultural heritage, without political cohesion, the country would disintegrate under the pressure of fissiparous forces, they accorded the highest priority to the ensurance of the unity and integrity of the country". [3]

Moreover, the founding fathers were aware that several regions or areas of India were economically and industrially far behind in relation to others, a situation which exists even today. Revenue-raising capacities and revenue needs of various States also differ. To reduce these economic disparities, a policy of regional balanced development was necessary, and which could be effectively implemented by a financially and otherwise strong Centre.

9.4 Commission on Centre-State Relations, 1988

Government of India appointed in 1983 a Commission on Centre State Relations under the Chairmanship of Mr. Justice R.S. Sarkaria, a retired judge of the Supreme Court. The Commission was set up to review the whole gamut of Centre-State relations in their legislative, administrative, and financial aspects.

The monumental report of the Commission, submitted in 1988, basically accepted the existing framework of the Constitution. It disfavoured any major changes in the provisions of the Constitution including the financial arrangements. It stood for a strong Centre to preserve the unity and integrity of the country.

An important recommendation of the Commission pertained to the residuary power of legislation under the Constitution. Article 248 read with Entry 97 of List I (Union List) of the Seventh Schedule vests in Parliament the residuary powers of legislation with respect to any matter not enumerated in List II (State List) or List III (Concurrent List). Such residuary powers include the power of making any law imposing a tax not mentioned in these Lists.

Regarding residuary powers of legislation, the Commission recommended, "that residuary power of legislation in regard to taxation should advisedly remain with Parliament. But, the residuary field other than that of taxation may be transferred to the Concurrent List...The Constitution may be suitably amended to give effect to this recommendation". [4]

Thus, the Commission recommended partial transfer of Entry 97 to the Concurrent List. Unfortunately, no action has been taken so far to implement this recommendation of the Commission.

As regards financial relations between the Centre and the States, the Commission recommended as follows.

1. The Commission disfavoured any major modification in the basic scheme of the Constitution dividing the fields of taxation between the Centre and the States.
2. It rejected almost all the suggestions to shift the taxation powers of the Centre to the States. Such suggestions pertained mainly to the shifting of terminal taxes on goods and passengers carried by railways, estate duty, and banking etc.
3. The Commission was not in favour of making the devolution of funds from the Centre to the States automatic. In its view the existing division of functions between the Finance Commission and the Planning Commission was reasonable and must

continue.

4. In its opinion the terms of reference of the Finance Commission should be drawn up in consultation with State Governments.
5. Significantly, the Commission recommended the sharing of corporation tax between the Centre and the States. Most other suggestions for enlarging the divisible pool were turned down.
6. It recommended legislation to levy consignment tax and constitutional amendment to enable levy of tax on advertisements in broadcasting.
7. As regards agricultural income tax, the Commission observed that as opinions are divided the matter should be examined further in depth.
8. The Commission recommended the setting up of an expert committee to examine taxation reforms and resource mobilisation.
9. Some other recommendations of the Commission included: review of the royalty paid to the States, modernisation of treasury systems, making available foreign borrowings by States from the banks, the issue of tax free municipal bonds, and assistance for natural calamities, shifting of additional excise duty from fabric to yarn, and setting up of special courts for economic offences.

To sum up, although the term *federation* has nowhere been used in the Indian Constitution, the federal character of the Constitution is one of its salient features. Constitution has provided for a structure of governance which is essentially federal in nature. It contains all the usual features of a federation, namely two tier government, division of powers, supremacy of Constitution, independent judiciary and bicameralism. However, the Indian Constitution also contains a large number of unitary or non-federal features, viz. a strong Centre, single constitution, single citizenship, integrated judiciary, appointment of State Governors by the Centre, all-India services, emergency provisions, and so on.

Article 1 of the Constitution describes India as a *Union of States* which implies two things: 1. Indian federation is not the result of an agreement by the States. 2. No state has the right to secede from the federation. Hence, the Indian constitution is often described as *federal in form but unitary in spirit*.

Within this basic framework of federalism, the constitution has given overriding powers to the Central Government. States must exercise their executive power in compliance with the laws made by the Central Government and must not impede on the executive power of the Union. Governors are appointed by the Central Government to oversee the States. The Centre can even take over the executive of the States on the issues of national security or breakdown of constitutional machinery of the State. Considering the overriding powers given to the Central Government, Indian federation has often been described as *quasi-federation.*

Federalism with the cultural and ethnic pluralism has given the country's political system great flexibility, and therefore the capacity to withstand stress through accommodation. However, continuation of the same requires not simply federalism, but co-operative and constructive federalism. A strong Centre is necessary for strong States and vice versa is the essence of cooperative federalism.

Indian federation should be seen in the context of its democratic system of governance at the national, state and local levels and the pluralities of its culture in terms of ethnic, linguistic, religious and other diversities which cut through the States.

India's federal polity ensures that governance is distributed spatially and a strong Central Government enables that the *unity amidst diversity* is maintained. It is through federation that the country mobilizes all its resources to maintain its harmony and integrity and marches ahead to progress.

It has been a trend in Indian political history that so long as the Central and State Governments are ruled by the same political party, the co-operative framework works very well. However, when different political parties are in power at the Centre and the States—and more recently when coalition governments are in power—there are signs of stresses and tensions in inter-governmental relations.

The post-Independence changing dynamics and the varied experiences that India has had—like rise of regional parties, formation of coalition Governments, active role of the Judiciary—have shaped the trajectory of federalism by swinging the pendulum from co-operative to confrontationist and vice versa.

Endnotes

1. Government of India, *Report of the Commission on Centre-State Relations* (Chairman: Justice R. S. Sarkaria) Part I, 1988, p. 8.
2. It is noteworthy that Article 246A of the Constitution confers concurrent powers to both Parliament and State Legislatures to make laws with respect to goods and services tax (GST).
3. *Report of the Commission on Centre-State Relations, op. cit.*, p. 7.
4. *Ibid.*, p. 31.

10

Centralisation of Revenues and the Need for and Channels of Transfers to States

10.1 Centralisation of Revenues

As per the current constitutional provisions, some most productive sources of revenue have been assigned to the Centre from the point of view of administrative convenience, uniformity and efficiency. Thus, income tax, the main source of direct tax revenue, is levied under the Income Tax Act, 1961. Entities chargeable to tax under the Act are of two types: (i) non-corporate entities, and (ii) corporate entities. Non-corporate entities mainly consist of individuals and firms and their taxation is called personal income tax.

In the field of indirect taxes, the chief source of revenue is the central goods and services tax (CGST) component of GST plus Centre's share in integrated goods and services tax (IGST). Besides, the Constitution grants exclusive powers to the Central Government to impose duties of customs. By virtue of Entry 83 of List I (Union List) in the Seventh Schedule of the Constitution of India, the Central Government is empowered to impose 'duties of customs including export duties'.

States, on the other hand, have no direct taxes of revenue significance. Land revenue, which formed the bulwark of States' tax revenue during the pre-Independence period and even in the early post-Independence years, has declined in importance over the years. In some States, land revenue has been abolished altogether. Agricultural income tax, which could have been an important source of revenue for the States, has remained negligible till date.

As regards indirect taxes, the main source of revenue for the states is the state goods and services tax (SGST) component of GST plus the share of importing State in the IGST. In addition to this, the States also levy duties of excise on alcoholic liquors for human consumption. [1] They also levy sales tax/VAT on the following five petroleum products: (a) petroleum crude, (b) high speed diesel, (c) motor spirit (commonly known as petrol), (d) natural gas and (e) aviation turbine fuel. [2]

Similarly, while borrowing (internal and external) powers of the Centre are unlimited, those of the States are subject to following restrictions: (i) it cannot borrow outside India; (ii) it can borrow within the territory of India subject to the following conditions: (a) limitations as may be imposed by the State Legislature, (b) consent of the Union Government to raise fresh loan if the Union has guaranteed an outstanding loan of the State, (c) consent of the Union to raise fresh loan if a Union loan to the State remains outstanding.

Constitutional provisions regarding taxation and borrowing powers of the Centre and the States, place the former in a commanding position. Not only the major sources of tax revenue belong to the Centre, its borrowing powers are also unlimited.

Moreover, the Central Government enjoys the exclusive right to print currency. At the same time, the major responsibility for the delivery of social services to the population has been vested with the States, and has now been devolved further downward to the panchayti raj institutions (PRIs). Given this situation, therefore, a very substantial responsibility falls on the Central Government to ensure that the overall flows of resources from the Centre to the States is adequate to meet the revenue needs of the states. Moreover, it should also be ensured that the relatively backward states are enabled to achieve a level of service delivery at par with the more advanced States. This involves issues of the fiscal capacity available to states to raise revenues, the extent to which such capacity is actually being utilized and the specific difficulties that the states face which result in increased unit costs of service delivery.

10.2 Need for Inter-governmental Transfers

Though the Constitution creates a dual polity based on divided governmental powers and functions, this division is not watertight. As the Administrative Reforms Commission, 1968, observed, "Exact correspondence of resources and functions is not possible to secure in any federal situation but in India the balance is tilted rather heavily in favour of the Centre and the outstanding feature of the financial relationship between the Centre and the States consequently is that the former is always the giver and the latter the receivers. The favourable position given to the Centre in regard to financial resources reflects the strong-centre theme running through the Constitution and many feel that this has been an important factor in keeping the country united". [3]

Emergence of imbalances between functional responsibilities and financial resources of different tiers of government is a characteristic feature of all federations, particularly of those whose economies are more dynamic. Even in older federations (like the United States, and Canada), financial conflicts between the national and sub-national governments persist and their once-for-all solution is difficult to find. The mismatch between functions and taxation powers occurs partly because of changing responsibilities of governments at different levels and partly because of the dominant position of federal government in regard to taxation powers, which is often by design. Therefore, vertical imbalances in terms of resources and expenditure responsibilities emerge between different levels of government calling for transfer of resources from the Centre to the States. This is the familiar problem of federal finance.

Thus, intergovernmental transfers are an inherent part of a multi-level fiscal system. Such transfers are justified on horizontal equity considerations.

10.3 Channels of Central Transfers to the States

Recognising the fact that the financial resources of the States may prove inadequate for undertaking welfare, maintenance, and development activities, the framers of India's Constitution did make elaborate, *albeit* complex, arrangements relating to flow of funds from the Centre to the States. The disequilibrium between proliferating functional responsibilities of the States and their own resources is corrected by Central transfers effected through various channels.

In an explicit recognition of vertical and horizontal imbalances, the Indian Constitution embodies the following enabling and mandatory provisions to address them through the transfer of resources from the Centre to the States.

1. Duties levied by the Union but collected and appropriated by the States (Article 268).
2. Taxes levied and collected by the Union but assigned to the States (Article 269).
3. Sharing of the proceeds of all Union taxes between the Centre and the States under Article 270. This is the main task of the Finance Commission.
4. Statutory grants-in-aid of the revenues of States under Article 275. This is also looked after by the Finance Commission.
5. Grants for any public purpose under Article 282. These grants were given by the Planning Commission (now abolished) for State Plans. [4]
6. Loans for any public purpose (Article 293).
7. Discretionary transfers for Centrally-sponsored schemes, relief from natural calamities, and relief and rehabilitation of displaced persons. [5]

Apart from these direct transfers, resources also flow to the states indirectly through the following channels.

1. Establishment/expansion of Central public sector enterprises.
2. Subsidised lending by banking and financial institutions.
3. Subsidised borrowing by the states from the Central Government and the banking system.

These may be called invisible transfers or subterranean transfers.

10.4 Claims and Counter-claims for Financial Resources

Regarding the magnitude of Central transfers to the States, it is natural to expect claims and counter claims by the two levels of the Government. The States have often complained that resources allocated to them are inadequate to enable them to discharge their responsibilities. They complain against widening gap between their own resources and needs, a trend indicating their increasing dependence on the Centre for resources. They assert that their resources should be commensurate with their obligations and responsibilities. Similarly, the Centre also feels constrained at the widening gap between its resources and needs, as reflected in the budgetary deficits. Since the early 1980s, the Centre has been running considerable deficit on its revenue account. Its commitments towards defence, subsidies, and interest payments claim a major chunk of its resources and there is little hope of any respite on these accounts in the near future.

To sum up, in a federal set-up, fiscal transfers are effected through tax devolutions and grants, often supplemented by loans from the Centre to the States. In line with the practice followed in other countries with federal structures, fiscal transfers in India are guided by the principle of *equalisation*, which neutralises insufficiency in fiscal capacity across States. Therefore, the objective of fiscal transfers is to correct vertical and horizontal imbalances—the former referring to imbalance between means and responsibilities of the Centre and the States and the latter pertaining to differences in resource capabilities among States.

In recognition of problems relating to vertical and horizontal imbalances, the Constitution of India has made several provisions to bridge the resource gap between the Centre and the States. Under the current system of transfers in India, tax devolution plays a dual role of correcting vertical as well as horizontal imbalances while grants-in-aid are primarily targeted towards achieving a degree of equalisation among states.

The Central Government raises the major part of combined resources and a significant part of that is transferred to the States to ensure vertical equity in the distribution of resources. Centralisation of revenues and adjustments thereafter is a characteristic feature of most federations of the world. Hence, to view Central transfers to the States as indicative of the latter's dependence on the former is erroneous because a significant part of the transfers takes place under constitutional provisions and in accordance with predetermined formulas.

Endnotes

1. Alcohol for human consumption is outside the purview of GST. According to clause 12A of Article 366 of the Constitution, *goods and services tax* means any tax on supply of goods, or services or both except taxes on the supply of the alcoholic liquor for human consumption. Clause 12A was inserted by section 14 of the Constitution (One Hundred and First Amendment) Act, 2016. Thus, in the case of alcohol for human consumption, States continue to levy the taxes presently being levied, i.e. State excise duty and sales tax/VAT.
2. By virtue of Article 279A(5) of the Constitution, the five petroleum products are part of the GST regime: However, the date on which GST would be levied on these petroleum products is yet to be decided by the Goods and Services Tax Council (GST Council), the constitutionally established joint forum of the Centre and the States. Thus, the levy of GST on the five petroleum products would continue to hang in balance till notified at a future date on the recommendations of the GST Council.
3. Administrative Reforms Commission, *Report of the Study Team on Centre-State Relationships*, Vol. I, 1968, p. 15.
4. The Planning Commission was set up in March 1950 by a resolution of the Government of India. It prepared the blueprint of economic plans in consultation with the States and in accordance with the guidelines provided by the National Development Council (NDC).
   Planning Commission, which for all practical purposes was a political body, made an assessment of the existing resources of the individual states and the country as a whole and set objectives in various fields and formulated plans for economic development in the light of requirements of each state. Article 282 of the Constitution of India provides that the Centre or a State may make grants for any public purpose. With the establishment of the Planning Commission in 1950, the Central Government invoked Article 282 for making grants to the states for plan purposes. Ever since the launching of the First Five Year Plan on April 1, 1951, these grants occupied an important place in Central financial transfers to the States.
   Grants given under Article 282 were a subject matter of controversy. These grants were intended by the Constitution makers to meet unforeseeable emergencies (like droughts, famines, and other natural calamities) and were not envisaged as part of normal Centre-State financial relations. Thus, Central grants to States to help settle persons displaced as a result of the partition of the country was a typical example of the purpose contemplated by Article

282. These grants, meant for emergency purposes, were kept outside the purview of the Finance Commission which otherwise was entrusted with all the major questions of Centre-State financial relations.

Some experts felt that the Planning Commission was an unintended channel for transferring resources to the States because the founding fathers envisaged a pre-eminent role for the Finance Commission in dealing with problems of fiscal federalism. They never anticipated the rise of the Planning Commission and the National Development Council with enormous powers in the matter of allocation of resources to the State Governments. In view of the dominant role of the Planning Commission, the effectiveness of the Finance Commission had been circumscribed, its role being restricted to non-Plan expenditure of State budgets. Therefore, it was often suggested that for healthy inter-governmental financial relations, the Finance Commission should decide grants-in-aid to each State under Article 282 of the Constitution. The Planning Commission could assist the Finance Commission by drawing up a priority list of projects, their costs, locational feasibility and other technical matters.

Planning Commission was scrapped by the Cabinet on August 13, 2014. It was replaced by NITI Aayog which was formed on January 1, 2015. NITI Aayog is a policy think-tank of the Government of India.

5. **Centrally-sponsored Schemes:** In view of their national importance, these schemes are launched by the Centre and implemented by the State Governments with Central assistance. The Central Ministries concerned propose and formulate these schemes. The States execute these schemes under the technical guidance and supervision of the Centre which also issues guidelines regarding the contents, coverage, expenditure pattern, and staffing of such schemes. The assistance is given for these schemes on a matching basis and the provision for it is made in the budgets of the Central Ministries. For example, in the agricultural sector, these schemes pertain to propagation of research and improved technology, disease control, preserving ecological balance, support to specific crops like pulses, cotton, jute etc.

   The States are generally unhappy with their inadequate involvement in the formulation of Centrally-sponsored schemes which mainly pertain to subjects included in the State List. Sponsoring of these schemes by the Centre is also considered an intrusion into subjects reserved for States.

   The States have also complained against Centrally-sponsored schemes on the ground that the system of matching grants involved in the schemes favours the richer States because they are better placed to provide matching funds to avail Central assistance. Such schemes induce the States to divert their limited resources to areas which may occupy low priority in the investment scheme of a State.

   The number of Centrally-sponsored schemes has reduced in recent years as the share of states in Centre's tax revenues has increased.

11

Fiscal Federalism and the Role of Finance Commission

11.1 Evolution of Fiscal Federalism in India

India's present fiscal structure is the result of a gradual evolution, along decentralised lines, dating back to December 14, 1870 when the resolution of Lord Mayo, Viceroy of India, was issued. The Mayo resolution explained the scheme by which the Government of India envisaged enlargement of the powers and responsibilities of the Provinces.

The next landmark in the history of Centre-State financial relations was the Montague-Chelmsford Report on Constitutional Reforms which led to the passing of the Government of India Act, 1919. This Act sought to secure for the Provinces a greater degree of financial independence by abolishing the *divided heads* and effecting a complete separation between the Central and Provincial heads of revenue.

The Government of India Act, 1935 was a watershed in the evolution of Centre-State financial relations. The Act was a step towards consolidation and enhancement of Provincial autonomy in matters of resources and functions. It laid the foundations for the structure of Centre-State relations as incorporated in the present Constitution of India.

The partition of the country gave rise to new problems of financial adjustments, particularly in relation to the divided Provinces of Bengal and Punjab.

Drafting of the Constitution of independent India provided another opportunity to review the financial relations between the Centre and the States. For the purpose of incorporating financial provisions in the Draft Constitution, the President of the Constituent Assembly constituted an Expert Committee of three members under the chairmanship of Shri N.R. Sarker.

Prior to Independence in 1947, Princely States had remained outside the fiscal and financial system of the rest of the country except for certain arrangements entered into with them by the Government of India regarding such matters as maritime customs, central excises, posts and telegraph and railways. The scheme of the Government of India Act, 1935, contemplated the accession of these States to the Indian federation. Under it, the Princely States were to accede in regard to foreign relations, defence and communications, with an option to accede in regard to other Central subjects also. This followed an extensive examination of the problems connected with the assimilation of States of varying sizes and having different kinds of relationship with the Centre into a workable system of financial relations with the proposed federation. As it happened, the provisions of the Government of India Act, 1935, relating to federation never came into operation.

It was in the 1950-51 budget speech that the Finance Minister announced the constitution of the First Finance Commission, an epoch-making arrangement for the evolution of sound fiscal federalism in India. The First Finance Commission was set up in November 1951 and it submitted its report in December 1952 for the period 1952-57. Since then fourteen more Finance Commissions have submitted their reports, the last being the Fifteenth Commission.

Recommendations of the Finance Commission constitute the core of fiscal federalism in India. Finance Commission is a unique feature of the Indian Constitution without parallel in the existing federal constitutions of the world. Reports of the Finance Commissions provide in-depth insights into problems and their solutions in the highly complex area of federal finance. These Reports examine in detail contemporary issues in Centre-State financial relations and recommend measures to solve them.

11.2 Appointment and Duties of the Finance Commission

Vertical and horizontal imbalances are common features of most federations and India is no exception to this. The constitution assigns taxes with a nation-wide base to the Union to make the country one common economic space unhindered by internal barriers to the extent possible. States being closer to people and more sensitive to the local needs have been assigned functional responsibilities involving expenditure disproportionate to their assigned sources of revenue resulting in vertical imbalances.

Horizontal imbalances across States are on account of factors, which include historical backgrounds, differential endowment of resources, and capacity to raise resources. Unlike in most other federations, differences in the developmental levels in Indian States are very sharp.

In addition to provisions enabling transfer of resources from the Centre to the states, a distinguishing feature of the Indian Constitution is that it provides for an institutional mechanism to facilitate such transfers. The institution assigned with such a task is the Finance Commission.

Although the Constitution provides for Central transfers, it neither indicates the share of the states in the divisible taxes nor prescribes any principles for the distribution of states' share among the States themselves. Framers of the Constitution consciously avoided permanent formulae in this regard in view of expected changes in the spheres of taxation and public expenditure. Thus, the precise manner of sharing taxes and the actual determination of grants is left to the deliberations of the Finance Commission which is appointed by the President (under Article 280) every quinquennium, or earlier if necessary.

Article 280 reads as follows, "(1) The President shall, within two years from the commencement of this Constitution and thereafter at the expiration of every fifth year or at such earlier time as the President considers necessary, by order constitute a Finance Commission which shall consist of a Chairman and four other members to be appointed by the President.

(2) Parliament may by law determine the qualifications which shall be requisite for appointment as members of the Commission and the manner in which they shall be selected.

(3) It shall be the duty of the Commission to make recommendations to the President as to:

(a) the distribution between the Union and the States of the net proceeds of taxes which are to be, or may be, divided between them under this Chapter and the allocation between the States of the respective shares of such proceeds;

(b) the principles which should govern the grants-in-aid of the revenues of the States out of the Consolidated Fund of India;

(bb) the measures needed to augment the Consolidated Fund of a State to supplement the resources of the Panchayats in the State on the basis of the recommendations made by the Finance Commission of the State;

(c) the measures needed to augment the Consolidated Fund of a State to supplement the resources of the Municipalities in the State on the basis of the recommendations made by the Finance Commission of the State; and

(d) any other matter referred to the Commission by the President in the interests of sound finance.

(4) The Commission shall determine their procedure and shall have such powers in the performance of their functions as Parliament may by law confer on them".

Note: Sub-clause (bb) was inserted by the Constitution (Seventy-third Amendment) Act, 1992. Sub-clause (c) was inserted by the Constitution (Seventy-fourth Amendment) Act, 1992. Sub-clause (c) was re-lettered as sub-clause (d) by the Constitution (Seventy-fourth Amendment) Act, 1992. [1]

Thus, in terms of clause (3) of Article 280, the main responsibilities of the Finance Commission are the following:

1. To evolve a scheme of transfer of financial resources from the Centre to the States so as to ensure financial equilibrium at the two levels of Government during the period of its award.
2. To design formulae to allocate resources so transferred among the States.
3. To determine the principles and quantum of grants-in-aid to States which are in need of such assistance.
4. To recommend measures needed to augment the Consolidated Fund of a State to supplement the resources of the panchayats/municipalities in the State on the basis of the recommendations made by the Finance Commission of the State.

These constitutionally mandated functions are mentioned in the Presidential Order constituting a Finance Commission. Hence they are the same for all the Finance Commissions and mentioned as such in the terms of reference (ToR) of different Finance Commissions.

In addition to the substantive functions, any other matter can be referred to a Finance Commission in the interest of sound finance under Article 280(3)(d) of the Constitution. It has become customary to mention certain considerations in the Presidential Order appointing a Commission, which the Commission may consider, among others, while making its recommendations. The Presidential Order listing out the main functions, additional matters and considerations constitutes the ToR of a Finance Commission.

As the Sixth Finance Commission remarked, "The purpose of Finance Commission, as envisaged in the Constitution, is primarily to facilitate a periodical assessment of the fiscal needs of the States and the formulation on an objective basis of proposals for transfer of resources from the Centre to the States through devolution of taxes and grants-in-aid. But an incidental and by no means insignificant advantage of the appointment of a Finance Commission has generally been to rekindle interest in issues pertaining to financial relations between the Centre and the States and to promote an enlightened national debate on the several facets of our federal fiscal set up". [2]

The task of a Finance Commission is by no means easy as it has to judge the conflicting claims, needs, and resources of the Centre and the States and evolve a scheme of transfers which would balance the needs and resources of the two layers of the Government.

Broadly speaking, the procedure adopted by the Finance Commission to fulfil its duties is as follows:

1. Preparing estimates of revenue and expenditure of the Central Government for the period of its award.
2. Forecasting own current revenues of the States and current expenditures.
3. Deciding the total amount of transfers from the Centre to the States so as to maintain the desired equilibrium in the finances of the two tiers of the Government.
4. Breaking down total amount of transfers into tax devolution and grants-in-aid to States.
5. Devising formula for distribution of tax devolution among the states.
6. Filling the post-devolution gaps with grants.

Transfer of resources from the Centre to the states is designed to correct vertical imbalances while the distribution of such resources among the states (with wide differentials in fiscal capabilities and needs) aims at correcting horizontal imbalances.

The years of establishment, years of reporting, periods of award, and the names of Chairmen of various Finance Commissions are given in Table 11.1.

Finance Commission is a unique feature of the Indian Constitution having no parallel in the existing federal constitutions of the world. As the Commission on Centre-State Relations, 1988 observed, "Unlike the Commonwealth Grants Commission of Australia*, the Indian Finance Commission is a Constitutional body and the objectivity in its role has been facilitated by keeping it outside the Union executive. Compared with its Australian counterpart, the Indian Finance Commission has a greater scope inasmuch as it recommends sharing of tax proceeds also, besides the grants-in-aid, and advises on other matters referred to it in the interest of sound finance. The absence of clear Constitutional provisions for revenue sharing created many problems in other federations and they had to evolve a variety of arrangements to overcome them. For example, in Canada, tax-rental arrangements were resorted to. In Australia, the Australian Commonwealth Grants Commission was set up to consider allocation of grants among the claimant States. Specific purpose grants, with strict enforcement conditions, came into existence in countries like USA". [3]

**The Australian Commonwealth Grants Commission recommends special purpose grants to the claimant States, but the general grants are determined largely on the basis of negotiations at the political level. In India, the Finance Commission has replaced political bargaining by objective criteria in regard to devolution of resources, ensuring at the same time flexibility in revenue-sharing.*

Table 11.1: Chronology of Finance Commissions in India

Finance Commission	Year and Month of Establishment	Year and Month of Reporting	Period of Award	Name of the Chairman
First	November 1951	December 1952	1952-53 to 1956-57	K.C. Neogy
Second	June 1956	September 1957	1957-58 to 1961-62	K. Santhanam
Third	December 1960	December 1961	1962-63 to 1965-66	A.K. Chanda
Fourth	May 1964	August 1965	1966-67 to 1968-69	P.V. Rajamannar
Fifth	February 1968	July 1969	1969-70 to 1973-74	Mahavir Tyagi
Sixth	June 1972	October 1973	1974-75 to 1978-79	K. Brahmananda Reddy
Seventh	June 1977	October 1978	1979-80 to 1983-84	J.M. Shelat
Eighth	June 1982	April 1984	1984-85 to 1988-89	Y.B. Chavan
Ninth	June 1987	July 1988* and December 1989#	1989-90* and 1990-91 to 1994-95#	N.K. P. Salve
Tenth	June 1992	November 1994	1995-96 to 1999-00	K.C. Pant
Eleventh	July 1998	July 2000	2000-01 to 2004-05	A.M. Khusro
Twelfth	November 2002	November 2004	2005-06 to 2009-10	C. Rangarajan
Thirteenth	November 2007	December 2009	2010-11 to 2014-15	Vijay Kelkar
Fourteenth	January, 2013	December 2014	2015-16 to 2019-20	Y.V. Reddy
Fifteenth	November 2017	December 2019* and November 2020#	2020-21* and 2021-22 to 2025-26#	N.K. Singh

* First Report; # Second Report

Source: *Finance Commission Reports.*

Award of a Finance Commission generates considerable interest in issues pertaining to financial relations between the Centre and the States. So far, fourteen Finance Commissions have given their reports since the commencement of the constitution. The Fifteenth Finance Commission is expected to give its report in October 2019.

There have been major changes in the public finances of the Union and the States since the establishment of First Finance Commission in 1951. A number of new matters have been refereed to the Commissions in consonance with these developments. How the different Finance Commissions have discharged their responsibilities in the ever changing fiscal situation is explained in the following paragraphs.

11.3 Powers and Procedures

The Finance Commission consists of a chairman and four members. To enable the Finance Commission to discharge its responsibilities in an effective manner, the Constitution vests the Finance Commission with power to determine its procedures.

Under clauses (2) and (4) of Article 280 of the Constitution, the qualifications which shall be requisite for appointment as Members of the Commission and the manner in which they shall be selected have to be determined by Parliament by law and the Commission shall have such powers in the performance of their functions as Parliament may by law confer on them.

The Constitution authorises the Commission to determine their procedure, while the Finance Commission (Miscellaneous Provisions) Act, 1951, has conferred on the Commission all the powers of a Civil Court under the Code of Civil Procedure, 1908. The Commission have also been empowered to require any person to furnish information on such points or matters as, in the opinion of the Commission, may be useful for, or relevant to, any matter under the consideration of the Commission. The powers conferred on the Commission are set out in detail in Section 8 of the Act mentioned earlier.

The recommendations of Finance Commissions are based on a detailed assessment of the financial position of the Central and State Governments. For this purpose, the Commissions visit the State Capitals and hold discussions with government leaders and officials. Discussions are also held with public finance experts and studies are commissioned on specific topics.

Under Article 281 of the Constitution, the report of the Finance Commission, together with the Explanatory Memorandum on the action taken on the recommendations of the Commission, is laid on the Table of the House by the Government.

11.4 Nature of Finance Commission Recommendations

Article 280(3) requires the Finance Commission to make recommendations to the President who is to lay the same under Article 281 before each House of Parliament. It is nowhere laid down in the Constitution that recommendations of the Commission shall be binding upon the Government of India. They are, therefore, non-justiciable. However, to safeguard the interests of the States in the Union taxes which are divisible, the Constitution provides (Article 274) that no bill or amendment which: (i) varies the rate of tax in which the States are interested; (ii) affects the principles on which moneys are distributable; or (iii) imposes any surcharge on any such tax for the purpose of the Union, shall be introduced or moved in the Parliament except on the recommendation of the President.

Though the President is not bound to accept the recommendations of the Finance Commission, they are generally accepted in view of the quasi-judicial nature of the Commission. There are some instances of partial acceptance of such recommendations. For example, the Centre did not accept the entire set of recommendations of the Eighth Finance Commission relating to the first year (1984-85) of the five year period covered by it. The Centre held the view that by the time the report was submitted (April 30, 1984), the Central and the State budgets had been passed and it was late to reopen the estimates. However, it was widely felt that this decision of the Government was in violation of the spirit of Article 280 of the Constitution.

Endnotes

1. As per the amended clause (3) of Article 280, the Finance Commission is duty bound to assess the resources required to be transferred from the Consolidated Fund of India to the State Government for passing on to the panchayats/municipalities. This assessment has to be based on the recommendations of State Finance Commissions (SFCs) which enjoy complete freedom in this regard.

   Now that it has to consider the needs of local bodies also, the Finance Commission has to ensure vertical equity in the distribution of resources not only between the Centre and the Sates but also between the States and the local bodies. By making the Finance Commission responsible for ensuring equitable distribution of resources at three levels instead of two, the Constitutional amendments distracted it from its traditional primary task of ensuring vertical fiscal equity as between the Centre and the States, and horizontal fiscal equity as among the States.

   It is also well-known that while the States are unanimous in demanding an increase in their share of the divisible pool of Central taxes, their approach to the principles for determination of relative shares of the States differs widely. In their memoranda to the Finance Commission, the States suggest a variety of conflicting criteria for the distribution of States' share inter se. Each State suggests a formula which it considers will benefit it and most, the richer States emphasising the *collection factor* and the poorer States the backwardness factor.

   The Finance Commission has to consider not only the memoranda of the State Governments but also the Reports of SFCs, which in turn are based on the financial assessments of hundreds of municipalities and thousands of panchayats. It has to perform a Herculean task to do justice to the work assigned to it. Generally, a Finance Commission takes one and a half years to complete its work. Now with the added burden of supplementing the resources of panchayats/municipalities, it will need more time. The old debate that Finance Commission should be converted from a quinquennial to a permanent body assumes relevance in this context.

   Through greater devolution, a Finance Commission may augment the Consolidated Fund of a State but how does it ensure supplementing the resources of the panchayats/municipalities. Recommendations of the Commission in this regard determine the efficacy of the Seventy-third and Seventy-fourth amendments.

A State Finance Commission has the power to decide the amount of assistance which may be needed from the Centre to supplement the resources of the municipalities of a State. It is plausible that a State Government may slacken its efforts to tap the potential available at its own level or the municipal level to contain expenditure and/or raise resources and instead put the burden on the national exchequer. If this happens, the National Finance Commission would find itself in the cobwebs of conflicting and exaggerated claims of not only Central and State Governments but also of thousands of municipalities through the SFCs.

It may be recalled that since the recommendations of the State Finance Commissions were not available to the Tenth Finance Commission, the latter was in doubt whether it could recommend measures for augmenting State resources for the purpose of supplementing the resources of panchayats and municipalities. To resolve the dilemma, it decided to make ad hoc provision of specific grants to States.

The Eleventh Finance Commission, which was the first to deal with the provisions of the Seventy-third and Seventy-fourth amendments on a full-fledged basis, had an enormous responsibility of assessing the financial needs of local bodies and recommending the scale of assistance to be given to them.

2. *Report of the Sixth Finance Commission*, 1973, p. 5.
3. Government of India, *Report of the Commission on Centre-State Relations* (Chairman: Justice R.S. Sarkaria) Part I, 1988, p. 254.

12

Finance Commission and Vertical Distribution of Resources

Though a federal system provides for divided governmental functions and powers, imbalances often, rather invariably, arise between functional responsibilities and financial resources at different tiers of the government. These imbalances are attributable to different revenue-raising capacities and revenue needs of various federating units. Therefore, vertical imbalances of resources and expenditure responsibilities emerge between different levels of the government, calling for transfer of resources from the centre to the states.

12.1 Itemised Sharing of Revenue between the Centre and the States Prior to Constitution (Eightieth Amendment) Act, 2000

Initially, the Constitution provided for the sharing of only two Central taxes with States. Article 270 permitted mandatory sharing of the net proceeds of income tax levied and collected by the Union with the States. Article 272 provided for sharing of Union excise duties, if Parliament by law so provided. This position continued till the Eightieth Amendment of the Constitution in 2000 which provided for sharing of the proceeds of all Union taxes and duties with the States, except surcharges on Central taxes and earmarked cesses. This was done taking into account the recommendation of the Tenth Finance Commission (X-FC) to enable the States to derive the advantage of sharing the buoyancy of all Central taxes, to ensure greater certainty in the resource flows to the States and to facilitate increased flexibility in tax reforms.

Thus, tax sharing recommended by the first ten Finance Commissions was restricted to the proceeds of income tax and Union excise duties.

12.1.1 Sharing of Income Tax Revenue: By virtue of Entry 82 of List I of the Seventh Schedule of the Constitution, the Central Government is empowered to levy 'taxes on income other than agricultural income'. Before the Eightieth Amendment of the Constitution, these were compulsorily shareable between the Centre and the States under Article 270(1) of the Constitution. However, the proceeds attributable to Union Territories, taxes payable in respect of Union emoluments, and corporation tax were kept out of the divisible pool in accordance with the provisions contained in clauses (2), (3) and (4) of Article 270. Similarly, surcharge levied for purposes of the Union under Article 271 was also excluded from the divisible pool. The Finance Commission was required to make recommendations on the following matters pertaining to income tax.

1. Determination of the percentage of net proceeds of income tax to be assigned to the States.
2. Formula for the allocation of States' share among the States.
3. Determination of the net proceeds attributable to Union Territories.

The share of the States in the net proceeds of income tax increased gradually ever since the recommendations of the First Finance Commission (I-FC) which fixed it at 55 percent. Second Finance Commission (II-FC), Third Finance Commission (III-FC), and Fourth Finance Commission (IV-FC) enlarged the share to 60 percent, 66.66 percent, and 75 percent respectively. III-FC and the IV-FC recommended the increase in the States' share to make good the loss sustained by the States on account of non-inclusion of corporation tax in the divisible pool beginning 1959. Fifth Finance Commission (V-FC) did not recommend any further increase in the States' share. Sixth Finance Commission (VI-FC) raised the States' share from 75 percent to 80 percent which was further increased to 85 percent by Seventh Finance Commission (VII-FC), making the Central Government virtually a collecting agency on behalf of the State Governments. Eighth Finance Commission (VIII-FC) and the Ninth Finance Commission (IX-FC) retained it at 85 percent. Tenth Finance Commission (X-FC) reduced the share of States in the net proceeds of income tax from 85 percent to 77.5 percent.

In reducing the share of the States in the net proceeds of income tax, X-FC was guided by the following two considerations, "(i) that the authority that levies and administers the tax should have a significant and tangible interest in its yield and (ii) that any change in the share on this account should not materially affect the level of overall devolution to the States. In other words, any downward revision in the share of States in the net proceeds of income tax should be mirrored in a revenue equivalent increase in their share in the net proceeds of Union excise duties". [1] The Commission did recommend enlargement in the share of States in excise duties from 45 percent to 47.5 percent.

A. Controversies over Distribution of Income Tax Revenue: Major controversies between the Centre and the States regarding distribution of revenue from income tax were the following.

(a) Corporation Tax: By virtue of Entry 85 of List I read with Article 270(4)(a), the receipts from corporation tax belong exclusively to the Central Government. Consequent upon the simplification in the scheme of company taxation in 1959, the income tax paid by companies was reclassified as corporation tax. As an offshoot of this definitional change, company taxation ceased to be mandatorily shareable with the States as per provision of Article 270.

Ever since, States had been pressing for the inclusion of corporation tax in the divisible pool, particularly in view of its buoyant revenue. In the face of explicit Constitutional provision precluding revenue from corporation tax being shareable with the States, the Finance Commissions had gradually increased the share of States in the truncated divisible pool. The Centre had opposed the inclusion of corporation tax in the divisible pool on the ground that the disadvantage to the States due to definitional change in 1959 had been made good by Finance Commissions by enhancing their share in income tax which went up to 85 percent and remained there till the recommendations of X-FC.

Taking note of this situation, the Commission on Centre-State Relations, 1988, observed, "It is a fundamental principle of taxation that the taxing authority should have interest in its proceeds. In order to maintain this principle and giving a more meaningful choice to the Union among fiscal alternatives, it is necessary to enlarge the base of devolution to the States but with a lower percentage share in individual taxes. This can be done by bringing into the divisible pool a major Union tax but still keeping a sizeable revenue source for exclusive utilisation by the Union". [2] Therefore, the Commission recommended that the net proceeds of corporation tax could be made permissibly shareable with the States through an appropriate amendment of the Constitution. Simultaneously, it made it clear that in the event of inclusion of corporation tax in the divisible pool, necessary adjustments will have to be made by suitably lowering shares of the States in income tax and Central excise duties. Some State Governments also argued on these lines. For example, the Government of Maharashtra suggested to IX-FC that the share of the States in income tax could be reduced to 75 percent provided 20 percent of the receipts from corporation tax were assigned to the States. IX-FC, however, refused to examine the question of corporation tax because it was not referred to it by the President.

(b) Surcharge on Income Tax: The Constitution provides under Article 271 for the levy of a surcharge on income tax wholly for the purpose of the Centre. Surcharge was levied in 1951 and continued uninterrupted (*albeit* with different nomenclatures like special surcharge, additional surcharge etc.) when it was withdrawn in 1985 following the recommendations of VIII-FC. However, surcharge on income tax was reintroduced in 1987 for drought purposes and the same was replaced by an employment surcharge in 1989. Surcharge was abolished by the Finance Act, 1994. It was re-imposed subsequently.

In fact, surcharge on income tax has remained almost a regular source of revenue for the Centre much against the spirit of the Constitutional provision. States have all along pleaded before successive Finance Commissions for the inclusion of surcharge in the divisible pool. The Commission on Centre-State Relations, 1988, was firmly of the view that surcharge on income tax should not be levied by the Central Government except for a specified purpose and for a strictly limited period only. VIII-FC and IX-FC opined that a surcharge continued indefinitely could be regarded an additional income tax and, therefore, shareable with the States. X-FC emphasised that the surcharge on income tax should not be levied except to meet emergent requirements for a limited period. Thus, although the explicit Constitutional provision favours the Centre, the levy of surcharge remains an irritant in Centre-State relations till date.

(c) Miscellaneous Receipts: Another point of controversy pertained to the receipts from penalties and interest recoveries under the head miscellaneous receipts. VIII-FC was of the view that such receipts should form part of the divisible pool of income tax. Unfortunately, the Centre did not accept this recommendation, maintaining that interest and penalties, though payable under the Income Tax Act, are distinct from income tax. IX-FC disagreed with this view of the Centre and cited several judgements of the Supreme Court to prove that there was no essential difference between tax and penalties related to it. X-FC also opined that receipts on account of interest recoveries and penalties form part of the divisible pool and should be shared with the States. It recommended that this should be done with effect from April 1, 1995.

In most European countries fines and penalties associated with a tax are part of the receipts from that tax. According to OECD, "Receipts from fines and penalties paid for infringement of regulations identified as relating to a particular tax and interest on payments overdue in respect of a particular tax are recorded together with receipts from that tax". [3] The stand taken by the Central Government in this regard is untenable.

(d) Cost of Collection: Apportionment of the cost of collection between income tax and corporation tax was another contentious issue between the Centre and the States. The cost of collection was deducted from the proceeds of income tax while working out the share of States. On the suggestion of VIII-FC, an expert committee was set up in 1985 which apportioned the cost of collection in the ratio of 1:7 between corporation tax and non-corporation income tax.

Following the observations made by IX-FC in its First Report, the Government of India constituted another expert Committee in 1989 to examine the allocation of the cost of collection between income tax and corporation tax. The Committee, which included representatives of the State Governments, made a detailed study in this regard and fixed the ratio at 1:6.5 which was accepted and used by X-FC.

12.1.2 Sharing of Union Excise Duties: Excise duties, levied by the Centre under entry 84 of List I in the Seventh Schedule of the Constitution, occupied a predominant place in the overall transfer of resources from the Centre to the States. These duties belonged to the category of taxes which may be divided between the Centre and the States (Article 272) and the subject-matter of this division fell within the purview of the Finance Commission [Article 280(3)(a)].

The sharing of excise duties was permissive and therefore different from the compulsory assignment to the States of the whole proceeds of taxes under Article 269 and compulsory sharing of the proceeds of income tax under Article 270. Hence, the States did not enjoy a constitutional right to claim a share out of the revenues from Central excises. It was for the Parliament to decide whether the States should at all be given such a share and in taking this decision it may consider recommendations of the Finance Commission made in this regard. This permissive provision in the Constitution aimed at providing additional resources to the States in the event of necessity to augment transfers which could be effected under other provisions of the Constitution.

Successive Finance Commissions had taken the view that permissive sharing, contemplated under Article 272, was not only justified but even necessary in view of the growing financial needs of the States for developmental and other essential services. Therefore, ever since April 1, 1952, the States had been getting a share in the proceeds of Central excises. In fact, successive Finance Commissions had increasingly relied upon excise duties in their schemes of revenue transfers with the result that these duties found an important place in the revenue accruals of the State Governments.

Understandably, there was near unanimity among the States to press for a higher proportion of excise revenue for distribution among themselves. This was thought necessary to impart viability and to introduce elasticity to finances of the States. However, Finance Commissions paying due regard to requirements of the States on the one hand and needs of the Centre on the other evolved their own sharing schemes considering the overall transfer of resources from the Centre to the States.

The sharing of excise revenue between the Centre and the States started on a rather low profile with the award of I-FC which recommended distribution of 40 percent of excise revenue from 3 commodities (tobacco, matches, and vegetable products) among the States in proportion to their population. In making this recommendation, the Commission was guided by its desire to widen the field of divisible taxes so that a balanced scheme of distribution could be evolved for the benefit of the States. The division of excise revenue, however, was restricted to the above three commodities because the Commission thought it inadvisable to divide too many excises to begin with, particularly in view of the relatively small yield from some of the items. As regards the selection of excises for division, the Commission preferred commodities: (a) which were of common and widespread consumption, (b) which yielded a sizeable sum of revenue for distribution, and (c) which possessed reasonable stability of yield. The selected commodities, namely tobacco, matches, and vegetable products were found to be the most suitable for the purpose.

Following the award of I-FC, a number of States urged upon II-FC to bring all excise duties under the distribution scheme. Such a sweeping suggestion did not find favour with that Commission which striking a note of compromise, preferred to widen the range by increasing the number of items to be shared from 3 to 8. These were: tobacco, matches, vegetable products, sugar, coffee, tea, paper, and vegetable non-essential oils. The Commission, however, decreased the share of States in distributable duties from 40 percent to 25 percent keeping in view the sum it proposed to transfer to the States from Central excises in its overall scheme of devolution. However, the reduction in the share was more than made good by the widening of the coverage of divisible duties and each State received a larger sum from this source than before.

States again pleaded before III-FC for inclusion of all excisable commodities in the distributable pool. In support of this demand the States argued that the expanding coverage of Central excises and their increasing incidence had adversely affected the revenue potential of sales tax. Accepting this demand of the States in principle the Commission observed, "The viability of the States could best be secured by a larger devolution of the Union excise duties and this should be effected by providing for the participation of the States, by conventions, in the proceeds of all Union excises. It would give a great deal of psychological satisfaction to the States and dissipate any suspicion that the Union is pursuing a policy of excessive centralisation of resources." [4] However, the Commission considering its own scheme of transfers, recommended for distribution among the States 20 percent of the excise revenue from commodities which each yielded in 1960-61 revenue of ₹ 50 lakh or more. The number of such commodities was 35.

In their representations to IV-FC, the States again argued for a share out of the proceeds of excise duties on all commodities including the commodities which might be brought under the excise net during the quinquennium relevant for the Commission's award. Accepting the States' view, the Commission recommended the sharing of the proceeds of all excise duties between the Centre and the States in the ratio of 80:20. V-FC and VI-FC merely carried forward the recommendations of the Fourth Finance Commission in this regard.

VII-FC drastically increased the share of States in excise duties from 20 percent to

40 percent, making them the most important shareable tax between the Centre and the States. In doing so, the Commission was guided by the objective of leaving as many of the less affluent States as possible with a surplus on revenue account. It preferred bulk of fiscal transfers by way of tax shares than grants-in-aid. VIII-FC further enhanced the share of States in excise duties to 45 percent, out of which 5 percent was set aside for distribution among those States which continued to have deficits even after the devolution of taxes and loans as recommended by it. IX-FC retained the share of States at 45 percent but used 5 percent and 7.425 percent from it for post-devolution deficits, in its First, and Second Reports respectively. In other words, the portion of the net proceeds of excise duties from which all States received a share was 40 percent for VIII-FC, it remained so in the one year (1989-90) report of IX-FC but it was reduced to 37.575 percent in the Second Report of the same Commission for the period 1990-95.

X-FC raised the share of States in the net proceeds of Union excise duties from 45 percent to 47.5 percent, keeping in view the decrease in the States' share of the net proceeds of income tax from 85 percent to 77.5 percent recommended by it. Out of 47.5 percent, 7.5 percent was kept apart for distribution among deficit States.

From the foregoing account of the sharing of excise revenue between the Centre and the States, it is clear that in the wake of recommendations of the successive Finance Commissions, the States had come to claim an increasingly larger proportion of excise revenue over the years. The underlying philosophy in this respect was to enlarge States' share in a buoyant source of Central tax revenue. This development, however, had taken place contrary to what the framers of the Constitution had envisaged. As already noted, the permissive sharing of excise proceeds was intended to supplement, in the event of necessity, transfer of resources under other provisions of the Constitution. However, the supplementary source had become by far the biggest source of revenue transfer. This development was partly attributed to significant structural changes in the Indian tax system since Independence. For example, the expansion in the range of commodities subject to excise duties and the increasing incidence of such duties had considerably reduced the scope for sales tax levied by the States and it was therefore desirable that the States had a substantial interest in the proceeds of Central excises.

A. **Areas of Controversy:** Distribution of excise revenue between the Centre and the States was beset with controversies some of which were the following.

(a) Special Duties of Excise: Special duties were in the form of surcharges on basic duties and were levied on certain goods for the first time in 1963 in the wake of Chinese aggression. These were earmarked exclusively for the Centre and were not shareable with the States. States had all along contended that proceeds of special excises should also be shared with them. While the Constitution specifically mentioned in Article 271 that surcharges on income taxes were exclusively for the use of the Centre, there was no such provision for surcharges on excise duties. Their sharing was disallowed only in the Finance Acts and could always be reviewed by the Parliament, particularly in the light of the recommendations of Finance Commissions in this regard.

IV-FC had taken the view that it was open to it to suggest that proceeds of special duties of excise should also be made shareable with the States. However, on practical considerations, it did not favour bringing the proceeds of special duties of excise within the sharing scheme. The Commission, however, suggested that the recourse to special excises by the Central Government should be an exception rather than the rule.

V-FC found no justification to exclude special duties of excise from the divisible pool and recommended their inclusion in the scheme of sharing of excise revenue from 1972-73 onwards. As a consequence, special duties of excise got merged with basic duties from April 1, 1972.

In the meantime, the Central Government devised another method to augment excise revenue exclusively for its own purpose. It had introduced regulatory duties of excise in 1961 for the purpose of empowering the Executive to vary rates of duties on any item within certain limits.

This provision had remained dormant till 1970-71 in the sense that revenue from regulatory duties was either nil or negligible during all these years and therefore it did not attract the attention of either the States or the Finance Commissions. The situation, however, changed significantly when in the wake of large influx of refugees from Bangladesh and conflict with Pakistan, the Central Government imposed in 1971 regulatory duties of excise on such items as steel, iron and steel products, copper, zinc, and aluminium. Furthermore, the regulatory duties were replaced by auxiliary duties (i.e. special duties) under the Finance Act, 1973 and it was specifically laid down in the Act that the auxiliary duties were for the purposes of the Centre, meaning thereby that proceeds there from were not to be shared with the States.

The States resented this arrangement, apprehending that continuance of auxiliary duties as a separate entity may encourage the Centre to raise additional revenue increasingly through auxiliary duties rather than the shareable basic duties. Upholding the States' view, VI-FC recommended the merger of revenue from auxiliary duties in the divisible pool. Consequently, auxiliary duties of excise, wherever applicable, were merged with the basic duties under the Finance Act of 1977.

To forestall any future ambiguity as regards division of revenue from special duties of excise between the Centre and the States, VII-FC categorically stated that revenue from excise duties, whether they were designated special or regulatory or by any other name, should also be included in the divisible pool. VIII-FC and IX-FC endorsed this view and recommended that the divisible pool should include all excise duties including special excise duties but excluding earmarked cesses and duties collected under the Additional Duties of Excise (Textiles and Textile Articles) Act, 1978.

(b) Earmarked Cesses: States also insisted for the inclusion of earmarked cesses and the additional excise duties under the Act of 1978 in the divisible pool. These were cesses on commodities which were not subject to excise duty like iron ore, and coal. Then there were items which were subject to regular excise duties along with cesses like tea, sugar, and paper. Additional excise duties on textiles were also a kind of earmarked levy meant to finance controlled cloth and *Janata* cloth schemes. Like surcharge on income tax, cesses had also become permanent feature of excise taxation, and since they reduced the scope for regular excise duties, the States wanted their merger in the divisible pool. VIII-FC and IX-FC examined the question of the inclusion of cesses in the divisible pool but were content to observe that their number should be kept to the minimum.

X-FC was more forthright in its views on this issue. It observed, "As regards the inclusion of revenues from the cesses in the divisible pool, it may be mentioned that a cess is levied on a specified commodity and is governed by a special Act of Parliament with the stipulation that it should be utilised for the development of the specific industry, the products of which bear the cess. The proceeds of such cesses cannot, therefore, be shared with the States". [5]

(c) Administered Prices: Another contentious issue pertained to frequent hikes in administered prices by the Centre. States desired that the Centre should raise resources by increasing excise duties instead of administered prices so that they could share the resources so raised. VIII-FC distinguished between hike in administered prices to meet the increase in cost of production and for raising revenue. If revenue raising was the objective, then excise duties should be preferred. IX-FC endorsed this view.

12.2 From Itemised to Globalized Sharing of Revenue between the Centre and the States after the Constitution (Eightieth Amendment) Act, 2000

As already noted, prior to Constitution (Eightieth Amendment) Act, 2000, income tax and Union excise duties were the only taxes shared with the States. Taxes on income and Union excise duties were shared with States under Article 270 and 272 respectively. The aforesaid amendment, done on the recommendations of the X-FC, altered the pattern of sharing of Central taxes between the Centre and the States significantly. It substituted a new Article for Article 270 and omitted the old Article 272. The new Article 270 provides for the sharing of the net proceeds of all Union taxes and duties with the States. However, the surcharge levied for purposes of the Union under Article 271 is excluded from the divisible pool. [6]

XI-FC was the first to make recommendations in accordance with the new provisions of the Constitution. [7] On the basis of the analysis and assessment of the budgetary requirements of the Centre and the States, XI-FC fixed the share of States at 28 percent of the net proceeds of shareable Central taxes/duties for distribution amongst all such States where the Central tax/duty was leviable for each of the five years starting from April 1, 2000. In addition, 1.5 percent of the net proceeds of shareable Central taxes/duties in a year was recommended for distribution amongst such States which did not levy sales tax on sugar, tobacco and textiles during that year, thus totalling 28 + 1.5 = 29.5 percent of the net proceeds of all Union taxes and duties. The distribution of this 1.5 percent among the States was to be done in the same manner as the distribution of 28 percent of the net proceeds.

XII-FC increased the share of States in shareable Central taxes from 29.5 percent to 30.5 percent.

XIII-FC further increased the States' share in net proceeds of Union taxes from the current level of 30.5 percent to 32 percent during its award period 2010-2015.

XIV-FC fixed it at 42.0 percent. It also recommended that a commensurate reduction takes place in Central Assistance to State Plans, which flowed through Centrally-sponsored Schemes and Block Grants. These recommendations reflected the demand from the States for an increase in flows in the form of tax devolution and a reduction in Centrally-sponsored Schemes, in terms of both numbers and outlays.

XV-FC fixed the share of states in central taxes at 41 percent. This was less than the 42 percent share recommended by the XIV-FC. The adjustment of 1 percent was to provide for the newly formed union territories of Jammu and Kashmir, and Ladakh from the resources of the Centre.

12.3 Overall Ceiling

XI-FC for the first time, introduced the concept of overall ceiling on total Central transfers to States from all channels on the revenue account. The indicative ceiling recommended by the Commission was 37.5 percent of the gross revenue receipts of the Centre. This was raised to 38 percent by XII-FC. This indicative ceiling was based on the then prevailing level of transfers on the revenue account. The recommendation of the indicative ceiling was prompted by considerations relating to macro-economic and fiscal stability. XIII-FC increased it to 39.5 percent.

Endnotes

1. *Report of the Tenth Finance Commission*, December 1994, pp. 21-22.
2. Government of India, *Report of the Commission on Centre-State Relations* (Chairman: Justice R.S. Sarkaria) Part I, 1988, p. 274.
3. Organisation for Economic Co-operation and Development, *Revenue Statistics of OECD Countries: 1965-85* (Paris, 1988), p. 38.
4. *Report of the Finance Commission, 1961,* p. 21.
5. *Report of the Tenth Finance Commission*, December 1994, p. 22.
6. The divisible pool is that portion of gross tax revenue which is distributed between the Centre and the States. The divisible pool consists of all taxes, except surcharges and cesses levied for specific purpose, net of collection charges.
7. At the time of finalisation of recommendations and preparation of the report of XI-FC, the Constitution (Eightieth Amendment) Act, 2000 was enacted by the Parliament which had a bearing on the work of the XI-FC. The amendments made in the Constitution necessitated changes in the terms of reference of the XI-FC. These were modified by the Presidential Order dated June 19, 2000. By this Order, para 7 of the terms of reference was deleted. This para required the XI-FC to suggest changes, if any, in the principles governing the devolution amongst the States of the net proceeds of the additional excise duties leviable under the Additional Duties of Excise (Goods of Special Importance) Act, 1957 in lieu of the sales tax formerly levied by the State Governments, and the grants to be made available to the States in lieu of the tax under the repealed Railway Passenger Fares Act, 1957. Thus, the Report submitted on July 7, 2000, addressed the original terms of reference (excluding paragraph 7). The Constitution (Eightieth Amendment) Act, 2000 provides for sharing of the net proceeds of all Union taxes and duties with the States.

13

Finance Commission and Horizontal Distribution of Resources

After making recommendations regarding states' share in Union taxes, it is the task of the Finance Commission to recommend its inter se distribution amongst States, along with grants-in-aid.

13.1 Inter Se Distribution of States' Share in Central Taxes Prior to Constitution (Eightieth Amendment) Act, 2000

As already noted, prior to Constitution (Eightieth Amendment) Act, 2000, income tax and Union excise duties were the only taxes shared with the States.

13.1.1 Inter Se Distribution of States' Share in Income Tax: Prior to the recommendations of VIII-FC, population was the dominant factor in the distribution scheme. The weightage given to the population factor varied between 80 percent and 90 percent and that for the *contribution factor* between 10 percent and 20 percent.

Although the VIII-FC and IX-FC retained the share of States in the proceeds of income tax at 85 percent, they changed the formula for the distribution of States' share *inter se* drastically. VIII-FC recommended the following formula.

1. 10 percent of the net proceeds of income tax to be distributed among the States on the basis of assessment of income tax.
2. 90 percent of the net proceeds to be distributed among the States on the following criteria:

- 25 percent on the basis of population in 1971,
- 25 percent on the basis of inverse of per capita income of the State multiplied by 1971 population, and
- 50 percent on the basis of distance of per capita income of the State from the highest per capita income State (i.e. Punjab) multiplied by the 1971 population of the concerned State.

The formula of IX-FC was as follows.

1. 10 percent on the basis of contribution.
2. 45 percent on the basis of distance of per capita income of a State from that of the State with the highest per capita income multiplied by the 1971 population.
3. 22.5 percent on the basis of the population of the State in 1971.
4. 11.25 percent on the basis of a composite index of backwardness compiled by the Commission.
5. 11.25 percent on the basis of the inverse of per capita income multiplied by the population of the State in 1971. [1]

X-FC adopted the following indices for determining the *inter se* shares of the States in the shareable proceeds of income tax.

1. 20 percent on the basis of population in 1971.
2. 60 percent on the basis of distance of per capita income. [2]
3. 5 percent on the basis of *area adjusted* formula. [3]
4. 5 percent on the basis of index of infrastructure, and
5. 10 percent on the basis of tax effort.

The prominent weight given to the *distance factor* by VIII-FC, IX-FC and X-FC tilted the devolution scheme in favour of backward States and therefore was generally welcomed.

Table 13.1 summarises the recommendations of various Finance Commissions regarding the distribution of income tax revenue between the Centre and the States and the principles followed for the distribution of States' share among themselves.

Table 13.1: Recommendations of Various Finance Commissions Regarding Distribution of Income Tax Revenue between the Centre and the States and the Principles Followed for the Distribution of States' Share among Themselves.

		Bases of distribution among the states (percent)		
Finance Commission and period of award	States' share in income tax (percent)	Population	Contribution	Other factors
First (1952-57)	55.0	80.0	20	--
Second (1957-62)	60.0	90.0	10	--
Third (1962-66)	66.0	80.0	20	--
Fourth (1966-69)	75.0	80.0	20	--
Fifth (1969-74)	75.0	90.0	10	--
Sixth (1974-79)	80.0	90.0	10	--
Seventh (1979-84)	85.0	90.0	10	--
Eighth (1984-89)	85.0	22.5	10	67.5
Ninth (1990-95)*	85.0	22.5	10	67.5
Tenth(1995-2000)	77.5	20.0	--	80.0

* A separate report was submitted for the year 1989-90.
Sources: *Reports of Finance Commissions.*

13.1.2 Inter se Distribution of States' Share in Union Excise Duties: In connection with the distribution of the States' share of excises as between different States, it is interesting to note the observations of VI-FC, "While there was near unanimity among the States in demanding an increase in the share of Union excise duties, there were naturally wide divergences in their approach to the principles for determination of relative shares of the States in the divisible pool. Each State was inclined to put forward a formula that would favour it most". [4]

I-FC distributed the States' share of excise duties among the States on the basis of States' respective population. II-FC also preferred distribution largely on the basis of population. III-FC, while agreeing to population being the major factor, also took into account other factors like the relative financial weakness of the States, disparity in the levels of development, percentage of scheduled castes and tribes, and population of backward classes. However, it did not specify either the exact manner of distribution or the weightage assigned to different indices of economic backwardness.

IV-FC accepted population as a general measure of the needs of States and distributed 80 percent of the States' share on the basis of population. The remaining 20 percent was distributed on the basis of social and economic backwardness of the States which was assessed on the basis of the following factors.

1. Per capita gross value of agriculture production.
2. Per capita value added by manufacture.
3. Percentage of workers (as defined in the Census) to the total population.
4. Percentage of enrolment in classes I to V to the population in age group 6-11.
5. Population per hospital bed.
6. Percentage of rural population to total population.
7. Percentage of population of scheduled castes and tribes to total population.

However, the Commission did not indicate the exact manner in which the above mentioned factors were combined.

V-FC distributed 80 percent of the States' share of excise duties on the basis of population and the remaining 20 percent on the basis of socio-economic backwardness. Two-thirds of the 20 percent was distributed among States whose per capita income was below the average per capita income of all States in proportion to the shortfall of the States' per capita income from all States' average multiplied by population of the respective States. The remaining one-third of the 20 percent was distributed according to an integrated index of backwardness on the basis of the following six criteria.

1. Population of the scheduled tribes.
2. Number of factory workers per lakh of population.
3. Net irrigated area per cultivator.
4. Length of railway and surfaced roads per 100 sq. km.
5. Ratio of the number of school going children as compared to those of school going age.
6. Number of hospital beds per 1,000 population.

VI-FC, after having considered the long list of indicators of backwardness suggested by the States concluded, "Even a cursory look at the list would show that most of the indicators put forward by the States refer either to characteristics that are themselves the causes of low per capita income or to characteristics that are direct or indirect consequences of low per capita income". [5] Therefore, it adopted per capita income as the sole criterion in assessing the relative economic position of the States. This approach of the Commission was partly the result of the difficulty it felt in assigning weightage among different indicators of economic backwardness. The Commission distributed 75 percent of the States' share of excise duties on the basis of population and the remaining 25 percent on the basis of economic backwardness. The distribution of weightage for backwardness was recommended in relation to the 'distance' of a State's per capita income from that of the State with the highest per capita income multiplied by the population of the State concerned in 1971. Thus, VI-FC rejected the approach of V-FC which had classified the States into two categories, rich and poor: States with per capita income above the national average being regarded rich, and those below the average as poor. According to VI-FC, this approach of its predecessor had affected most adversely those States whose per capita income was just above the dividing line.

VII-FC evolved its own overall indicators of backwardness, viz. per capita income and the proportion of people below the poverty line, in preference to partial indicators like level of schooling, health services, population of scheduled castes and tribes, and road mileage as adopted by previous Commissions. It determined the shares of States in the divisible pool of excises by giving equal weights (i.e. 25 percent each) to the following four factors.

1. Population.
2. Inverse of per capita State Domestic Product (SDP).
3. Percentage of the poor in each State. [6]
4. A revenue equalisation formula evolved by the Commission. [7]

Thus, VII-FC not only significantly enhanced the share of States in excise proceeds but also drastically changed the principles of allocation of excise revenue among the States.

VIII-FC was guided by the following three overriding considerations while deciding the criteria for allocating shares of excise duty among the States.

1. That the formula should be progressive in the sense that it should allocate a larger share to those States which have relatively lower per capita incomes or which are otherwise backward and financially weak.
2. The formula should be simple.
3. Firm and reliable data should be available for applying the formula.

Based on these considerations, the Commission recommended the distribution of States' share (45 percent) among the States in the following manner.

(a) 40 percent on the following bases (or the same formula as recommended by it for the distribution of 90 percent of the States' share in income tax),

- one-fourth (i.e. 25 percent) on the basis of 1971 population,
- one-fourth (i.e. 25 percent) on the basis of the inverse of per capita income of the State multiplied by 1971 population,
- the remaining 50 percent on the basis of distance of per capita income of the State from that of the State with the highest per capita income (i.e. Punjab).

(b) The remaining 5 percent was set aside for distribution among the States which had deficits after taking into account their shares from the devolution of all taxes and duties.

IX-FC retained the share of States in excise duties at 45 percent and recommended its distribution among the States in the following manner.

(a) 37.575 percent on the following bases:

- 29.94 percent on the basis of 1971 population.
- 14.97 percent on the basis of Income Adjusted Total Population.
- 14.97 percent on the basis of the index of backwardness.

- 40.12 percent on the basis of distance of per capita income of a State from that of the State having the highest per capita income (i.e. Punjab).

(b) The remaining 7.425 percent was distributed among the States with deficits, after taking into account their shares from various taxes and duties. [8]

X-FC recommended the distribution of States' share (47.5 percent) among the States in the following manner.

(a) 40 percent on the following bases (or the same formula as recommended by it for the distribution of States' share in income tax).

- 20 percent on the basis of population in 1971.
- 60 percent on the basis of distance of per capita income.
- 5 percent on the basis of *area adjusted* formula.
- 5 percent on the basis of index of infrastructure.
- 10 percent on the basis of tax effort.

(b) The remaining 7.5 percent of the net proceeds of excise duties was distributed among the deficit States in accordance with the shares specified by the Commission.

Table 13.2 summarises the recommendations of successive Finance Commissions regarding the distribution of excise revenue between the Centre and the States and the bases for allocating the States' share *inter se.*

Table 13.2: Recommendations of Various Finance Commissions Regarding Distribution of Central Excise Revenue between the Centre and the States and the Bases for Allocating the States' share *inter se.*

		Bases of distribution among the states (percent)		
Finance Commission and period of award	Coverage (number of commodities)	States' share in excise revenue (percent)	Population	Other factors
First (1952-57)	3	40	100	--
Second (1957-62)	8	25	90	10
Third (1962-66)	35	20	Major factor	Weightage not stated
Fourth (1966-69)	All	20	80	20
Fifth (1969-74)	All	20	80	20
Sixth (1974-79)	All	20	75	25
Seventh (1979-84)	All	40	25	75
Eighth (1984-89)	All	45	25	75
Ninth (1990-95)*	All	45	29.94	70.06
Tenth(1995-2000)	All	47.5	20	80

* A separate report was submitted for the year 1989-90.

Sources: *Reports of Finance Commissions.*

A. Varying Emphasis on Criteria Adopted: The foregoing account of the principles adopted by Finance Commissions to distribute States' share of excise duties among the States brings out the following points.

1. Proposal for devising the distribution scheme on the basis of consumption of excisable goods did not find favour with the Finance Commissions. The argument of some of the States that consumption of excisable goods reflected the *contribution* that each State made to the total excise proceeds was rejected because the purpose of sharing excise duties was not to return to the States what was collected from them.
2. Distribution in proportion to sales tax collections, justified on the ground that the levy of excise duties limited the scope for mobilisation of resources by the States in the form of sales tax, was also disfavoured by the Finance Commissions. However, this argument of the States was taken care of in the overall sharing of excise revenue between the Centre and the States.
3. Finance Commissions generally accepted population as a criterion for determining the share of each State in excise revenue. Population was assigned predominant weightage, ranging between 80 to 100 percent, by the first six Finance Commissions. However, VII-FC, VIII-FC, IX-FC, and X-FC gave more weightage to backwardness factor in their distribution schemes. Population as a criterion was supported on the ground that it represented the needs of the States and proceeds of excises should be so distributed among the States that each got according to its needs. It was further argued that in the case of some commodities, population was a rough index of total consumption and therefore the proposal for devising the distribution scheme on the basis of consumption of excisable goods was partly taken care of. The undue emphasis on population criterion as a measure of general needs of the States by earlier Finance Commissions was somewhat unjustified. In India, States differ widely in respect of per capita income, geographical area, nature of the terrain, and population distribution over the area. Thus, it is not always that the populous States are poor or that the less populous States are rich. Under these circumstances, population may be taken as one of the determinants of the needs of a State but it cannot be considered an adequate measure of that need.
4. Beginning with III-FC, relative economic backwardness was also accepted as a legitimate criterion in the distribution scheme. For this purpose, different Finance Commissions evolved their own indicators for measuring relative economic backwardness. The richer States had often argued against the adoption of backwardness as a criterion on the ground that excise duties should be related exclusively to non-discriminatory criteria such as population or consumption and that any special help to the backward States should be rendered through the mechanism of grants-in-aid under Article 275 of the Constitution. This view was rejected by the Finance Commissions.
5. Adoption of the backwardness criterion, though laudable, was assigned relatively low weightage (20 to 25 percent) by III-FC, IV-FC, V-FC, and VI-FC and therefore did not serve the needs of the backward States adequately. Thus, there was not only a

late realisation of the need to adopt backwardness criterion but the weightage assigned to it was also low. However, VII-FC, VIII-FC, IX-FC, and X-FC gave predominant weightage to the backwardness factor though indices of backwardness were obtained rather haphazardly and to some extent arbitrarily.

13.2 Inter Se Distribution of States' Share in Central Taxes after the Constitution (Eightieth Amendment) Act, 2000

XI-FC marked the beginning of the distribution formula when all the Union taxes became shareable with States. It carried forward the shift in favour of equity considerations in the formula for the inter se distribution of States' share in all Union taxes. Its recommendation to reduce the weightage given to population to 10 percent and to assign a weightage of 62.5 percent to per capita income distance had resulted in the reduction of shares of high income and middle-income States in tax devolution. This evoked a sharp reaction from these States, despite the fact that the Commission assigned a combined weightage of 12.5 percent to tax effort and fiscal discipline. The contention of these States was that the better performing States were being penalized under the dispensation of the Finance Commissions and that this was creating a moral hazard for States to remain profligate and not to improve their fiscal situation. Though a need was felt to reward the States for better performance, it gathered momentum in the wake of the recommendation of the XI-FC according higher weightage to equity.

XII-FC increased the weight to population from 10 to 25 percent and reduced the weight assigned to distance of per capita income from 62.5 percent to 50 percent. Furthermore, the Commission doubled the weightage assigned to efficiency parameters like tax effort and fiscal self sufficiency.

XIII-FC adopted the following bases of distribution of States' share inter se: population (25 percent), area (10 percent), fiscal capacity distance (47.5 percent and fiscal discipline (17.5 percent). [9]

XIV-FC distributed States' share inter se on the following criteria: 1971 population (17.5 percent), 2011 population (10 percent), fiscal capacity/income distance (50 percent), area (15 percent) and forest cover (7.5 percent).

XV-FC distributed States' share inter se on the following criteria: 2011 population (15 percent), income distance (45 percent), geographical area (15 percent), forest and ecology (10 percent), demographic performance (12.5 percent), and tax effort (2.5 percent).

13.3 Grants-in-aid of Revenues

The architects of the Constitution probably realised that even with a share in the proceeds of divisible taxes, some States might still need financial assistance. Accordingly, they made provision for annual grants-in-aid of revenues under Article 275(1) to such States as may be in need of assistance. Also, the Centre is required to give grants-in-aid to the States for the welfare of Scheduled Tribes and for raising the level of administration in Scheduled Areas and separately for Assam. These provisions which set apart a portion of Central revenues for the benefit of States indicate flexibility of India's Constitution in terms of distribution of financial resources between the Centre and the States.

13.3.1 Background: The Government of India Act, 1935, and the Constitution contain provisions under which assistance may be given to the States by way of grants. Section 142 of the Government of India Act provided for the payment of such sums as might be prescribed by His Majesty in Council as grants-in-aid of the revenues of such Provinces as His Majesty might determine to be in need of assistance, while Section 150 gave the Centre or a Province power to make grants for any purpose.

Article 275(1) of the Constitution, in its substantive part, is worded similarly to Section 142 of the Government of India Act, 1935, while Article 282, except for the substitution of *any public purpose* for *any purpose,* also follows the wording of Section 150 of the Government of India Act, 1935. Thus, Article 282 permits the Union or a State to make grants for any public purpose notwithstanding that the purpose is not one with respect to which Parliament or the Legislature of a State, as the case may be, may make laws.

Thus, even after the transfer to the States of a share of divisible taxes, the resources of some of the States may remain inadequate to meet their needs. Therefore, the Constitution provides for grants-in-aid by the Centre to such States as are in need of assistance. Two types of grants are provided by the Centre to the States: the first under Article 275 which are routed through the Finance Commission, and the Second under Article 282 which have traditionally been determined by the Planning Commission.

13.3.2 Principles of Grants-in-aid of Revenues: Under Article 275 of the Constitution, Finance Commissions are mandated to recommend the principles as well as the quantum of grants to those States which are in need of assistance and that different sums may be fixed for different States. Thus, one of the pre-requisites for grants is the assessment of the needs of the States.

Grants recommended by the Finance Commissions are predominantly in the nature of general purpose grants meeting the difference between the assessed expenditure on the revenue account of each State and the projected revenue including the share of a State in Central taxes.

The expression *grants-in-aid of the revenues* has not been defined in the Constitution of India. [10]

Article 280(3)(b) requires the Finance Commission to make recommendations as to the principles which should govern the grants-in-aid of the revenues of the States under Article 275(1). I-FC enunciated the following principles for giving grants to the States.

A. Budgetary Needs: As budgetary needs are an important criterion for determining the eligibility of a State for a grant-in-aid as well as for the assessment of the amount of the grant-in-aid, the budget has necessarily to be the starting point of an examination of fiscal need. In using the budget as a basis for this purpose, several adjustments are, however, necessary in the State budgets. These adjustments should, in the first place, reduce all budgets to a comparable basis. Adjustments are called for in respect of any abnormal or unusual and non-recurrent items of receipts or expenditure which may vitiate comparisons unless these are excluded. Besides such adjustments, which should be made for the purpose of arriving at what might be broadly termed a normal budget, certain other allowances mentioned below have also to be made.

B. Tax Effort: The extent of self-help of a State should determine the eligibility for, as well as the amount of, help from the Centre. This requires an assessment of the general scope for additional taxation in the States and of their tax effort. The point may be made that differences in relative taxation from State to State are of no relevance for the purpose of determining the degree of Central assistance to various States, as such assistance should be based primarily on the comparative poverty or affluence of the States, as judged by indices of their relative *per capita* incomes. This argument seems to miss the rationale of taking the relative tax effort of States into consideration.

A State which is prepared to raise the maximum amount of revenue through taxation is better entitled to Central assistance than a State which does not itself act sufficiently in the same direction. In respect of a State in the letter class, there is no guarantee that the benefit of external assistance will, in fact, accrue to the weaker sections of the community for whom it would be intended. Assistance to such a State may have the effect of postponing action by the State to increase its own taxation. Such assistance from outside may thus go to relieve those who are comparatively well off from the necessity of contributing more to State revenues rather than help to increase public expenditure for the benefit of the general mass of the people. It may be observed that it is only in clear cases of inadequate taxation that this should affect the quantum of assistance a State would otherwise be qualified to get.

C. Economy in Expenditure: An allowance should be made for possibilities of economy in expenditure. The principle of self-help also implies that a State should utilise its existing resources to good account before it makes a claim for assistance from the Centre. It should be emphasised that it is not the purpose of any system of grants-in-aid to diminish the responsibility of the State Governments to balance their own budgets. The method of extending financial assistance should be such as to avoid any suggestion that the Central Government have taken upon themselves the responsibility for helping the States to balance their budgets from year to year. If the amount of grants-in-aid were to be merely in proportion to the financial plight of a State, a direct premium might be placed on impecunious policies and a penalty imposed on financial prudence. On the other hand, if a State is eligible for a grant on other grounds, it should not be precluded from this benefit, merely because its budget is in order as a result of its sound financial management.

D. Standard of Social Services: An important purpose of grants-in-aid is to help in equalising standards of basic social services. The standards of social services in a State may be a criterion for grant-in-aid. Thus, of two States whose budgets, with the adjustments already indicated, point to the need for an equal amount of assistance, the one with a significantly lower level of social services should, in our view, qualify for a higher amount of assistance than the other with a relatively high level of such services. Alternatively, in marginal cases, a State with a high level of such services may become ineligible, while another State with a low level of services is eligible for a grant. Factors like the area of a State in relation to its population, economic backwardness etc. would be reflected in the level of social services and the standard of development of a State, and would be taken into account accordingly under this principle.

E. Special Obligations: Grants-in-aid may be given to help a State to meet special burdens or obligations of national concern, though within the State sphere, if they involve an undue strain on its finances. Certain States may have special obligations or burdens likely to continue for a period of years, i.e. commitments arising out of abnormal conditions. These would justify assistance by way of grants-in-aid to the States concerned. The circumstances necessitating assistance may, for example, include the consequences of partition, such as the disruption of the institutional framework of a State, the strain on the economy and administration of a State, and its increased responsibility in respect of security.

F. Broad Purposes of National Importance: Independently of the budgetary criterion, grants may be given to further any beneficent service of primary importance in regard to which it is in the national interest to assist the less advanced States to go forward. It is, in our view, desirable to provide grants-in-aid for a broad purpose, selected with reference both to the importance of the service assisted and to the practicability of measuring, from time to time, the standard of the service on the basis of reliable indices.

13.3.3 Approach of Various Finance Commissions: Despite these guidelines, the Finance Commissions have distributed these grants, by and large, on the basis of budgetary needs of the States, i.e. to cover non-Plan gap on revenue account variously described as *budgetary gap*, *financial need*, *revenue gap*, *fiscal needs* etc.

The first eight Finance Commissions confined themselves to the non-Plan revenue accounts of the States. They determined the grants equal to deficit of each State so that the non-Plan revenue accounts of all the States were balanced or left with a surplus every year. This was called the *gap-filling approach* (or more appropriately *net gap filling approach*) meaning that the deficits on non-Plan revenue account which remained after tax devolution were covered through grants. The *gap-filling approach* adopted by successive Finance Commissions was to some extent attributable to the terms of reference issued to them. The main disadvantage of the *gap filling approach* was that it encouraged wasteful expenditure and discouraged revenue efforts on the part of State Governments.

The shortcomings of the *gap-filling approach* led the Centre to ask IX-FC to adopt a normative approach to make the States more revenue conscious. This Commission broke new grounds in at least two areas. As is well-known, this Commission assessed revenue receipts of the States normatively and also applied certain norms to assess expenditures. Therefore, it recommended grants to fill the *normative gaps* as opposed to traditional *budgetary needs*. Secondly, it dealt with the total revenue account (i.e. including Plan revenue account) and worked to eliminate deficits in the revenue account as a whole. [11]

Reverting back to the *gap-filling approach*, X-FC recommended grants-in-aid equal to the amount of residual deficits, emerging after taking into account the transfers pertaining to taxes and duties, for each of the years during 1995-96 to 1999-2000. Hence, no State has a post-devolution deficit on the non-Plan revenue account in the terminal year. The total amount of grants on account of non-Plan revenue deficit for the period 1995-2000 was ₹ 7,582 crore.

XI-FC recommended the following grants-in-aid to the states:

1. Grants-in-aid to Cover Non-Plan Gap on Revenue Account.
2. Grants-in-aid for Upgradation of Standards of Administration and Special Problems of States.
3. Grants to States for Financing Local Bodies.

XII-FC disfavoured the then existing system of imposing a 70:30 ratio between loans and grants for extending plan assistance to non-special category states (10:90 in the case of special category states). Instead, it recommended that the centre should confine itself to extending plan grants to the states, and leave it to the states to decide how much they wish to borrow and from whom.

XIII-FC recommended total non-plan revenue grant of ₹ 51,800 crore over the award period for eight states. A performance grant of ₹ 1,500 crore was recommended for three Special Category States.

XIV-FC recommended a total revenue deficit grant of ₹ 1,94,821 during its award period for 11 states.

XV-FC recommended various amounts of revenue deficit grants, sector-specific grants, state-specific grants and grants to local bodies.

It is noteworthy that while a State cannot be denied a part of a shared Central tax even if it has no demonstrated financial need, grants are given upon genuine financial needs of the States. It is possible that even before tax devolution from the Centre, some high-income States have a surplus in their non-Plan revenue account. VII-FC identified Punjab, Haryana, Gujarat, Tamil Nadu, and Karnataka as such States. Thus, grants-in-aid along with shared taxes serve as a levelling up force to promote regional balanced development. From this, it may also be inferred that States as a whole are not affected whether transfers are made by one means (shareable taxes) or another (grants). It is the total amount transferred which is important for them. However, the sources of transfer become important when it comes to individual States because the formulae applied for various transfers are different. It is not possible to adopt a single formula for all transfers in view of the differing nature of taxes, duties, and grants.

Endnotes

1. The use of 1971 census data was considered appropriate because some States fared better in implementing the family planning programme between 1971 and 1981. Adoption of the 1981 census figures would have been detrimental to the interest of the States which are promoting this desirable national objective.
2. According to X-FC, "the respective 'distances' are multiplied by the population of the States, and the share of a State is obtained by dividing the product by the sum of such products for all the States. This procedure of multiplying an index by respective populations and deriving shares according to such products has been called scaling" (*Report of the Tenth Finance Commission*, 1994, p. 23).

3. Although X-FC used area as a factor, it made certain adjustments at the upper and lower ends. Thus, it ensured that no State received a share higher than 10 percent at the upper end and no State received a share less than 2 percent at the lower end.
4. *Report of the Sixth Finance Commission, 1973,* p. 15.
5. *Ibid.*, p. 16.
6. The Commission used the per capita State Domestic Product in a comparable series at State current prices by adopting the annual average for the triennial 1973-76. The poverty percentage in each State was taken as the proportion of people below an augmented poverty line in the State to the aggregate poor population in all the States. The augmented poverty line was the minimum per capita consumption expenditure level for 1970-71 on the well-known Dandekar-Rath criterion plus the State budget expenditure per capita on selected public services in that year.
7. For the revenue equalisation principle, the per capita revenue potential of each State with reference to the average per capita SDP for the triennial 1973-76 was computed. The per capita average of each State's own tax and non-tax revenue for 1975-76 and 1976-77 were regressed on the average per capita income of the States to derive the estimated values of per capita revenue of each State. The distance of the per capita revenue thus estimated for each State from the maximum estimated per capita revenue among all the States (i.e. Punjab) was multiplied by the estimated population of the State as on March 1, 1976. The percentage of the product of the distance of the per capita revenue so estimated from that of Punjab and the population for each State in the total of these products for all the States gave the share of each State in the component of the divisible pool based on revenue equalisation formula. The adoption of this formula was recognition of the fact that States which are less favourably placed with regard to their resource potential are helped to take steps for the betterment of the people living in those States.
8. To put it differently, the 45 percent share of the States was distributed among the States on the following bases: (i) 25 percent on the basis of 1971 population. (ii) 12.5 percent on the basis of Income Adjusted Total Population. (iii) 12.5 percent on the basis of the index of backwardness. (iv) 33.5 percent on the basis of distance of per capita income of a State from that of the State having the highest per capita income (i.e. Punjab). (v) The remaining 16.5 percent was distributed among the States with deficits, after taking into account their shares from various taxes and duties. The weights given in the text were derived by multiplying the weights given above by a factor of (100/83.5).
9. The index of fiscal discipline is arrived at by comparing improvements in the ratio of own revenue receipts of a state to its total revenue expenditure relative to the corresponding average across all states.
10. On this issue, I-FC observed, "It is possible to argue that the term *grants-in-aid of the revenues* should be construed as confining it to such grants as are intended for the augmentation of the revenues of the receiving State without any limitation as to how the money so made available should be spent. We consider that the problem has to be viewed in the larger perspective of securing an equitable allocation of resources among the units. We are, therefore, of the view that the scope of Article 275 or Article 280(3)(b) should not be limited solely to grants-in-aid which are completely unconditional grants directed to broad but well defined purposes could reasonably be considered as falling within their scope. In enunciating the principles which should govern grants-in-aid of the revenues of the States we accordingly propose to cover both general grants and grants for broad purposes". (*Report of*

the First Finance Commission, 1952, p. 91.

11. In India, budgets of the Central and State Governments are divided into revenue budget and capital budget under provisions of Articles 112 and 202 of the Constitution respectively. After the commencement of the Five Year Plans, the revenue budgets of the Governments came to be sub-divided into Plan and non-Plan budgets, particularly on the expenditure side. Traditionally, Plan side was considered by the Planning Commission and the non-Plan side by the Finance Commission. However, implementation of Plan projects led to new expenditures on non-Plan revenue account. Moreover, the Constitution in no way restricts the Finance Commission's jurisdiction to only non-Plan side of the budget. This constitutional position was confirmed when the Government in its terms of reference asked IX-FC that Plan and non-Plan sides of the revenue accounts should be considered together in assessing receipts and expenditures of the Centre and the States or to assess the total revenues and total revenue expenditures of the Central and State Governments without making a distinction between Plan and non-Plan. The consideration of the Plan component of the revenue budget by IX-FC was a major departure from the past practice and in a way also an encroachment on the territory of the Planning Commission. It marked a turning point in the controversy regarding the role and authority of the Finance Commission versus the Planning Commission or the scope of Article 275 versus Article 282. For details of the controversy regarding the scope of Article 275, see *Second Report of the Ninth Finance Commission*, 1989, p. 28.

14

Constitution (One Hundred and First Amendment) Act, 2016, Goods and Services Tax (GST) and the Changed Landscape of Fiscal Federalism in India

Enactment of the Constitution (One Hundred and First Amendment) Act, 2016 and the subsequent introduction of Goods and Services Tax (GST) from July 1, 2017 marked a clear departure from the initial scheme of distribution of taxation powers between the Centre and the States envisaged in the Constitution.

14.1 From Mutually Exclusive to Concurrent Powers of Taxation

Prior to enactment of the Constitution (One Hundred and First Amendment) Act, 2016, taxation powers between the Centre and the States were clearly demarcated in the Constitution of India with no overlaps between their respective domains. In other words, there were no concurrent powers of taxation (or joint occupancy of tax fields) by the two levels of government. The absence of joint occupancy of tax fields successfully minimised double taxation, tax rivalry between the Centre and the States, and duplicate tax administration.

Broadly speaking, the important sources of indirect tax revenue for the Centre were customs duty, excise duty (except on alcoholic liquors) and service tax. States collected the major part of their indirect tax revenue from tax on sales and purchases, excise duty on alcoholic liquors, octroi or entry tax, electricity duty and taxes on luxuries, entertainments and amusements.

In the case of inter-State sales, the Centre had the power to levy Central Sales Tax (CST), though the tax was collected and retained entirely by the originating States.

In fact, taxes with inter-State base and those in the case of which all-India uniformity in rates was desirable—to facilitate industry and trade—were vested in the Central Government. Taxes which were location-specific and related to subjects of local consumption were with the States.

The Constitution (One Hundred and First Amendment) Act, 2016 inserted Article 246A in the constitution which now confers concurrent powers to both Parliament and State Legislatures to make laws with respect to goods and services tax (GST). The dual GST imposes tax on the same taxable event—supply of goods and services—simultaneously by the Centre and the States. Both the Centre and the States are empowered to levy GST across the value chain from the stage of manufacturing to consumption. The credit of GST paid on inputs at every stage of value addition is available for the discharge of GST liability on the output, thereby ensuring that GST is charged only on the value addition component at each stage. This mechanism has ensured that there is no *tax-on-tax* on goods and services.

By amalgamating a large number of Central and State taxes into a single tax and allowing set-off of prior-stage taxes, GST has mitigated the ill effects of *cascading* or *pyramiding* and paved the way for a common national market. Introduction of GST would make India's products competitive in the domestic and international markets. GST is not merely a tax reform. It is also a reform that would revolutionize the way business is conducted in India.

Since major Central and State indirect taxes have got subsumed under GST, the multiplicity of taxes has been substantially reduced which, in turn, is expected to decrease the operating costs of the indirect tax system. With GST in place, the burden of Central sales tax (CST) has also been removed. The uniformity in tax rates and procedures across the country will go a long way in reducing compliance costs.

As already stated, introduction of GST has concurrently empowered the Centre and the States to levy and collect it. The assignment of concurrent jurisdiction to the Centre and the States for the levy of GST requires a unique institutional mechanism that would ensure that decisions about the structure, design and operation of GST are taken jointly by the two levels of government. Goods and Services Tax Council (GST Council) is the institutional mechanism for this purpose with constitutional force.

14.2 Compensation to States for the Loss of Revenue Due to GST Implementation

14.2.1 Need for Compensation: In the pre-GST era, when goods were sold within the State, then sales tax (later VAT) was levied, collected and appropriated by the concerned state. In case goods were sold in the course of inter-State trade, then Central Sales Tax (CST) was levied by the Central Government but the revenue was collected and appropriated by the exporting State (State of origin) where production or sale took place rather than the State where consumption happened (importing State).

Switchover from origin-based sales tax/VAT to destination-based GST was a thorny issue in the designing of the new tax. Many manufacturing States expressed concerns over the loss of revenue on account of such a shift. To allay their fears, it was decided to compensate states which may suffer revenue loss consequent upon the introduction of GST.

14.2.2 Constitutional Provisions and the Law for Compensation to States: Despite the sincere attempts made by the Empowered Committee (EC) of State Finance Ministers [1] on the determination of revenue neutral GST rates, it was difficult to estimate accurately as to how much the States would gain from service taxes and how much they would lose on account of removal of cascading effect, payment of input tax credit and phasing out of CST. In view of this, it was essential to provide adequately for compensation for loss that might emerge during the process of implementation of GST. The payment of this compensation was ensured in terms of special grants to be released to the States on the basis of neutrally-monitored mechanism. Section 18 of the Constitutional (One Hundred First Amendment) Act, 2016—reproduced below—incorporated provisions for such compensation.

"Compensation to States for Loss of Revenue on Account of Introduction of Goods and Services Tax: Parliament shall, by law, on the recommendation of the Goods and

Services Tax Council, provide for compensation to the States for loss of revenue arising on account of implementation of the goods and services tax for a period of five years".

As a follow up, Goods and Services Tax (Compensation to States) Act, 2017 was enacted to levy compensation cess for providing compensation to the States for the loss of revenue arising on account of implementation of GST with effect from July 1, 2017, for a period of 5 years or for such period as may be prescribed on the recommendations of the GST Council.

Compensation to the affected states is provided through GST compensation cess which is levied—on top of the peak rate of GST (28 percent)—on a few specified goods (which are mainly luxury and demerit items), viz. *paan masala*, tobacco, coal, aerated waters, and motor cars to create a fund for compensating states.

In the very First Meeting of GST Council held on September 22-23, 2016, it was decided, *inter alia*, that Financial year 2015-16 would be the base year for compensating the States in case of any revenue loss to States following the implementation of GST.

Growth rate of revenue for a state during the 5 year period is assumed to be 14 percent.

The base year tax revenue consists of revenue from: (a) state VAT, (b) Central sales tax, (c) entry tax, octroi, local body tax, (d) taxes on luxuries and (e) taxes on advertisements etc. In other words, revenue from all taxes of a state—subsumed under GST—in 2015-16 is the base year revenue. However, any revenue among these taxes related to supply of alcohol for human consumption, and five specified petroleum products, is not accounted as part of the base year revenue.

14.3 GST and Co-operative Federalism

Tax revenue is generally the main source of financing public expenditure at different levels of the government. In most democratic countries, taxation powers of central, state and local governments are mentioned in the constitution itself. Taxation powers of the government at different levels may be mutually exclusive or overlapping. The joint occupancy of tax fields often causes friction not only between the federal and provincial governments but also among the provinces themselves. This conflict concerns the manner in which the tax capacity of a particular tax base is shared between the two levels, i.e. how the tax room is apportioned.

In this connection, it is pertinent to note the relevance of co-operative federalism. To quote, "The essence of a co-operative federalism is that the Centre and the State Governments should be guided by the broader national concerns of using the available resources for the benefit of the people. Co-operative federalism encourages the Government at different levels to take advantage of a large national market, diverse and rich natural resources and the potential of human capabilities in all parts of the country and from all sections of the society for building a prosperous nation. Co-operative federalism makes it possible to raise all the available resources by the Government at different levels in a co-ordinated way and channel them for use for the common good of the people. This requires a harmonious relationship and co-operative spirit between the Centre and the States and among the States themselves. While a healthy competition among the States for evolving efficient and socially desirable policies and programmes is welcome, any competition which nullifies each other's advantages in development and erodes the resource base of the States should be avoided. Co-operative federalism is intended to ensure a minimum bundle of basic services and a nationally acceptable level of living for all the people of the country". [2]

GST has charted out a new course for co-operative federalism in India, focusing on mutual understanding and accommodation between the Centre and States as regards the structure of taxation of goods and services. It is pertinent to note that in all the 35 meetings of the GST Council held so far, all decisions have been taken unanimous or through consensus. In other words, no occasion has arisen so far that required voting to decide any matter. It may be recalled that economic reforms initiated in 1991 did not seek to consult the states. In contrast, every state was taken on board at every stage of the implementation of GST.

Highlighting the significance of GST Council, *Economic Survey, 2017-18* observed, "India has created one of the most effective institutional mechanisms for cooperative federalism, the GST Council. At a time when international events have been marked by a retreat into economic nativism and the attendant seizing of control, Indian states and the centre have offered up a refreshing counter-narrative, voluntarily choosing to relinquish and then pool sovereignty for a larger collective cause.

Co-operative federalism is of course not a substitute for states' own efforts at furthering economic and social development. But it is a critical complement, needed to tackle a wide array of difficult structural reforms that involve the states. For example, the "co-operative federalism technology" of the GST Council could be used to create a common agricultural market, integrate fragmented and inefficient electricity markets, solve interstate water disputes, implement direct benefit transfers (DBT), make access to social benefits portable across states, and combat air pollution". [3]

14.4 Enhanced Need for Co-operative Federalism in the 21st Century

India is making strides in the global sphere and this momentum cannot be maintained and carried forward without shared partnership of the State Governments in the development process. Hence, whenever development programmes are touched by international agreements, the well-conceived demands of states should be met in order to promote truly co-operative, co-ordinative and multi-dimensional centre-state relations.

Environmental challenges of global nature like climate change do not recognise state frontiers. Pollution and conservation issues reflect the uncomfortable tension between decision-making process of the governments at the centre-state-local levels. Disaster management transcends inter-state boundaries too.

Terrorism, militancy, organised crimes, rehabilitation of internally displaced persons, all require that the country as a whole comes together and the institutional bodies under State Governments help the Centre by collectively making available the necessary information and resources.

Globalisation has reinforced the need for concurrence between the geographical, climatic, environmental and technological diversities so that they may link with global processes. The experiences felt at the global level are also being felt at the local level.

Regrettably, sporadic voices of autonomy and separatism have vitiated the political and social fabric of the federal structure. Some ill-informed political leaders view all problems from a narrow parochial outlook. This not only weakens the nation but also makes the land fertile for the growth of terrorism and insurgency.

It has been argued that GST has led to loss of fiscal autonomy for states as it has curbed their ability to levy new taxes, change the existing tax rates or give exemptions to any class of goods or services. However, this criticism is outweighed when seen in the light of benefits of GST. GST has provided an all-India unified, uniform and harmonized indirect tax system to the country. It has ensured uniform exemption lists, uniform tax rates and uniform collection procedures throughout the country. It has paved the way for a common national market. The country has moved from an inefficient and fragmented indirect tax system to an efficient and unified tax regime in the form of GST. The old system was mainly manual and opaque while the new system is technology-based and hence transparent.

GST has successfully ensured tax harmony (instead of tax rivalry) not only between the Centre and the States but also among the States themselves.

Both the Centre and the States must attend to the task of preserving India's unity through constructive co-operative federalism which requires a great deal of commitment.

To sum up, post-GST, taxation powers of the Centre and the States overlap and the two tiers of the government will have to agree on GST rates, exemption lists, compliance procedures and other matters related to the smooth functioning of the new tax. The implementation of GST is the single most important tax reform undertaken since Independence in 1947 with far reaching fiscal consequences for the federal polity of India.

Endnotes

1. While declaring its intention to introduce GST from April 1, 2010, the Central Government had indicated that the Empowered Committee (EC) of State Finance Ministers would work with the Central Government to prepare a road map for the introduction of GST. Hence, EC—which had formulated the design of State level VAT—prepared a report on a Model and Road Map for GST.
2. Government of India, Planning Commission, *Ninth Five Year Plan* (1997-2002), Volume I, p. 241.
3. Government of India, Ministry of Finance, *Economic Survey, 2017-18*, Volume I, p. 3.

15

First Finance Commission (I-FC): 1952-53 to 1956-57

Highlights of the Report	
Chairman	Shri K.C. Neogy
Members	Shri V.P. Menon Justice R. Kaushalendra Rao Dr. B.K. Madan Shri M.V. Rangachari, Member-Secretary
Year and month of establishment	November 1951
Year and month of reporting	December 1952
Period of award	1952-53 to 1956-57
Main Recommendations	
1. States' share in income tax fixed at (percent): 55 2. Bases of distribution of States' share in income tax inter se (percent): Population: 80; Contribution: 20; Other factors: Nil 3. States' share in Union excise duties fixed at (percent): 40 (from 3 commodities) 4. Bases of distribution of States' share in Union excise duties inter se (percent): Population: 100; Other factors: Nil	

I-FC was constituted by an Order of the President dated November 22, 1951. It was charged with the duty of making recommendations to the President as to: (a) the distribution between the Union and the States of the net proceeds of taxes which are to be, or may be divided between them under the provisions of the Constitution and the allocation between the States of the respective shares of such proceeds, (b) the principles which should govern the grants-in-aid of the revenues of the States out of the Consolidated Fund of India, (c) any other matter referred to the Commission by the President in the interest of sound finance.

The task of I-FC was by no means a simple one. It had to grapple with problems created by the Partition of the country in 1947. In its own words, "The three years that followed the advent of Independence witnessed a transformation in the political, economic and financial background. The partition divided three Provinces while large areas comprised in the former Indian States were merged with Provinces or formed into new political units as Part B and Part C States. The developments during these years added appreciably to Central expenditure. After Independence, defence involved additional commitments. Besides, Independence gave a natural stimulus to expansion of social services and called for large additional outlays on nation-building activities, while the deficit position of the country in regard to food in an inflationary context rendered necessary the continuance of subsidies on foodgrains". [1]

15.1 Financial Assistance to States: Approach of I-FC

In drawing up the scheme of assistance to the States, I-FC kept three main considerations in view.

1. Additional transfer of resources from the Centre must be such as the Centre could bear without undue strain on its resources, taking into account its responsibility for such vital maters as the defence of the country and the stability of its economy.
2. Principles for the distribution of revenues between the States and the determination of grants-in-aid must be uniformly applied to all the States.
3. Scheme of distribution should attempt to lessen the inequalities between States.

During the course of discussions a number of State Governments drew the attention of I-FC to the finances required for meting expenditure on capital schemes. As the I-FC was primarily concerned with the distribution of revenues between the Centre and the States and the determination of grants-in-aid of the revenues of the States, which have to come from Central revenues, it made no recommendations in regard to grants for meeting the capital requirements of the States.

15.2 Devolution and Distribution of Income Tax

15.2.1 Determination of the Share of States: I-FC considered it undesirable to concentrate on income tax as a balancing factor in the adjustment of resources between the Centre and the units. It believed that an increase in the States' share of this tax should not be used as a major factor in the devolution of further revenues to the States. On the other hand, the State Governments had put forward an almost unanimous demand for an increase in the States' share of income tax. On a consideration of all the circumstances, it came to the conclusion that some increase in the share assignable to the States was justified although it could not be of the order suggested by the majority of State Governments. It accordingly recommended that the percentage of the net proceeds of income tax to be allocated to the States be raised from 50 percent to 55 percent.

15.2.2 Distribution of the Share of States Inter Se: Various bases were suggested for the distribution of income tax among the States, the more important of which were the following.

1. Collection of income-tax in the various States.
2. Amount of income-tax realised in respect of incomes, wherever earned, of individuals resident in the different States.
3. Collection of income-tax in the various States adjusted with reference to the origin of the income.
4. Relative population of each State.
5. Relative volume of industrial labour in each State.
6. Relative per capita income of the States.
7. Needs of different States according to various criteria, e.g. area of sparseness of population, economic backwardness or the inverse relative per capital income of each State.

The first three factors primarily sought to relate the distribution to the respective contributions of the different States to the total proceeds, and were intended to provide the most adequate or convenient measure of such contribution. At the other end were factors like the area of a state in relation to its population, economic backwardness and inverse relative per capita income which were specialised measures of needs. Between these categories fell suggestions for the adoption of such factors as population, industrial labour etc. which were supposed to reflect both the needs and, to an extent, the contribution of the States.

The percentage share of the net proceeds of income tax assigned to the States was recommended to be distributed among the States in the manner shown in Table 15.1.

Table 15.1: Percentage Shares of the States in the Net Proceeds of Income Tax Assigned to the States as Recommended by the First Finance Commission

S. No.	State	Percent	S. No.	State	Percent
1.	Assam	2.25	9.	Orissa	3.50
2.	Bihar	9.75	10.	PEPSU*	0.75
3.	Bombay	17.50	11.	Punjab	3.25
4.	Hyderabad	4.50	12.	Rajasthan	3.50
5.	Madhya Bharat	1.75	13.	Saurashtra	1.00
6.	Madhya Pradesh	5.25	14.	Travancore-Cochin	2.50
7.	Madras	15.25	15.	Uttar Pradesh	15.75
8.	Mysore	2.25	16	West Bengal	11.25

*PEPSU = Patiala and East Punjab States Union

Source: *Report of the First Finance Commission*, 1952, pp. 76-77.

15.3 Devolution and Distribution of Union Excise Duties

15.3.1 Determination of the Share of States: The first issue before I-FC in this regard was whether the States should be given a share in all the Union excises or in only one or more selected excises. It considered it inadvisable, at any rate to begin with, to divide too many excises, particularly as the yield from some of them was relatively small, and that it was desirable to restrict the division to a few selected excises. The selected excises should be such as are levied on commodities which are of common and widespread consumption and which yield a sizeable sum of revenue for distribution. There should also be reasonable stability of yield and comparative immunity of the duties selected from fluctuations related to changes in the customs tariff. Taking all these factors into account, it came to the conclusion that duties on tobacco (including cigarettes, cigars etc.), matches and vegetable products were the most suitable for distribution. It, therefore, recommend that 40 percent of the net proceeds of these duties be allocated to the States.

15.3.2 Distribution of the Share of States Inter Se: The question of determining the mode of distribution still remained. The resources of the States required to be strengthened. At the same time, the scheme of distribution needed to be balanced and equitable as a whole. Considering all these factors, it recommended the distribution of the excise duties on a per capita basis. In other words, States' share of the excise duties was distributed among them on the basis of population.

The manner of distribution of the share of the net proceeds of the three excises suggested by I-FC for allocation to the States (Table 15.2) represents the percentages of the population of the different States in accordance with the Census of 1951.

Table 15.2: Distribution of States' Share of Excise Duties on Tobacco, Matches and Vegetable Products among the States Recommended by the First Finance Commission

S. No.	State	Percent	S. No.	State	Percent
1.	Assam	2.61	9.	Orissa	4.22
2.	Bihar	11.60	10.	PEPSU*	1.00
3.	Bombay	10.37	11.	Punjab	3.66
4.	Hyderabad	5.39	12.	Rajasthan	4.41
5.	Madhya Bharat	2.29	13.	Saurashtra	1.19
6.	Madhya Pradesh	6.13	14.	Travancore-Cochin	2.68
7.	Madras	16.44	15.	Uttar Pradesh	18.23
8.	Mysore	2.62	16	West Bengal	7.16

*PEPSU = Patiala and East Punjab States Union
Source: *Report of the First Finance Commission*, 1952, p. 83.

15.4 Grants-in-aid of Revenues

I-FC formulated certain principles which should regulate the assessment of fiscal needs and, in doing so, it defined also their scope. It considered that the budgetary needs of the States should first be estimated by a detailed examination of the forecasts of revenue and expenditure submitted and then these should be reduced to a comparable basis by the exclusion of abnormal, unusual and non-recurring items of expenditure. Adjustments in this analysis should be made to take account of the extent of tax effort made by each State individually; and also the measure of economy it had effected in administration. This would help a broad judgement on the quantum of assistance that would be justified. It, however, felt that this analysis should not, by itself, limit grants-in-aid, but that the level of social services reached in a State and any special disabilities arising out of its constitution should entitle it to a further moiety of assistance. It added that grants should also be made for broad purposes of national importance to bring up deficient States to an acceptable minimum level.

Taking a liberal meaning of the term *grants-in-aid of the revenues,* I-FC enunciated principles which should govern grants-in-aid of the revenues of the States to cover both general grants and grants for broad purposes. In the case of specific grants, the following factors were taken into account.

1. Deficiency of States' resources in relation to functions.
2. Concern of the Central Government in seeing that welfare services (e.g. education, health etc.) and developmental activities (e.g. roads) are maintained at a certain minimum standards throughout the country.
3. Interest of the Central Government in developing some activities which State Governments, left to themselves, might neglect (e.g. unemployment insurance, social security etc.).
4. Possibility of improving the quality of performance in the sphere of social services, owing to the superior technical advice available to the higher level of government.
5. Desirability of some co-ordination of standards which can be achieved thereby.

As regards the policy and the role of grants from a higher level of government to a lower level of government, I-FC opined, "The most important factors that appear to have influenced policy in the field of conditional grants are the increasing adaptation of these grants on the one hand to the ability or fiscal capacity of the units and on the other to their relative need for the specific services concerned. The former factor leads to the varying of the requirement to *match* the federal grant with a State contribution so as to reduce the State contribution in the case of financially weaker States. The principle of need is, of course, innate in the purpose of grant, and implies that States with a deficiency of the particular service which is assisted, e.g. education or roads, would receive a proportionately greater measure of assistance than those which are relatively better served.

As regards the relative role of unconditional and conditional grants in the scheme of financial assistance by the federal authority, there is no clear lead in the experience of other federations, there being no single system of universal applicability in regard to this sector of federal financial relations. It appears that each country has tried to find for itself the system or combination of systems which best fits the facts of its political, economic and administrative conditions.

We believe that both the methods of conditional and unconditional grants should have their part to play in the scheme of assistance by the Centre. Unconditional grants should reinforce the general resources of the State Governments, which they would be free to allocate among competing purposes according to their best judgement, subject to the usual administrative and parliamentary checks. Grants for broad purposes may be given to stimulate the expansion of particular categories of services rather than specified schemes under those categories". [2]

In line with its thinking, it enunciated the following principles for giving grants to the States. Firstly, in determining the eligibility of a State for grants-in-aid, its budgetary needs would be an important criterion. In studying the budgetary needs of a State, receipts from shared Central taxes would be taken into account, adjustments would be made for unusual or non-recurring items of revenue and expenditure and due allowance would be made for failure to maximise tax effort or to economise expenditure. Secondly, grants-in-aid should help equalise the standards of basic social services in the various States. Thirdly, grants-in-aid may be given to promote any beneficent service of primary importance in regard to which it is in national interest to assist the less advanced States to get forward.

In assessing the needs of the States and formulating its recommendations in regard to the sums to be paid as grants-in-aid, it considered the budgetary position of the States and the probable amount which would accrue to them under its plan for the devolution of revenue from income tax and Union excises. It took into account the additional burdens arising out of the partition of the country which had been placed upon some of the States. It also kept in view the need for assisting to some extent, the less developed States by the provision of special grants which would enable them to raise the standards of one of the important social services.

With the above philosophy in mind, I-FC came to the conclusion that Madras, Uttar Pradesh, Bihar, Madhya Pradesh, Hyderabad, Rajasthan, Madhya Bharat and the Patiala and East Punjab States Union (PEPSU) could not be considered as being in need of assistance. Bombay, West Bengal, Orissa and Saurashtra were categorised as marginal cases, while Punjab and Assam were considered in need of assistance. It recommended following annual grants for various States: West Bengal (₹ 80 lakh), Orissa (₹ 75 lakh), Saurashtra (₹ 40 lakh), Punjab (₹ 1.25 crore), Assam (₹ 1 crore), Mysore (₹ 40 lakh) and Travancore-Cochin (₹ 45 lakh).

15.5 Permanent Secretariat for the Finance Commission

In a significant recommendation, which has not found favour with successive governments at the Centre, I-FC felt the need for a small permanent office to continuously monitor and record developments in the Central and State finances and other indicators which could be of use for the work of a finance commission. It observed, "Our experience as the first Commission has impressed us with the need for a small organisation being set up, preferably as part of the secretariat of the President, to make a continuous study of the finances of the State Governments so that whenever the Commission are constituted in the future, they will have sufficient material available to them at the very commencement of their enquiry. This organisation should work in close liaison with the Finance Ministry and should make a study of the budgets of the State Governments, the changes in their finances from time to time, the rates of taxes in operation, the effects of the further measures of taxation undertaken by them, the working of their commercial enterprises and their effect on the State finances and cognate matter. [3]

Endnotes

1. *Report of the First Finance Commission*, 1952, p. 45.
2. *Ibid.*, pp. 95-96.
3. *Ibid.*, p. 110.

16

Second Finance Commission (II-FC): 1957-58 to 1961-62

Highlights of the Report	
Chairman	Shri K. Santhanam
Members	Shri Ujjal Singh Shri L.S. Misra Shri M.V. Rangachari Dr. B.N. Ganguli
Year and month of establishment	June 1956
Year and month of reporting	September 1957
Period of award	1957-58 to 1961-62
Main Recommendations	
1. States' share in income tax fixed at (percent): 60 2. Bases of distribution of States' share in income tax inter se (percent): Population: 90; Contribution: 10; Other factors: Nil 3. States' share in Union excise duties fixed at (percent): 25 (from 8 commodities) 4. Bases of distribution of States' share in Union excise duties inter se (percent): Population: 90; Other factors: 10	

II-FC, set up under Article 280 of the Constitution, was constituted by an Order of the President dated June 1, 1956.

In addition to making recommendations as to the matters specified in sub-clauses (a) to (c) of clause (3) of Article 280, II-FC was asked to make recommendations as to the following matters.

1. Sums which may be prescribed under Article 273 as grants-in-aid of the revenues of the States of Assam, Bihar, Orissa and West Bengal, in lieu of assignment of any share of the net proceeds in each year of export duty on jute and jute products to those States.
2. States which are in need of assistance by way of grants-in-aid of the revenues of those States under Article 275, and the sums to be paid to those States, having regard, among other considerations to: (i) the requirements of the Second Five Year Plan and (ii) the efforts made by those States to raise additional revenue from the sources available to them.
3. Principles which should govern the distribution under Article 269 of the net proceeds in any financial year of estate duty in respect of property other than agricultural land, levied by the Government of India in the States within which such duty is leviable.
4. Modifications, if any, in the rates of interest and the terms of repayment of the loans

made to the various States by the Government of India between the August 15, 1947 and March 31, 1956.

16.1 Devolution and Distribution of Income Tax

As usual the States were unanimous in suggesting an increase in the percentage of the net proceeds assigned to them. As regards the principles of distribution of the States' share there was a wide divergence of opinion.

II-FC first dealt with the determination of the share of the net proceeds to be assigned to the States. In its opinion, income tax had ceased to be an expanding source of revenue it once was. In the changing pattern of Union taxation, income tax could not be a major factor in the devolution of further revenues to the States. However, it felt that some increase in the States' share of this tax was justified in view of the unanimous desire of the States. After a careful review of the matter in all its aspects, it came to the conclusion that the percentage of the net proceeds assigned to the States should be raised from 55 to 60. Some States had suggested the inclusion of corporation tax, the tax on Union emoluments and the surcharge on income tax levied for Union purposes in the divisible pool. II-FC expressed its inability to consider these suggestions as they were against the provisions of the Constitution.

Turning to the problem of distribution of the share assigned to the States, it considered two principles, namely population and collection, on the basis of which the States' share was distributed.

Population found the widest measure of support among the States while collection had been urged by the two industrially advanced States of Bombay and West Bengal. In all previous schemes of distribution, some weight had been given to collection but this had been reduced in favour of population. In the opinion of the II-FC this had been a move in the right direction. Considering that income tax was paid by an infinitesimal portion of the population and that the bulk of the tax arose out of business incomes which was derived from the country as a whole, the principle of collection could no longer be considered an equitable basis of distribution. While there might be a case for weightage being given to collection in the restricted field of personal income tax, it came to the conclusion that collection should be completely abandoned in favour of population as the basis of distribution.

However, II-FC did not desire to cause a sudden break in the continuity and hence recommended that the distribution of the States' share should be 10 percent on the basis of collection and 90 percent on the basis of population.

In this, as in all other matters, where population had to be taken into account as a factor in the distribution of taxes, the Commission adopted the population figures of the 1951 census as the only practicable basis. The manner of distribution of the States' share in the net proceeds of income tax is shown in Table 16.1. It further recommended that 1 percent of the net proceeds of the income tax be prescribed as the net proceeds attributable to Union territories.

Table 16.1: Percentage Shares of the States in the Net Proceeds of Income Tax Assigned to the States as Recommended by the Second Finance Commission

S. No.	State	Percent	S. No.	State	Percent
1.	Andhra Pradesh	8.12	8.	Mysore	5.14
2.	Assam	2.44	9.	Orissa	3.73
3.	Bihar	9.94	10.	Punjab	4.24
4.	Bombay	15.97	11.	Rajasthan	4.09
5.	Kerala	3.64	12.	Uttar Pradesh	16.36
6.	Madhya Pradesh	6.72	13.	West Bengal	10.08
7.	Madras	8.40	14.	Jammu and Kashmir	1.13

Source: *Report of the Second Finance Commission*, 1957, p. 41.

16.2 Devolution and Distribution of Union Excise Duties

Prior to April 1, 1952, no duty of excise was shared between the Union and the States. I-FC broke new ground when it recommended that, with effect from 1952-53, 40 percent of the net proceeds of the excise duties on matches, tobacco and vegetable products should be distributed among the States in proportion to their population. This recommendation was accepted by the government and embodied in the Union Duties of Excuse (Distribution) Act, 1953. In the case of Jammu and Kashmir, after its financial integration with India from April 1, 1954, sums equivalent to 40 percent of the net proceeds of these excise duties levied and collected by the Government of India in that State were paid to it, under an agreement entered into with that State, until April 1, 1957, when that State came within the scheme of distribution of the II-FC.

With taxes on income ceasing to be an expanding source of revenue, it was obvious that any further substantial devolution of revenues to the States by sharing of taxes had to come from Union excises. The coverage and yield of these duties had expanded considerably after Independence. The State Governments were asked for their suggestions in regard to the range of dutiable commodities which could be shared between the Union and the States, the proportion to be allocated to the States and the principles which should govern the distribution of the States' share.

All States asked for an increase in the number of commodities the duties on which should be shared. It was urged by a number of States that all excise duties should be shared. II-FC considered these suggestions and came to the conclusion that it is neither necessary nor expedient to make such a sweeping change. However, it felt the need to widen the range by increasing the number of duties to be shared. Accordingly, it decided to expand the existing list of three duties, viz. duties on matches, tobacco and vegetable products, by adding the duties on sugar, tea, coffee, paper and vegetable non-essential oils. As to the States' share of these duties, keeping in view the sum it proposed to transfer to the States from Union duties of excise in its overall scheme of devolution, it recommended that it should be 25 percent. The reduction in the share allocated to the

States out of the duties on tobacco, vegetable products and matches was more than made good by the widening of the range of divisible duties and each State received a larger sum from this source than previously.

As regards distribution of the States' share of the divisible excises, it noted that I-FC had suggested consumption of the taxed commodities as a suitable basis for distribution but, in the absence of any reliable data of consumption, it recommended population as indicating the nearest measure of consumption. I-FC also suggested that arrangements should be made for the collection of statistics of consumption of the more important commodities subject to excise. Such statistics were still not available. Hence, II-FC also adopted population as the sole basis for distribution. However, it made a small correction in favour of the poorer by recommending that 90 percent of the States' share of the divisible Union excise duties should be distributed on the basis of population, the balance of 10 percent being used for adjustments.

In short, it recommended that: (a) 25 percent of the net proceeds in any financial year of the Union duties of excise on matches, tobacco (including manufactured tobacco), vegetable products, tea, coffee, sugar, paper and vegetable non-essential oils be paid to the States and (b) this amount be distributed among them in the following manner shown in Table 16.2.

Table 16.2: Distribution of States' Share of Excise Duties among the States Recommended by the Second Finance Commission

S. No.	State	Percent	S. No.	State	Percent
1.	Andhra Pradesh	9.38	8.	Mysore	6.52
2.	Assam	3.46	9.	Orissa	4.46
3.	Bihar	10.57	10.	Punjab	4.59
4.	Bombay	12.17	11.	Rajasthan	4.71
5.	Kerala	3.84	12.	Uttar Pradesh	15.94
6.	Madhya Pradesh	7.46	13.	West Bengal	7.59
7.	Madras	7.56	14.	Jammu and Kashmir	1.75

Source: *Report of the Second Finance Commission*, 1957, p. 44.

16.3 Grants-in-aid of Revenues

The grants-in-aid, which the II-FC recommended were much larger than the grants-in-aid paid to the States in the past. This was mainly due to the fact that, in the past, the requirements of the States for development were not fully taken into account, while II-FC did so. It should, however, be understood that the sums recommended by it, while justified in the context of the Second Five Year Plan (1956-57 to1960-61), did not indicate permanent requirements of the States for their ordinary budgetary needs.

By the devolution of revenue which II-FC proposed, the States received a significant measure of assistance which enabled them to implement the Second Five Year Plan. In this connection, II-FC observed, "We wish to emphasise that they cannot depend wholly on this; they will still have to help themselves by raising at least the additional revenue expected of them towards the execution of the current plan, by securing all possible economies in administrative expenditure and by maximising their revenue through the tightening up of the machinery for collection and by the recovery of overdue arrears". [1] Table 16.3 records the amounts of grants-in-aid recommended by II-FC for various States.

As to the question whether these grants should be conditional or not, it maintained, "Since our scheme of devolution involved substantial transfer of resources for implementing the revenue portion of the plan, which for most States is reflected in the grants-in-aid recommended for them, we considered whether we should make any part of the grants-in-aid conditional on such implementation. We would have liked to do so, if the assistance provided under our scheme had represented the major part of the expenditure. Under our scheme, the States will be receiving a little less than a third of the outlay and a little over a third will come by way of specific assistance from the Union under the plan; for the balance they will have to raise their own resources. We have, therefore, decided not to impose any condition on the grants-in-aid recommended by us". [2]

Table 16.3: Grants-in-aid Recommended by the Second Finance Commission for Various States

(₹ crore)

State	1957-58	1958-59	1959-60	1960-61	1961-62	Total
Andhra Pradesh	4.00	4.00	4.00	4.00	4.00	20.00
Assam	3.75	3.75	3.75	4.50	4.50	20.25
Bihar	3.50	3.50	3.50	4.25	4.25	19.00
Kerala	1.75	1.75	1.75	1.75	1.75	8.75
Madhya Pradesh	3.00	3.00	3.00	3.00	3.00	15.00
Mysore	6.00	6.00	6.00	6.00	6.00	30.00
Orissa	3.25	3.25	3.25	3.50	3.50	16.75
Punjab	2.25	2.25	2.25	2.25	2.25	11.25
Rajasthan	2.50	2.50	2.50	2.50	2.50	12.50
West Bengal	3.25	3.25	3.25	4.75	4.75	19.25
Jammu & Kashmir	3.00	3.00	3.00	3.00	3.00	15.00
Total	**36.25**	**36.25**	**36.25**	**39.50**	**39.50**	**187.75**

Source: *Report of the Second Finance Commission*, 1957, p. 50.

16.4 Distribution of Estate Duty

Estate duty was first levied in India in 1953 and the total collections up to March 31, 1957 amounted to ₹ 4.75 crore. Pending Parliamentary legislation, the net proceeds had been provisionally distributed among the States in the same ratio as the States' share of the divisible pool of income tax.

A variety of suggestions were made by the States in regard to the principles of distribution. Estate duty being a tax on property, the basis of location would be the most appropriate principle of distribution. It is, however, not possible to apply this principle in the case of the part relating to movable property, which may be included in an estate, and in respect of it some general principle of distribution such as population is inescapable. Keeping these limitations in mind, II-FC made the following recommendation.

1. Out of the net proceeds of the duty in any financial year, a sum equal to one percent be retained by the Union as proceeds attributable to Union territories.
2. Balance be apportioned between immovable property and other property in the ratio of the gross value of all such properties brought into assessment in that year.
3. Sum thus apportioned to immovable property be distributed among the States in proportion to the gross value of the immovable property located in each State.
4. Sum apportioned to property other than immovable property be distributed among the States in proportion to their population.

On the basis of above principles, the percentage share of each State was worked out as shown in Table 16.4. This scheme of distribution took effect from the financial year 1957-58.

Table 16.4: Percentage Shares of States in Estate Duty Recommended by the Second Finance Commission

S. No.	State	Percent	S. No.	State	Percent
1.	Andhra Pradesh	8.76	8.	Mysore	5.43
2.	Assam	2.53	9.	Orissa	4.10
3.	Bihar	10.86	10.	Punjab	4.52
4.	Bombay	13.52	11.	Rajasthan	4.47
5.	Kerala	3.79	12.	Uttar Pradesh	17.71
6.	Madhya Pradesh	7.30	13.	West Bengal	7.37
7.	Madras	8.40	14.	Jammu and Kashmir	1.24

Source: *Report of the Second Finance Commission*, 1957, p. 52.

16.5 Miscellaneous

In its study of the expenditure of State Governments in recent years, II-FC was struck by the dislocation caused to the finances of many of them by unforeseen expenditure on natural calamities like famine, droughts and floods and it felt the need for making some regular provision to meet this type of expenditure. In its estimate of the committed expenditure of the States, it included a margin for enabling them to set apart annually from their revenue sizeable sums to be accumulated in a fund for meeting expenditure on natural calamities. Table 16.5 records the annual amounts, based roughly on the average annual expenditure over the last decade, allowed by II-FC for individual States.

Table 16.5: Annual Amounts Recommended by the Second Finance Commission to Meet Expenditure on Natural Calamities

S. No.	State	Amount (₹ lakh)	S. No.	State	Amount (₹ lakh)
1.	Andhra Pradesh	75	8.	Mysore	30

contd...

2.	Assam	25	9.	Orissa	50
3.	Bihar	100	10.	Punjab	40
4.	Bombay	40	11.	Rajasthan	40
5.	Kerala	10	12.	Uttar Pradesh	50
6.	Madhya Pradesh	15	13.	West Bengal	80
7.	Madras	50	14.	Jammu and Kashmir	10
	Total				**615**

Source: *Report of the Second Finance Commission*, 1957, p. 66.

Endnotes

1. *Report of the Second Finance Commission, 1957*, pp. 47-48.
2. *Ibid.*, p. 50.

17

Third Finance Commission (III-FC): 1962-63 to 1965-66

Highlights of the Report	
Chairman	Shri A.K. Chanda
Members	Shri P. Govinda Menon Shri Dwijendra Nath Roy Professor M.V. Mathur Shri G.R. Kamat, Member-Secretary
Year and month of establishment	December 1960
Year and month of reporting	December 1961
Period of award	1962-63 to 1965-66
Main Recommendations	
1. States' share in income tax fixed at (percent): 66 2. Bases of distribution of States' share in income tax inter se (percent): Population: 80; Contribution: 20; Other factors: Nil 3. States' share in Union excise duties fixed at (percent): 20 (from 35 commodities) 4. Bases of distribution of States' share in Union excise duties inter se (percent): Population: Major factor; Other factors: Weightage not stated.	

In addition to the matters under Article 280 of the Constitution, III-FC was required to make recommendations regard to

1. States which are in need of assistance by way of grants-in-aid of their revenues under Article 275, and the sums to be paid to those States other than the sums specified in the provisos to clause (1) of that article, having regard, among other considerations, to: (i) the requirements of the Third Five Year Plan, and (ii) the efforts to be made by those States to raise additional revenue from the sources available to them,
2. changes, if any, to be made in the principles governing the distribution amongst the States under Article 269 of the net proceeds in any financial year of estate duty in respect of property other than agricultural land,
3. changes, if any, to be made in the principles governing the distribution among the States under Article 269 of the net proceeds in any financial year of taxes on railway fares and
4. changes, if any, to be made in the principles governing the distribution of the net proceeds in any financial year of the additional excise duties levied on each of the following commodities, namely: (i) cotton fabrics, (ii) rayon or artificial silk fabrics, (iii) woollen fabrics, (iv) sugar and (v) tobacco, including manufactured tobacco, in replacement of the States sales taxes formerly levied by the State Governments:

Provided that the share accruing to each State shall not be less than the revenue realised from the levy of sales tax in the financial year 1956-57 in that State.

III-FC was required to make recommendations for 4 years commencing with 1962-63.

17.1 Distribution of Estate Duty

Some of the States were content with the principles laid down by II-FC for the distribution of revenue from estate duty. However, some others suggested a revision on the lines submitted for the consideration of II-FC. After discussion with III-FC, all the States agreed that the principles enunciated by II-FC might be left undisturbed. Therefore, III-FC recommended the continuance of these principles which were as under.

1. Out of the net proceeds of the duty in each financial year, a sum equal to 1 percent be retained by the Union as proceeds attributable to Union territories.
2. Balance be apportioned between immovable property and other property in the ratio of the gross value of all such properties brought into assessment in that year.
3. Sum thus apportioned to immovable property be distributed among the States in proportion to the gross value of the immovable property located in each State.
4. Sum apportioned to property other than immovable property be distributed among the States in proportion to their population.

The percentages laid down by II-FC, however, needed revision on the basis of 1961 census. Revised percentages are shown in Table 17.1.

Table 17.1: Percentage Shares of States in Estate Duty Recommended by the Third Finance Commission

S. No.	State	Percent	S. No.	State	Percent
1.	Andhra Pradesh	8.34	9.	Maharashtra	9.16
2.	Assam	2.75	10.	Mysore	5.46
3.	Bihar	10.78	11.	Orissa	4.08
4.	Gujarat	4.78	12.	Punjab	4.71
5.	Jammu and Kashmir	0.83	13.	Rajasthan	4.67
6.	Kerala	3.92	14.	Uttar Pradesh	17.10
7.	Madhya Pradesh	7.51	15.	West Bengal	8.11
8.	Madras	7.80			

Source: *Report of the Third Finance Commission,* 1961, p. 14.

17.2 Devolution and Distribution of Income Tax

All the States pointed out that, as a result of a change brought about in the Income Tax Act by the Finance Act of 1959, the income tax paid by companies was classified as corporation tax and was thus excluded from the pool of income tax hitherto available for distribution. This, they represented, had deprived them of an expanding source of revenue to which they had hitherto a constitutional entitlement. The States argued that III-FC should take into account at least such part of the corporation tax as was attributable to this yield, if not the entire tax. Suggestion had also been made that the surcharge on income tax levied under Article 271, which had been in force for about the last 15 years, should be merged in the basic rates. It was urged that this would abate partly the impact of the loss sustained, as this would indirectly bring within the pool of distribution an excluded amount.

However, III-FC made it clear to the State Governments that the recommendations that it would make should necessarily be in accordance with the provisions of the Constitution and its terms of reference. While appreciating this position, all the States claimed that the percentage of the tax to be assigned to them should be substantially increased. On the considerations mentioned above, III-FC fixed the share of the States in the net proceeds of income tax at 66.66 percent.

As to the question of distribution of the share assigned to the States, widely divergent views were expressed, ranging from distribution entirely on the basis of collection to distribution wholly on the basis of population. In between, there were suggestions that population should be weighed to take account of the proportion of scheduled castes and tribes and backward classes in the population, that the area of the State should be a relevant consideration and that its backwardness should not be ignored. There were also suggestions that distribution should be based on considerations of population as also collection in various proportions.

III-FC was in general agreement with the approach of previous Finance Commissions that the relevant considerations were population and collection. It did not find it feasible to introduce other factors in the distribution of this tax. In all previous schemes of distribution, there had been a blending of these two principles, but in different proportions. While I-FC recommended that distribution of the States' share should be on the basis of 20 percent for collection and 80 percent for population, II-FC reduced the element of collection to 10 percent and expressed the view that in due course the factor of collection should be eliminated altogether and distribution be made entirely on the basis of population.

II-FC had recognised that there could be a case for weightage being given to collection in the restricted field of personal income tax. I-FC had also stated that there was all over the country a core of incomes which could be treated as of local origin. Hence, III-FC maintained, "In our view, while population should remain the main factor for the distribution of the net proceeds of income-tax amongst the States, the factor of contribution should receive adequate recognition. It has been urged before us by the industrial and urban States, in whose territory large amounts are collected by way of income-tax, that they should have an incentive and the wherewithal to maintain the environments which would preserve and promote industrial and trade activities. Since the Second Finance Commission made its recommendations, the taxes on income paid by companies have been excluded from the divisible pool. Bulk of this tax paid by companies would have accrued from income of all-India origin. With the exclusion of this element from the divisible pool, a higher percentage than before of the total yield of income-tax now represents tax derived from incomes of local origin. We consider, therefore, that a higher weightage should be given to the factor of contribution in the distribution of income-tax than that recommended by the Second Commission. We have also been impressed with the submission that the industrial States having larger collections have problems of their own. Large concentration of population, more particularly of industrial labour, creates problems of law and order and gives rise to an increased demand for the administrative and social services. Further, the unit cost of providing these services is larger in such areas than elsewhere, more particularly in the non-urbanised parts". [1]

Taking all these considerations into account, III-FC felt that it would be fair and equitable to restore the formula of I-FC for the distribution of income tax, namely 80 percent on the basis of population and 20 percent on the basis of collection. As regards the actual manner of distribution of the States' share in each year, it agreed with the earlier Commissions that it would be convenient both to the States and to the Union if the Shares were expressed as fixed percentages. Hence, it recommended that two-thirds, that is to say 66⅔ percent of the net proceeds in any financial year of taxes on income other than agricultural income, except in so far as those proceeds represent proceeds attributable to Union territories or to taxes payable in respect of Union emoluments, be assigned to the States and distributed among them in the manner given in Table 17.2. It further recommended that 2.5 percent of the net proceeds of the income tax be prescribed as the net proceeds attributable to Union territories.

Table 17.2: Percentage Shares of the States in the Net Proceeds of Income Tax Assigned to the States as Recommended by the Third Finance Commission

S. No.	State	Percent	S. No.	State	Percent
1.	Andhra Pradesh	7.71	9.	Maharashtra	13.41
2.	Assam	2.44	10.	Mysore	5.13
3.	Bihar	9.33	11.	Orissa	3.44
4.	Gujarat	4.78	12.	Punjab	4.49
5.	Jammu and Kashmir	0.70	13.	Rajasthan	3.97
6.	Kerala	3.55	14.	Uttar Pradesh	14.42
7.	Madhya Pradesh	6.41	15.	West Bengal	12.09
8.	Madras	8.13			

Source: *Report of the Third Finance Commission,* 1961, p. 19.

17.3 Devolution and Distribution of Union Excise Duties

Till April 1952, the proceeds of this duty were not brought into distribution and were retained wholly by the Union. I-FC broke new ground by recommending the sharing of the proceeds of duties on 3 commodities between the Union and the States. It was presumably influenced in this conclusion by the growing financial needs of the States in fulfilling a complementary role in the development of the national economy and the provision of a higher level of social services. II-FC expanded the list of duties to 8 commodities as in their view the taxes on income were ceasing to be an expanding source of revenue and increasing dependence should be placed for purposes of devolution on the growing source of excise revenue. The impact of planning on the States also called for a larger measure of devolution which could be suitably provided by using the permissive provisions of Article 272 more extensively.

On their part, the States again pleaded before III-FC for inclusion of all excisable commodities in the distributable pool. In support of this demand the States argued that the expanding coverage of Central excises and their increasing incidence had adversely affected the revenue potential of sales tax. Accepting this demand of the States in principle the Commission observed, "We consider that the inadequacy of resources that has developed in the States is attributable mainly to the planning process and this inadequacy may become more pronounced with the completion of each successive Plan for some years to come. The viability of the States could best be secured by a larger devolution of the Union excise duties and this should be effected by providing for the participation of the States, by convention, in the proceeds of all Union excises. It would give a great deal of psychological satisfaction to the States and dissipate any suspicion that the Union is pursuing a policy of excessive centralisation of resources". [2]

However, III-FC considering its own scheme of transfers, recommended for distribution among the States 20 percent of the excise revenue from commodities which each yielded in 1960-61 revenue of ₹ 50 lakh or more. The number of such commodities was 35, namely sugar, coffee, tea, tobacco, kerosene, refined diesel oils, diesel oil not otherwise specified, furnace oil, asphalt and bitumen, vegetable non-essential oils, vegetable products, pigments etc., soap, tyres and tubes, paper, rayon and synthetic fibres and yarn, cotton fabrics, silk fabrics, woollen fabrics, rayon or artificial silk fabrics, cement, pig iron, steel ingots, aluminium, tin plate and tin sheets, internal combustion engines, electric motors and parts thereof, electric batteries and parts thereof, electric lighting bulbs and fluorescent lighting bulbs, electric fans, motor vehicles, cycles, foot wear, cinematograph films exposed, and matches

As regards the distribution of the States' share of the divisible excises, I-FC had suggested that consumption of taxed commodities could provide a suitable basis for distribution, but in the absence of reliable data, it adopted population as the basis. Confronted with the same situation of non-availability of reliable statistics, II-FC felt that population was the best basis of adopt, more particularly, as distribution on consumption, even if the relevant data were available, would benefit the more urbanised and the financially stronger States. III-FC was of the view that while population should continue to be the major factor of distribution, the relative financial weaknesses of the States, the disparity in the levels of development reached, the percentage of scheduled castes and tribes and backward classes in their population etc. should also be taken into account in determining the share to be allocated to each State individually. In other words, it felt that in this permissive participation, an attempt should be made to bring all the States, as far as possible, to a comparable level of financial balance. It, therefore, recommended the distribution of the States' share among the States in the manner given in Table 17.3.

Table 17.3: Distribution of States' Share of Excise Duties among the States Recommended by the Third Finance Commission

S. No.	State	Percent	S. No.	State	Percent
1.	Andhra Pradesh	8.23	9.	Maharashtra	5.73
2.	Assam	4.73	10.	Mysore	5.82
3.	Bihar	11.56	11.	Orissa	7.07
4.	Gujarat	6.45	12.	Punjab	6.71
5.	Jammu and Kashmir	2.02	13.	Rajasthan	5.93
6.	Kerala	5.46	14.	Uttar Pradesh	10.68
7.	Madhya Pradesh	8.46	15.	West Bengal	5.07
8.	Madras	6.08			

Source: *Report of the Third Finance Commission,* 1961, p. 24.

17.4 Grants-in-aid of Revenues

Commenting on the principles enunciated by I-FC to distribute grants-in-aid of the revenues of the States, III-FC observed, "These principles are unexceptionable in themselves, but difficulties as appreciated by the First Commission arise in their application. The comparative determination of the tax efforts of the States cannot be in absolute terms. It has to be related to their tax potential, and this calls for a special study. Similarly, the assessment of the measure of economy effected or the degree of efficiency reached in a State's administration is a complicated exercise which, in any event, we could hardly undertake with the organisation and time at our disposal. Yet, without reliable and comparable information on these two essential ingredients of grants-in-aid, it is difficult to determine the quantum of assistance that would be necessary and justified. This and other considerations lead us to the suggestion that an independent Commission should be constituted to review, amongst other things, the financial relations which, in the new situation of planned development, should subsist between the Union and the States....In the enumeration of principles, the First Commission acknowledged that it was not sufficient to cover the amount of budgetary needs but also the fiscal needs arising out of development programmes undertaken. The Second Commission re-affirmed that fiscal needs should be considered in a comprehensive sense and that grants-in-aid should sub-serve the requirements of planned development. It added that the priorities and provisions in the Plan itself should determine the fiscal needs for development for the period of the Plan". [3]

On the considerations placed before it, III-FC recommended that the total amount of grants-in-aid should be of an order which would enable the States, along with any surplus out of the devolution, to cover 75 percent of the revenue component of their Plans. In determining the revenue component, it deducted in full the amount of additional tax to be raised by each State as incorporated in the Plan itself. In making this recommendation, it was influenced, amongst other things, by the fact that the Plan contains repetitive schemes of continuing character. The expenditure on these was unavoidable and was of the nature of committed expenditure.

III-FC had not intended to make any special-purpose grant, but during the course of discussions with the States, it was convinced that impetus should be given to the development of communications more extensively. There was the pressing need to open up backward areas, to break down barriers of isolation and stagnation, to develop social services and social sense, to mobilise economic resources, and above all, to bring about a feeling of oneness in the minds of the people of these regions with the rest of the community. It noted that due to financial stringency, the State Governments had made inadequate provision for the proper maintenance of existing roads and for new construction. It, therefore, felt that in the special circumstances an earmarked grant should be made for improvement of communications in the interests of national economy and national integration. It recommended a total sum of ₹ 36 crore for distribution for this purpose.

Endnotes

1. *Report of the Third Finance Commission*, 1961, p. 18.
2. *Ibid.*, p. 21.
3. *Ibid.*, pp. 28-29.

18

Fourth Finance Commission (IV-FC): 1966-67 to 1968-69

Highlights of the Report	
Chairman	Shri P.V. Rajamannar
Members	Shri Mohan Lal Gautam Shri D.G. Karve Professor Bhabatosh Datta Shri P.C. Mathew, Member-Secretary
Year and month of establishment	May 1964
Year and month of reporting	August 1965
Period of award	1966-67 to 1968-69
Main Recommendations	
1. States' share in income tax fixed at (percent): 75 2. Bases of distribution of States' share in income tax inter se (percent): Population: 80; Contribution: 20; Other factors: Nil 3. States' share in Union excise duties fixed at (percent): 20 4. Bases of distribution of States' share in Union excise duties inter se (percent): Population: 80; Other factors: 20	

IV-FC was constituted by the President in his Order dated May 5, 1964. In addition to the matters on which, under the provisions of sub-clauses (a) and (b) of clause (3) of Article 280 of the Constitution, it was required to make recommendations, IV-FC was also asked to make recommendations in regard to

1. States which are in need of assistance by way of grants-in-aid of their revenues under Article 275, and the sums to be paid to those States other than the sums specified in the provisos to clause (1) of that articles, having regard, among other considerations, to: (i) the revenue resources of those States for the five years ending with the financial year 1970-71 on the basis of the levels of taxation likely to be reached in the financial year 1965-66, (ii) the requirements of those States to meet the committed expenditure on maintenance and upkeep of Plan schemes completed during the Third Plan, (iii) any further expenditure likely to devolve upon those States for the servicing of their debt, (iv) creation of a fund out of the excess, if any, over a limit to be specified by the Commission of the net proceeds of estate duty on property other than agricultural land accruing to a State in any financial year, for the repayment of the State's debt to the Central Government and (v) the scope for economy consistent with efficiency, which may be effected by the States in their administrative expenditure.

2. Changes, if any, to be made in the principles governing the distribution amongst the States under Article 269 of the net proceeds in any financial year of estate duty in respect of property other than agricultural land.
3. Changes, if any, to be made in the principles governing the distribution amongst the States of the grant to be made available to the States in lieu of taxes on railway fares.
4. Changes, if any, to be made in the principles governing the distribution of the net proceeds in any financial year of the additional excise duties levied on each of the following commodities, namely: (i) cotton fabrics, (ii) silk fabrics, (iii) rayon of artificial silk fabrics, (iv) woollen fabrics, (v) sugar and (vi) tobacco (including manufactured tobacco) in replacement of the States' sales taxes formerly levied by the State Governments.

   Provided that the share accruing to each State shall not be less than the revenue realized from the levy of the sales tax for the financial year 1956-57 in that State.
5. Effect of the combined incidence of a State's sales tax and Union duties of excise on the production, consumption or export of commodities or products, the duties on which are shareable with the States, and the adjustments, if any, to be made in the State's share of Union excise duties if there is any increase in the State's sales tax on such commodities or products over a limit to be specified by the Commission.

18.1 Distribution of Estate Duty

A number of suggestions were made to IV-FC by the States in regard to the principles of distribution. The different suggestions were as under.

1. Distribution of estate duty wholly on the basis of population.
2. Distribution partly on the basis of collection and partly on the basis of location.
3. Distribution on the basis of population with weightage to Scheduled Castes and Scheduled Tribes.
4. Distribution on the basis of 80 percent population and 20 percent location.
5. Continuance of the existing scheme of distribution.

IV-FC expressed agreement with the principles laid down by its predecessors and recommended the continuance of the following principles. It, however, raised the share of Union Territories to 2 percent, taking into account population and the value of immovable property assessed in these territories in recent years.

1. Out of the net proceeds of the duty in each financial year, a sum equal to two percent be retained by the Union as proceeds attributable to Union territories.
2. Balance be apportioned between immovable property and other property in the ratio of the gross value of all such properties brought into assessment in that year.
3. Sum thus apportioned to immovable property be distributed among the States in proportion to the gross value of the immovable property located in each State.
4. Sum apportioned to property other than immovable property be distributed among the States in proportion to their population.

On the basis of the 1961 Census figures, the percentages were worked out as given in Table 18.1.

Table 18.1: Percentage Shares of States in Estate Duty Recommended by the Fourth Finance Commission

S. No.	State	Percent	S. No.	State	Percent
1.	Andhra Pradesh	8.34	9.	Maharashtra	9.16
2.	Assam	2.75	10.	Mysore	5.46
3.	Bihar	10.76	11.	Nagaland	0.09
4.	Gujarat	4.78	12.	Orissa	4.07
5.	Jammu & Kashmir	0.83	13.	Punjab	4.70
6.	Kerala	3.92	14.	Rajasthan	6.67
7.	Madhya Pradesh	7.50	15.	Uttar Pradesh	17.08
8.	Madras	7.80	16.	West Bengal	8.09
	Total				**100**

Source: *Report of the Fourth Finance Commission*, 1965, p. 13.

18.2 Grant in Lieu of Tax on Railway Passenger Fares

It may be recalled that the tax on railway passenger fares was imposed under the Railway Passenger Fare Act, 1957 and the II-FC was, for the first time, asked to make recommendations as to the principles which should govern the distribution under Article 269 of the Constitution of the net proceeds in any financial year of the tax. II-FC decided that the proceeds of the tax should be distributed among the States in the ratio of passenger earnings which may be determined with reasonable accuracy by allocating passenger earnings among States on the basis of railway route mileage within each State with due allowance for variation in density of traffic between the various railway zones and as between the various gauges in each zone. Thus, the earnings from passenger traffic of each zonal railway (excluding earnings from suburban services) were allocated by route mileage located in each State separately for each gauge. II-FC recommended that the proceeds of the tax be distributed in the ratio of State-wise earnings so worked out and indicated each State's share as a fixed percentage applicable for five years from 1957-58.

Railway Passenger Fares Act, 1957 was repealed 1961 and the tax was merged in the basic fares. The Central Government, however, decided to make an *ad hoc* grant of ₹ 12.50 crore per annum to the States in lieu of the tax for a period of five years from 1961-62 to 1965-66. III-FC which was asked to recommend principles on which the *ad hoc* grant should be distributed, recommended that the distribution should be on the principle of compensation to place the States broadly on the same footing as before and accordingly worked out the distribution of the sum of ₹ 12.50 crore per year.

IV-FC agreed that the distribution of this grant should be on the basis of compensation and that the percentage share of each State in which the tax is leviable should be worked out on the principles enunciated by II-FC. However, in its term of reference on the subject, IV-FC was asked to make recommendations regarding changes, if any, to be made in the principles governing distribution among States of the grant to be made available to the States in lieu of taxes on railway passenger fares, but the actual amount of grant to be distributed was not indicated. Therefore, instead of recommending the sums payable to each State, it considered it desirable to express the States' shares in percentages. In determining the percentage share (Table 18.2), it used the latest available statistics of railway route length in each State under each gauge and the average annual earnings from passenger traffic (excluding earnings from suburban traffic) for three years ending 1964 for which actuals were available.

Table 18.2: Percentage Share of Each State in Grant in Lieu of Tax on Railway Passenger Fares

S. No.	State	Percent	S. No.	State	Percent
1.	Andhra Pradesh	9.05	9.	Maharashtra	8.98
2.	Assam	2.79	10.	Mysore	3.98
3.	Bihar	9.99	11.	Nagaland	0.01
4.	Gujarat	7.11	12.	Orissa	2.12
5.	Jammu & Kashmir	---	13.	Punjab	7.43
6.	Kerala	1.85	14.	Rajasthan	6.40
7.	Madhya Pradesh	9.85	15.	Uttar Pradesh	18.23
8.	Madras	5.81	16.	West Bengal	6.40
	Total				**100**

Source: *Report of the Fourth Finance Commission*, 1965, p. 15.

18.3 Devolution and Distribution of Income Tax

IV-FC was asked to make recommendations in regard to the following three matters.

1. Percentage of the *net proceeds* of income tax to be assigned to the States.
2. Manner of distribution among the States of their share.
3. Percentage of the *net proceeds* which shall be deemed to represent proceeds attributable to Union territories.

Almost all the States urged upon IV-FC for an increase in the share to be assigned to them. They pointed out that as a result of the change in the classification of the income tax paid by companies brought about by the Finance Act, 1959, the rate of growth of the divisible pool had been adversely affected. It was further argued that what the framers of the Constitution had intended to be a flexible and expanding source of revenue to the States had ceased to have the significance that was once contemplated. Some of the States reiterated the views placed by them before the previous Finance Commissions that though the Government of India was competent to levy any surcharge, wholly for the purposes of the Union under Article 271, such a levy in the very nature of things, was intended to be a temporary measure to serve a particular situation. It was, therefore, urged that during normal times there should be no need for any surcharge exclusively for the Union. However, if at all such a surcharge was levied, it should as a matter of course be merged with the basic rates after a period of three years.

As regards the percentage of the States' share, while some States did not suggest any change in the existing percentage, some others suggested that the entire net proceeds be assigned to the States. The suggestions by other States fell between these two views. Another view was that the permanent solution to the shrinkage in the divisible pool was suitably to amend the Constitution so as to provide for inclusion of the proceeds from corporation tax in the divisible pool, alternatively the Centre should make good to the States by way of grants the loss on account of non-inclusion of corporation tax in the divisible pool.

After considering the claims put forward by the States, IV-FC expressed general agreement with the observation of III-FC that in the case of a divisible tax in which there was obligatory participation between the Union and the States, a sound principle to observe would be that all participating governments, more particularly the one responsible for levy and collection, should have a significant interest in the yield of that tax. Considering the various facts placed before it, IV-FC took the view that some further increase in the States' share was justified. Accordingly it recommended that 75 percent of the divisible pool of income tax should be allocated to the States for distribution among them.

As regards the principles of distribution of the States' share *inter se,* the views expressed by the States, as usual, were widely divergent. While some States wanted the share to be distributed entirely on the basis of population, another view was that the distribution should be solely on the basis of collection. The other suggestions made were that the distribution should be made taking into account the proper weightage to Scheduled Castes and Tribes, relative financial weakness and economic backwardness, inverse ratio of per capita income etc. IV-FC had no hesitation in rejecting some of the factors put forward by the States like area, backwardness and financial weakness and proportion of Scheduled Castes and Tribes in the population as proper bases for a scheme of distribution of the proceeds of income tax among the States. There remained only two factors which, IV-FC believed, were relevant, namely population and contribution. Taking these two factors of population and collection, there could be divergence of opinion as to the relative proportion to be assigned to these two factors. Eventually, it decided that the principle of distribution to individual States of their share in the divisible pool of income tax proceeds should be the same as recommended by I-FC and by III-FC, i.e. 80 percent on the basis of population and 20 percent on the basis of collection.

As regards the actual manner of distribution of the States' share in each year, it felt it convenient both to the States and to the Union if the shares were expressed as fixed percentages. Taking, therefore, the average of the collections of the three years ending with 1963-64, and the population figures according to the 1961 Census, the percentage share of each State in the distributable amount were worked out as given in Table 18.3. It also prescribed 2.5 percent of the net proceeds of the tax to represent proceeds attributable to Union territories.

18.4 Devolution and Distribution of Union Excise Duties

The first issue before IV-FC was whether the States should at all be given a share out of Union excises. It noted that under the Constitution the distribution of proceeds of Union excise duties between the Centre and the States was merely permissive and did not stand on the same footing as the compulsory assignment to the States of proceeds of taxes enumerated under Article 269 of the Constitution or compulsory distribution between the Centre and the States of the proceeds of income tax under Article 270 of the Constitution. Thus, the States did not have a constitutional right to claim a share out of the proceeds of Union excises. It was for the Parliament to decide if the States should at all be given a share. The factual position was that ever since 1952-53, the States had been getting a share out of Union excise proceeds. The first three Finance Commissions had taken the view that having regard to the growing requirements of funds by the States for developmental and other essential services, recourse to permissive sharing contemplated under Article 272 of the Constitution was not only justified but even necessary. This view was endorsed by IV-FC also.

Table 18.3: Percentage Shares of the States in the Net Proceeds of Income Tax Assigned to the States as Recommended by the Fourth Finance Commission

S. No.	State	Percent	S. No.	State	Percent
1.	Andhra Pradesh	7.37	9.	Maharashtra	14.28
2.	Assam	2.44	10.	Mysore	5.14
3.	Bihar	9.04	11.	Nagaland	0.07
4.	Gujarat	5.29	12.	Orissa	3.40
5.	Jammu & Kashmir	0.73	13.	Punjab	4.36
6.	Kerala	3.59	14.	Rajasthan	3.97
7.	Madhya Pradesh	6.47	15.	Uttar Pradesh	14.60
8.	Madras	8.34	16.	West Bengal	10.91
	Total				**100**

Source: *Report of the Fourth Finance Commission*, 1965, p. 20.

Having accepted that Union excises were to be shared with the States, the next question before the Commission was which of the excisable commodities should be selected for the distribution of proceeds and what percentage of the total proceeds on those commodities should be made over to the States?

The first two Finance Commissions confined the sharing scheme to a few selected items: I-FC to 3 items, viz. tobacco, matches and vegetable products and II-FC to 8 items, viz. tobacco, matches, vegetable products, sugar, tea, coffee, paper and vegetable non-essential oils. III-FC approach to the question of selection of items for sharing was different from that of the earlier Commissions. It accepted in principle the reasonableness of the demand of the States for participation in the proceeds of all Union excises. For purposes of distribution, however, it included only the commodities on which duties collected in 1960-61 amounted to ₹ 50 lakh or more. The number of such commodities was 35.

In their representations to IV-FC, the States almost unanimously argued that whatever reservations the last Finance Commission's distribution scheme had should go and that they should be entitled to a share out of the proceeds of excise duties on all commodities, including the commodities which might be taken up for the levy in the coming quinquennium.

Convinced by the arguments given by the States, IV-FC recommended that all existing Union excise duties as also those that might be levied in the coming five years should be shared between the Centre and the States.

On the question of the percentage of the proceeds of distributable excises, IV-FC took the view that in determining the over-all share of the States, due regard had to be given to the requirements of the States on the one hand and the needs of the Union Government on the other. Having considered the issue in this light and keeping in mind the estimates of yield from the existing excise duties in the coming quinquennium as also the requirements of the States, it came to the conclusion that the States' share out of the distributable excises be fixed at 20 percent of the net proceeds.

In regard to the principles for the distribution of the total of the States' share as among different States, there were divergent placed before it. After examining various viewpoints, it decided to take into account economic and social backwardness also as indicated by the following factors.

1. Per capita gross value of agricultural production.
2. Per capita value added by manufacture.
3. Percentage of workers (as defined in the Census) to the total population.
4. Percentage of enrolment in Classes I to V to the population.
5. Population per hospital bed.
6. Percentage of rural population to total population.
7. Percentage of the population of Scheduled Castes and Tribes to total population.

IV FC gave the factor of relative economic and social backwardness a weight equivalent to 20 percent. For the other factor, namely population, it recommended a weight equivalent to 80 percent. The percentage share of each State was worked out as shown in Table 18.4.

Table 18.4: Distribution of States' Share of Excise Duties among the States Recommended by the Fourth Finance Commission

S. No.	State	Percent	S. No.	State	Percent
1.	Andhra Pradesh	7.77	9.	Maharashtra	8.23
2.	Assam	3.32	10.	Mysore	5.41
3.	Bihar	10.03	11.	Nagaland	2.21
4.	Gujarat	4.80	12.	Orissa	4.82
5.	Jammu & Kashmir	2.26	13.	Punjab	4.86
6.	Kerala	4.16	14.	Rajasthan	5.06
7.	Madhya Pradesh	7.40	15.	Uttar Pradesh	14.98
8.	Madras	7.18	16.	West Bengal	7.51
	Total				**100**

Source: *Report of the Fourth Finance Commission*, 1965, p. 29.

18.5 Principles Governing Grants-in-aid of Revenues

The rules regarding grants-in-aid were considered by I-FC in detail and it recommended that budgetary needs of the States should be an important criterion for determining the assistance required by the States. However, in arriving at these needs, appropriate allowances have to be made based on a number of considerations as listed below.

1. Budgets should be reduced to a standard form by eliminating non-repetitive items.
2. Due consideration should be given to the tax efforts by the State and the extent to which the State itself had made efforts to raise resources in relation to its tax potential.
3. Allowance should be made for the scope for economy in expenditure.
4. System of grants-in-aid should be designed to avoid large disparities in the standards of basic social services.
5. Grants-in-aid may be given to help individual States to meet their special burdens, if such burdens are of national concern and if they are likely to cause undue strain on the States' finances.
6. Grants-in-aid may be given for broad national purposes with a view to further any beneficent service of primary importance in regard to which it is in the national interest to assist the less advanced States to go forward.

IV-FC agreed with the principles formulated by its predecessors except to the extent that it did not recommend the inclusion of plan grants and special purpose grants in grants-in-aid. In applying these principles and working out the grants-in-aid admissible to States, its terms of reference required it to have due regard to certain special considerations which were not specifically mentioned in the terms of reference to the earlier Commissions. Among these considerations were the expenditure devolving on the States for servicing of their debt, the creation of a fund out of part of the proceeds of estate duty, and the scope for economy consistent with efficiency which might be effected by the States in their administrative expenditure.

19

Fifth Finance Commission (V-FC): 1969-70 to 1973-74

Highlights of the Report	
Chairman	Shri Mahavir Tyagi
Members	Shri P.C. Bhattacharyya Shri M. Seshachalapathy Dr. D.T. Lakdawala Shri V.L. Gidwani
Year and month of establishment	February 1968
Year and month of reporting	July 1969
Period of award	1969-70 to 1973-74
Main Recommendations	
1. States' share in income tax fixed at (percent): 75 2. Bases of distribution of States' share in income tax inter se (percent): Population: 90; Contribution: 10; Other factors: Nil 3. States' share in Union excise duties fixed at (percent): 20 4. Bases of distribution of States' share in Union excise duties inter se (percent): Population: 80; Other factors: 20	

V-FC was constituted by an Order of the President dated February 29, 1968. It was asked to make recommendations as to the following matters.

1. Distribution between the Union and the States of the net proceeds of taxes which are to be, or may be, divided between them under Chapter 1 of Part XII of the Constitution and the allocation between the States of the respective shares of such proceeds.
2. Principles which should govern the grants-in-aid of the revenues of the States out of the Consolidated Fund of India and the sums to be paid to the States which are in need to assistance by way of grants-in-aid of their revenues under article 275 for purposes other than those specified in the provisos to clause (1) of that article and other than the requirements of the Five Year Plan, having regard, among other considerations, to: (i) the revenue resources of those States for the five years ending with the financial year 1973-74 on the basis of the levels of taxation likely to be reached at the end of the financial year 1968-69, (ii) the requirements on revenue account of those States to meet the expenditure on administration, interest charges in respect of their debt, maintenance and upkeep of Plan schemes completed by the end of 1968-69, transfer of funds to local bodies and aided institutions and other committed expenditure and (iii) the scope for better fiscal management as also for economy consistent with efficiency which may be effected by the States in their

administrative, maintenance, developmental and other expenditure.

3. Changes, if any, to be made in the principles governing the distribution amongst the States of the grant to be made available to the States in lieu of the repealed tax on railway passenger fares.
4. Changes, if any, to be made in the principles governing the distribution amongst the States under Article 269 of the net proceeds in any financial year of estate duty in respect of property other than agricultural land.
5. Desirability or otherwise of maintaining the existing arrangements under the Additional Duties of Excise (Goods of Special Importance) Act, 1957, in regard to the levy of additional duties of excise on sugar, textiles and tobacco in lieu of the States' sales taxes thereon, with or without any modifications and the scope for extending such arrangements to other items or commodities.
6. Irrespective of the recommendations made under item (e) above, the changes, if any, to be made in the principles governing the distribution of the net proceeds in any financial year of the additional excise duties leviable under the 1957 Act aforesaid on each of the following commodities, namely: (i) cotton fabrics, (ii) silk fabrics, (iii) woollen fabrics, (iv) rayon or artificial silk fabrics, (v) sugar and (vi) tobacco including manufactured tobacco, in replacement of the States' sales taxes formerly levied by the State Governments. Provided that the share accruing to each State shall not be less than the revenue realised from the levy of the sales tax for the financial year 1956-57 in that State.
7. Principles which should govern the distribution of the net proceeds of such additional items or commodities as may be recommended under item (e) above for levy of additional excise duties in lieu of the States' sales taxes thereon.
8. Scope for raising revenue from the taxes and duties mentioned in Article 269 of the Constitution but not levied at present.
9. Scope for raising additional revenue by the various State Governments from the sources of revenue available to them.
10. Problem of unauthorised overdrafts of certain States with the Reserve Bank and the procedure to be observed for avoiding such overdrafts.

19.1 Devolution and Distribution of Income Tax

V-FC made the following recommendations regarding income tax.

1. In respect of distribution of the unadjusted balance of advance tax collections up to the year 1966-67: (i) out of the amount of such advance tax collections, as determined by the Comptroller and Auditor-General of India, a sum equal to 2.5 percent thereof be deemed to be the portion which represent the proceeds attributable to Union territories, as constituted immediately prior to the Punjab Reorganisation Act, 1966, (ii) percentage of the amount of advance tax as determined by the Comptroller and Auditor-General of India except the portion attributable to Union territories, to be assigned to the States should be 75 percent, (iii) distribution among the States *inter se* of the share assigned to the States should be made on the basis of

the percentages recommended by the IV-FC, with appropriate adjustments in regard to the share of reorganised Punjab and Haryana States and Union territories in accordance with the Punjab Reorganisation Act, 1966 and (iv) share of each State should be paid to the State Government in three equal annual instalments during the year from 1971-72 to 1973-74.

2. In respect of distribution between the Union and the States of the net proceeds of income tax in the years 1967-68 and 1968-69, there should be no change in the distribution as prescribed in the Constitution (Distribution of Revenues) Order, 1965, in the event of the said net proceeds being certified by the Comptroller and Auditor-General of India on the revised basis.
3. In respect of the distribution of net proceeds of income tax in the financial year from 1969-70 to 1973-74: (i) out of the net proceeds of taxes on income in each financial year, a sum equal to 2.6 percent thereof be deemed to be the portion which represents the proceeds attributable to Union territories, (ii) percentage of the net proceeds of taxes on income, except the portion which represents proceeds attributable to Union territories, to be assigned to the States should be 75 percent and (iii) distribution among the States *inter se* of the share assigned to the States in respect of each financial year should be made on the basis of the following percentages (Table 19.1).

Table 19.1: Percentage Shares of the States in the Net Proceeds of Income Tax Assigned to the States as Recommended by the Fifth Finance Commission

S. No.	State	Percent	S. No.	State	Percent
1.	Andhra Pradesh	8.01	10.	Mysore	5.40
2.	Assam	2.67	11.	Nagaland	0.08
3.	Bihar	9.99	12.	Orissa	3.75
4.	Gujarat	5.13	13.	Punjab	2.55
5.	Haryana	1.73	14.	Rajasthan	4.34
6.	Jammu & Kashmir	0.79	15.	Tamil Nadu	8.18
7.	Kerala	3.83	16.	Uttar Pradesh	16.01
8.	Madhya Pradesh	7.09	17.	West Bengal	9.11
9.	Maharashtra	11.34			
	Total				**100**

Source: *Report of the Fifth Finance Commission*, 1969, p. 30.

19.2 Devolution and Distribution of Union Excise Duties

V-FC made the following recommendations in regard to the distribution of Union excise duties.

1. During each of the years 1969-70 to 1971-72 a sum equivalent to 20 percent of the net proceeds of Union duties of excise on all articles levied and collected in that

year, excluding special excises, regulatory duties and duties and cesses levied under special Acts and earmarked for special purposes, should be paid out of the Consolidated Fund of India to the States.

2. During the years 1972-73 and 1973-74, a sum equivalent to 20 percent of the net proceeds of Union duties of excise on all articles levied and collected in the respective year, including special excises, but excluding regulatory duties and duties and cesses levied under special Acts and earmarked for special purposes, should be paid out of the Consolidated Fund of India to the States.
3. Distribution among the States of the sum payable to the States in respect of each financial year should be made on the basis of the following percentages (Table 19.2).

Table 19.2: Distribution of States' Share of Excise Duties among the States Recommended by the Fifth Finance Commission

S. No.	State	Percent	S. No.	State	Percent
1.	Andhra Pradesh	7.15	10.	Mysore	4.65
2.	Assam	2.51	11.	Nagaland	0.08
3.	Bihar	13.81	12.	Orissa	4.72
4.	Gujarat	4.17	13.	Punjab	2.17
5.	Haryana	1.49	14.	Rajasthan	5.28
6.	Jammu & Kashmir	1.12	15.	Tamil Nadu	6.50
7.	Kerala	4.28	16.	Uttar Pradesh	18.82
8.	Madhya Pradesh	8.48	17.	West Bengal	6.84
9.	Maharashtra	7.93			
	Total				**100**

Source: *Report of the Fifth Finance Commission*, 1969, p. 37.

19.3 Additional Duties of Excise in Lieu of Sales Tax

V-FC made the following observations in regard to additional duties of exçise, "(a) It would not be desirable to maintain the existing arrangements in regard to the levy of additional duties of excise on textiles, sugar and tobacco, unless the Government of India, after discussing the matter further with the State Governments, can arrive at a general agreement for the continuance of the present scheme with suitable modifications; (b) While the arrangements are continued, the rates of duties may be made *ad valorem* as far as possible, and may be revised periodically so as to secure reasonable incidence having regard to the prevailing prices and the general level of sales taxes on similar items levied by the States; There is no scope at present for extending such arrangements to other items or commodities". [1]

It recommended the distribution of the net proceeds of the additional excise duties, during each financial year in which the existing arrangements continue, on the following basis.

1. A sum equal to 2.05 percent of such net proceeds be retained by the Union as attributable to Union territories.

2. A sum equal to 0.83 percent of such net proceeds be paid to the State of Jammu and Kashmir as its share.
3. A sum equal to 0.09 percent of such net proceeds be paid to the State of Nagaland as its share.
4. Out of the remaining balance of 97.03 percent of such net proceeds the sums specified (Table 19.3), representing the revenue realised in the financial year 1956-57 by each respective State from the levy of sales taxes on the commodities subject to additional excise duties, be paid as guaranteed amounts.
5. The balance be distributed among the States other than Jammu and Kashmir and Nagaland in accordance with their respective percentage shares of such balance as under (Table 19.4).
6. In case the existing arrangements are discontinued during the course of a financial year, the sums specified in clause (4) above, be reduced *pro rata* to the period for which the arrangements have continued.

Table 19.3: Distribution of Additional Excise Duties among the States Recommended by the Fifth Finance Commission

S. No.	State	Guaranteed amount (₹ Lakh)	S. No.	State	Guaranteed amount (₹ lakh)
1.	Andhra Pradesh	235.24	9.	Mysore	100.10
2.	Assam	85.08	10.	Orissa	85.10
3.	Bihar	130.16	11.	Punjab	96.07
4.	Gujarat	323.45	12.	Rajasthan	90.10
5.	Haryana	65.49	13.	Tamil Nadu	285.34
6.	Kerala	95.08	14.	Uttar Pradesh	575.81
7.	Madhya Pradesh	155.17	16.	West Bengal	280.41
8.	Maharashtra	637.77	17.		

Source: *Report of the Fifth Finance Commission*, 1969, p. 45.

Table 19.4: Distribution of the Remainder, if any, of Additional Excise Duties among the States

S. No.	State	Percentage distribution of excess amount	S. No.	State	Percentage distribution of excess amount
1.	Andhra Pradesh	8.13	9.	Mysore	6.00
2.	Assam	2.47	10.	Orissa	3.13
3.	Bihar	8.40	11.	Punjab	2.98

contd...

4.	Gujarat	6.33	12.	Rajasthan	4.42
5.	Haryana	1.70	13.	Tamil Nadu	9.63
6.	Kerala	4.84	14.	Uttar Pradesh	12.99
7.	Madhya Pradesh	6.34	15.	West Bengal	8.75
8.	Maharashtra	13.89			
	Total				**100.00**

Source: *Report of the Fifth Finance Commission*, 1969, p. 46.

19.4 Grants-in-aid of Revenues

After reviewing the recommendations of the earlier Commissions and taking into account its own scheme of devolution, V-FC recommended that the following States be paid the sums specified against each of them as grants-in-aid of their revenues in the respective years indicated (Table 19.5).

Table 19.5: Grants-in-aid of Revenues Recommended by the Fifth Finance Commission (₹ crore)

State	**Total in 5 years**	**1969-70**	**1970-71**	**1971-72**	**1972-73**	**1973-74**
Andhra Pradesh	65.01	15.54	14.27	13.00	11.73	10.47
Assam	101.97	20.80	20.60	20.39	20.19	19.99
Jammu & Kashmir	73.68	16.81	15.77	14.74	13.70	12.66
Kerala	49.65	9.93	9.93	9.93	9.93	9.93
Mysore	17.99	6.48	5.04	3.60	2.16	0.71
Nagaland	77.95	17.40	16.49	15.59	14.69	13.78
Orissa	104.67	24.51	22.72	20.94	19.14	17.36
Rajasthan	51.49	12.36	11.33	10.30	9.27	8.23
Tamil Nadu	22.82	6.61	5.59	4.56	3.54	2.52
West Bengal	72.62	22.29	18.41	14.52	10.64	6.76
Total	**637.85**	**152.73**	**140.15**	**127.57**	**114.99**	**102.41**

Source: *Report of the Fifth Finance Commission*, 1969, p. 66.

Endnote

1. *Report of the Fifth Finance Commission*, 1969, pp. 44-45.

20

Sixth Finance Commission (VI-FC): 1974-75 to 1978-79

Highlights of the Report	
Chairman	Shri K. Brahmananda Reddy
Members	Justice Syed Sadat Abul Masud Dr. B.S. Minhas Dr. I.S. Gulati Shri G. Ramachandran, Member-Secretary
Year and month of establishment	June 1972
Year and month of reporting	October 1973
Period of award	1974-75 to 1978-79
Main Recommendations	
1. States' share in income tax fixed at (percent): 80 2. Bases of distribution of States' share in income tax inter se (percent): Population: 90; Contribution: 10; Other factors: Nil 3. States' share in Union excise duties fixed at (percent): 20 4. Bases of distribution of States' share in Union excise duties inter se (percent): Population: 75; Other factors: 25	

VI-FC was constituted by the President in his Order dated June 28, 1972 to make recommendations as to the following matters.

1. Distribution between the Union and States of the net proceeds of taxes which are to be, or may be divided between them under Chapter I of Part XII of the Constitution and the allocation between the States of the respective shares of such proceeds.
2. Principles which should govern the grants-in-aid of the revenues of the States out of the Consolidated Fund of India and the sums to be paid to the States which are in need of assistance by way of grants-in-aid of their revenues under Article 275 of the Constitution for purposes other than those specified in the provisos to clause (1) of that article having regard, among other considerations, to: (i) the existing practice in regard to determination and distribution of Central assistance for financing State Plans, (ii) the revenue resources of those States for the five-years ending with the financial year 1978-79 on the basis of the levels of taxation likely to be reached at the end of the financial year 1973-74, (iii) the requirements on revenue account of those States to meet the expenditure on administration taking also into account such provision for emoluments of Government employees, teachers and local body employees as obtaining on a specified date as the Commission deem it proper in the light of the States' capacity and needs, interest charges in respect of their debt,

transfer of funds to local bodies and aided institutions and other committed expenditure, (iv) adequate maintenance and upkeep of capital assets and maintenance of Plan schemes completed by the end of 1973-74, the norms, if any, on the basis of which specified amounts are allowed for the maintenance of different categories of capital assets being indicated by the Commission, (v) the requirements of States which are backward in standards of general administration for upgrading the administration with a view to bringing it to the levels obtaining in the more advanced States over a period of ten years and (vi) the scope for better fiscal management and economy consistent with efficiency which may be effected by the States in their administrative, maintenance, developmental and other expenditure.

3. Changes, if any, to be made in the principles governing the distribution amongst the States of the grant to be made available to the States in lieu of tax under the repealed Railway Passenger Fares Tax Act, 1957.
4. Changes, if any, to be made in the principles governing the distribution amongst the States under Article 269 of the Constitution of the net proceeds of any financial year of estate-duty in respect of property other than agricultural land.
5. Changes, if any, to be made in the principles governing the distribution of the net proceeds in any financial year of the additional excise duties leviable under the Additional Duties of Excise (Goods of Special Importance) Act, 1957 on each of the following commodities; namely: (i) cotton fabrics, (ii) woollen fabrics, (iii) rayon or artificial silk fabrics, (iv) sugar and (v) tobacco including manufactured tobacco, in replacement of the States' sales taxes formerly levied by the State Governments. Provided that the share accruing to each State shall not be less than the revenue realised from the levy of sales tax for the financial year 1956-57 in that State.
6. Principles governing the distribution among the States of the grant to be made available to the States on account of wealth tax on agricultural property.

20.1 Devolution and Distribution of Income Tax

It may be recalled that I-FC had fixed the assignment of the net proceeds of income tax to the States at 55 percent which was enlarged progressively by the succeeding Commissions and placed at 75 percent by the IV-FC. V-FC retained the States' share of the net proceeds of income tax at 75 percent, despite the request of many State Governments for further enhancement. VI-FC recommended that the States' share of the net proceeds of income tax be raised from 75 to 80 percent during the period covered by its award.

As regards the manner of distribution among the States of the percentage of the net proceeds of income tax assigned to them, the views of the States were understandably divergent. While some of the relatively advanced States pressed for a higher weightage for the factor of contribution, the other States urged that the net proceeds of income tax should be distributed wholly on the basis of population. Some of the States also suggested weightage for other factors such as area, proportion of scheduled castes and scheduled tribes population.

All the earlier Finance Commissions had recognised population and contribution to be the only two relevant factors in the distribution of the proceeds of income tax among the States, though they had differed on the relative weightage to be accorded to these two factors. None of them had taken into account other considerations such as economic backwardness, area and proportion of scheduled castes and scheduled tribes population. VI-FC also endorsed this approach of its predecessors both because there were advantages in India's complex federal system in maintaining a reasonable measure of stability in the principles of distribution of shareable taxes and also because the country was seeking to mitigate the economic disabilities of some of the States through weightage for relative economic backwardness in the distribution of Union excise duties and through grants-in-aid for upgradation of standards of administrative and social services.

Accordingly, it recommended that during the period covered by its award, 90 percent of the States' share of the divisible pool of income tax should be distributed among them on the basis of population according to 1971 census and the remaining 10 percent on the basis of figures of assessment after allowing for reductions on account of appellate orders, revisions, refunds and rectification. All the previous Commissions had prescribed the respective shares of States worked out on the principles enunciated by them in terms of fixed percentages. For the sake of administrative convenience, VI-FC continued this practice.

It further recommended that 1.79 percent of the net proceeds of income tax might be taken to be the portion of such proceeds attributable to Union Territories. In short, it made the following recommendations in respect of the distribution of the net proceeds of income tax in each of the financial years from 1974-75 to 1978-79.

1. Out of the net proceeds of taxes on income in each financial year, a sum equal to 1.79 percent thereof be deemed to represent the proceeds attributable to Union Territories.
2. 80 percent of the net proceeds of taxes on income, except the portion representing the proceeds attributable to Union Territories, be assigned to the States.
3. Distribution among the States *inter se* of the share assigned to the States in respect of each financial year should be on the basis of the following percentages (Table 20.1).

20.2 Devolution and Distribution of Union Excise Duties

Sharing of Union excise duties with the States started on a rather modest scale with the award of I-FC which recommended sharing in respect of only 3 of the major commodities then subject to excise duties.

Consequent upon the recommendations of successive Finance Commissions, the share of the States in Union excise duties had progressively enlarged. By the time the V-FC was set up, the States were already sharing the proceeds of all Union excise duties excepting only special excise duties, regulatory duties of excise and cesses on commodities.

Almost all the States pressed for augmentation of their share in the divisible pool of Union excise duties. Striking a balance between the plea of the States for a substantial increase in the divisible pool and the needs of the Centre, VI-FC recommended that the States' share of all basic duties of excise should be retained at 20 percent during the period covered by its award. 20 percent of the net proceeds of auxiliary duties of excise were also made shareable from 1976-77 onwards. Revenues from cesses on excisable commodities, levied under special enactments and reserved for special purposes, continued to remain excluded from the divisible pool.

Table 20.1: Percentage Shares of the States in the Net Proceeds of Income Tax Assigned to the States as Recommended by the Sixth Finance Commission

S. No.	State	Percent	S. No.	State	Percent
1.	Andhra Pradesh	7.76	12.	Manipur	0.18
2.	Assam	2.54	13.	Meghalaya	0.18
3.	Bihar	9.61	14.	Nagaland	0.09
4.	Gujarat	5.55	15.	Orissa	3.73
5.	Haryana	1.77	16.	Punjab	2.75
6.	Himachal Pradesh	0.60	17.	Rajasthan	4.50
7.	Jammu & Kashmir	0.81	18.	Tamil Nadu	7.94
8.	Karnataka	5.33	19.	Tripura	0.27
9.	Kerala	3.92	20.	Uttar Pradesh	15.23
10.	Madhya Pradesh	7.30	21.	West Bengal	8.89
11.	Maharashtra	11.05			
	Total				**100.00**

Source: *Report of the Sixth Finance Commission*, 1973, p. 13.

While there was near unanimity among the States in demanding an increase in the share of Union excise duties, there were naturally wide divergences in their approach to the principles of determination of the relative share of the States in the divisible pool. Each State was inclined to put forward a formula that would favour it most.

After considering the conflicting claims of the States, VI-FC recommended that while the weightage for backwardness should be raised from 20 percent to 25 percent, the *inter se* distribution of this portion of Union excise duties should be in relation to the *distance* of a State's per capita income from that of the State with the highest per capita income multiplied by the population of the State concerned according to 1971 census. The balance of 75 percent of the States' share of the divisible pool of Union excise duties should be distributed on the basis of population of the States according to 1971 census. It worked out the relative shares of the States in terms of percentages according to the principles enunciated above. Distribution among the States was made in terms of percentages prescribed by it (Table 20.2).

20.3 Additional Duties of Excise

Commenting on the working of the scheme of additional excise duties in lieu of sales tax, VI-FC remarked, "The scheme of levy of additional excise duties in lieu of sales tax has now been in force for over 15 years. All available evidence indicates that the continuance of the scheme is welcomed by trade and industry who have in fact frequently pleaded for its extension to other commodities. But till quite recently, most of the State Governments would seem to have had reservations about the utility of the existing system. Dissatisfaction of the State Governments with the inadequate exploitation of the revenue potential of the additional excise duties on these commodities by the Union Government led the Government of India to request the last Finance Commission to investigate and report on the desirability or otherwise of continuing the scheme of levy of additional excise duties in replacement of sales tax. Later in the wake of the recommendations of the Fifth Finance Commission the whole question was considered by a representative group of Central and State Government officials. In the light of the proposals made by the group, the National Development Council at its meeting held on 28-12-1970 agreed to the continuance of the present arrangements subject to certain conditions. The main condition stipulated by the National Development Council for the continuance of the scheme was that the incidence of the additional excise duties should be stepped up to 10.8 percent of the value of the clearances within a period of two or three years. These recommendations were accepted by the Government of India and have since been implemented through successive Finance Acts". [1]

Table 20.2: Distribution of States' Share of Excise Duties among the States Recommended by the Sixth Financc Commission

S. No.	State	Percent	S. No.	State	Percent
1.	Andhra Pradesh	8.16	12.	Manipur	0.21
2.	Assam	2.71	13.	Meghalaya	0.19
3.	Bihar	11.47	14.	Nagaland	0.11
4.	Gujarat	4.57	15.	Orissa	4.06
5.	Haryana	1.53	16.	Punjab	1.87
6.	Himachal Pradesh	0.63	17.	Rajasthan	5.00
7.	Jammu & Kashmir	0.90	18.	Tamil Nadu	7.43
8.	Karnataka	5.45	19.	Tripura	0.30
9.	Kerala	3.86	20.	Uttar Pradesh	17.03
10.	Madhya Pradesh	8.15	21.	West Bengal	7.79
11.	Maharashtra	8.58			
	Total				**100.00**

Source: *Report of the Sixth Finance Commission*, 1973, p. 17.

It recommended that the net proceeds of the additional excise duties during each financial year be distributed on the following basis.

1. A sum equal to 1.41 percent of such net proceeds be retained by the Union as attributable to Union Territories.

2. The balance of 98.59 percent of such net proceeds be distributed among the States in accordance with their respective percentage shares of such balance as given in Table 20.3.

Table 20.3: Distribution of Additional Excise Duties among the States Recommended by the Sixth Finance Commission

S. No.	State	Percent	S. No.	State	Percent
1.	Andhra Pradesh	8.39	12.	Manipur	0.17
2.	Assam	2.47	13.	Meghalaya	0.17
3.	Bihar	9.36	14.	Nagaland	0.08
4.	Gujarat	5.91	15.	Orissa	3.59
5.	Haryana	1.94	16.	Punjab	2.68
6.	Himachal Pradesh	0.59	17.	Rajasthan	4.17
7.	Jammu & Kashmir	0.73	18.	Tamil Nadu	7.27
8.	Karnataka	5.62	19.	Tripura	0.25
9.	Kerala	3.58	20.	Uttar Pradesh	16.10
10.	Madhya Pradesh	6.98	21.	West Bengal	8.30
11.	Maharashtra	11.65			
	Total				**100.00**

Source: *Report of the Sixth Finance Commission*, 1973, p. 21.

20.4 Grant in Lieu of Tax on Railway Passenger Fares

In this connection the Commission observed, "The existing principles of distribution, which are substantially the same as those formulated by the Second Finance Commission, have stood the test of time. In the continuing absence of statistics on passenger earnings in each State on account of actual travel within its limits, the allocation of passenger earnings from non-suburban services from each gauge for each railway zone separately among the States according to route length lying within each State would be the most equitable basis for distribution of the grant. We have accordingly worked out the percentage shares of different States on the basis of statistics of gauge-wise route length of railways in each State and the actual passenger earnings from non-suburban traffic for each zonal railway for the four years ending 1971-72". [2]

The percentages worked out by the Commission are set forth in Table 20.4.

20.5 Distribution of Estate Duty

After considering various suggestions of the States, VI-FC was convinced that the principles of distribution enunciated by II-FC and endorsed by all the subsequent Commissions did not call for any change. It, therefore, held that no change was necessary in the then existing principles governing the distribution of the net proceeds of the duty among the States. Accordingly, it recommended as follows.

Table 20.4: Percentage Share of Each State in Grant in Lieu of Tax on Railway Passenger Fares

S. No.	State	Percent	S. No.	State	Percent
1.	Andhra Pradesh	8.01	12.	Manipur	---
2.	Assam	2.70	13.	Meghalaya	---
3.	Bihar	10.58	14.	Nagaland	0.01
4.	Gujarat	7.47	15.	Orissa	2.24
5.	Haryana	2.57	16.	Punjab	5.06
6.	Himachal Pradesh	0.17	17.	Rajasthan	6.59
7.	Jammu & Kashmir	0.02	18.	Tamil Nadu	5.14
8.	Karnataka	3.47	19.	Tripura	0.02
9.	Kerala	1.61	20.	Uttar Pradesh	19.85
10.	Madhya Pradesh	9.89	21.	West Bengal	5.73
11.	Maharashtra	8.87			
	Total				**100.00**

Source: *Report of the Sixth Finance Commission*, 1973, p. 23.

1. Out of the net proceeds of the estate duty in each financial year, a sum equal to 2.5 percent thereof be retained by the Union as being the proceeds attributable to Union Territories.
2. The balance of net proceeds be distributed among the States in accordance with the following principles: (a) such balance be first apportioned between immovable property and other property in the ratio of the gross value of all such properties brought into assessment in that year, (b) the sum thus apportioned to immovable property be distributed among the States in proportion to the gross value of the immovable property located in each State and brought into assessment in that year and (c) the sum apportioned to property other than immovable property be distributed among the States in proportion to the population of each State (Table 20.5).

Table 20.5: Percentage Shares of States in Estate Duty Recommended by the Sixth Finance Commission

S. No.	State	Percent	S. No.	State	Percent
1.	Andhra Pradesh	8.04	12.	Manipur	0.20
2.	Assam	2.70	13.	Meghalaya	0.19
3.	Bihar	10.41	14.	Nagaland	0.10
4.	Gujarat	4.93	15.	Orissa	4.05
5.	Haryana	1.86	16.	Punjab	2.50
6.	Himachal Pradesh	0.64	17.	Rajasthan	4.76

contd...

7.	Jammu & Kashmir	0.85	18.	Tamil Nadu	7.61
8.	Karnataka	5.41	19.	Tripura	0.29
9.	Kerala	3.94	20.	Uttar Pradesh	16.32
10.	Madhya Pradesh	7.70	21.	West Bengal	8.19
11.	Maharashtra	9.31			
	Total				**100.00**

Source: *Report of the Sixth Finance Commission*, 1973, p. 26.

20.6 Grants-in-aid of Revenues

Making a departure from the approach of the earlier Finance Commissions, VI-FC initiated process of enabling the States that were backward in standards of general administration to come up to a certain national minimum. For this purpose, it identified certain administrative and social services as to be of crucial importance and proposed that the State whose expenditure in per capita terms was below the all-States average should be enabled to come up to such an average by the last year of its award. Among these services, it considered primary education, medical and public health and welfare of scheduled castes, scheduled tribes and other backward classes to be of critical importance for the well-being of the people and particularly the weaker sections. It, therefore, thought it essential to devise suitable special safeguards against diversion of the funds so provided for improvement of these services to other purposes.

Endnotes

1. *Report of the Sixth Finance Commission*, 1973, p. 18.
2. *Ibid*., p. 23.

21

Seventh Finance Commission (VII-FC): 1979-80 to 1983-84

Highlights of the Report	
Chairman	Justice J.M. Shelat
Members	Dr. Raj Krishna Dr. C.H. Hanumantha Rao Shri H.N. Ray Shri V.B. Eswaran, Member-Secretary
Year and month of establishment	June 1977
Year and month of reporting	October 1978
Period of award	1979-80 to 1983-84
Main Recommendations	
1. States' share in income tax fixed at (percent): 85 2. Bases of distribution of States' share in income tax inter se (percent): Population: 90; Contribution: 10; Other factors: Nil 3. States' share in Union excise duties fixed at (percent): 40 4. Bases of distribution of States' share in Union excise duties inter se (percent): Population: 25; Other factors: 75	

VII-FC was constituted by an Order dated June 23, 1977 of the Vice-President acting as President. It was asked to make recommendations as to the following matters.

1. Distribution between the Union and the States of the net proceeds of taxes which are to be, or may be, divided between them and the allocation between the States of the respective shares of such proceeds.
2. Principles which should govern the grants-in-aid of the revenues of the States out of the Consolidated Fund of India and the sums to be paid to the States which are in need of assistance by way of grants-in-aid of their revenues under Article 275 of the Constitution for purposes other than those specified in the provisos of clause (1) of that article.

In making its recommendations on the various matters aforesaid, VII-FC was asked to adopt population figures of 1971 in all cases where population was regarded as a factor for determination of devolution of taxes and duties and grants-in-aid.

21.1 Distribution of Estate Duty

The duty was levied under the Estate Duty Act, 1953. [1] II-FC examined for the first time the principles which should govern the distribution of the net proceeds of the duty among the States. It held that the most appropriate principle of distribution would be the location of the property assessed to duty. It also observed that it would not be possible to apply the principle of location in the case of duty attributable to movable property, in respect of which it considered some general principle such as population. The latter Finance Commissions generally endorsed the principles recommended by the II-FC. Each of the Commissions had also specified the percentage of the net proceeds of the estate duty in a financial year to be retained by the Central Government as being the proceeds attributable to the Union Territories.

The principles laid down by the Sixth Finance Commission were the following.

1. Out of the net proceeds of the estate duty during each financial year, a sum equal to 2.5 percent thereof be retained by the Union as being the proceeds attributable to Union Territories.
2. The balance of net proceeds be distributed among the States in accordance with the following principles: (a) Such balance be first apportioned between immovable property and other property in the ratio of the gross value of all such properties brought into assessment in that year, (b) The sum thus apportioned to immovable property be distributed among the States in proportion to the gross value of the immovable property located in each State and brought into assessment in that year and (c) The sum apportioned to property other than immovable property be distributed among the States in proportion to the population of each State.

In their memoranda to VII-FC, most of the States suggested continuance of the above-mentioned principles of distribution. It accordingly recommended that the net proceeds of estate duty in respect of property other than agricultural land brought to assessment in each of the years from 1979-80 to1983-84, should be distributed among the States in proportion to the gross value of the immovable property as also property other than immovable property taken together located in each State, excepting in regard to property located abroad.

The Commission did not deem it necessary to determine the portion of the net proceeds of estate duty attributable to the Union territories, for the period of its award. This portion for each year, it recommended, should be determined in the same manner and on the same principles as for the determination of the shares of each State, taking the Union Territories as one unit for the purpose.

21.2 Additional Duties of Excise

It may be recalled that the additional duties of excise were levied by the Central Government in pursuance of a unanimous agreement recorded by the National Development Council (NDC) in December 1956. That agreement was that sales taxes levied in the States on mill-made textiles, tobacco including manufactured tobacco and sugar should be replaced by a surcharge on the Central excise duties on these articles and that the income derived therefrom should be distributed among the States on the basis of consumption. It also provided that the distribution among the States should assure to them the income derived by them at that time from their respective sales taxes. NDC had also agreed that the sharing and distribution among the States should be referred to the

Finance Commission. The aforesaid arrangement was in the nature of tax rental as noted by the earlier Commissions. Though the States had the constitutional right to levy sales tax on any of these articles, but by virtue of Sections 14 and 15 of the Central Sales Tax Act, which had declared these articles to be goods of special importance in inter-State trade and commerce, the rate of the tax could not exceed 4 percent.

The predecessors of VII-FC, which recommended the principles for distribution of the net proceeds of additional excise duties among the States, found that the most appropriate basis of distribution would be that of consumption of the articles in each State, since such a basis ensured to the States shares more or less equivalent to what they would have obtained if they had continued to levy and collect sales taxes. The Commissions had, however, faced the difficulty arising from lack of reliable statistics of consumption of these articles in each State. Each of them had therefore devised formulae which it considered would most closely approximate to the basic principle.

VII-FC made the following recommendations in this regard.

1. "There is no need to set apart any guaranteed amounts to the States out of the net proceeds of additional duties of excise as in our view there is no risk of the share of any States falling short of the revenue realised in the financial year 1956-57 in a State from the levy of the Sales tax on the commodities subject to additional duties of excise in lieu of sales tax.
2. Sikkim should have a share in the net proceeds of these duties except the duties on textiles on which the State levies sales tax.
3. A sum equal to 3.271 percent of the net proceeds of the additional duties of excise on sugar in each of the years from 1979-80 to 1983-84 should be retained by the Central Government as attributable to the Union territories and the balance of 96.729 percent of the net proceeds should be distributed among the States in the percentages shown (Table 21.1).
4. A sum equal to 2.192 percent of the net proceeds of additional duties of excise on textiles and on tobacco in each of the year from 1979-80 to 1983-84 be retained by the Central Government as attributable to the Union territories.
5. The balance of 97.808 percent of such net proceeds of the additional duties of excise on textiles and tobacco be distributed among the States in the percentages shown (Table 21.2)". [2]

Table 21.1: Distribution of Additional Duties of Excise on Sugar among the States Recommended by the Seventh Finance Commission

S. No.	State	Percent	S. No.	State	Percent
1.	Andhra Pradesh	5.245	12.	Manipur	0.143
2.	Assam	2.408	13.	Meghalaya	0.029
3.	Bihar	5.933	14.	Nagaland	0.115
4.	Gujarat	8.742	15.	Orissa	2.178

contd...

5.	Haryana	2.656	16.	Punjab	6.220
6.	Himachal Pradesh	0.860	17.	Rajasthan	4.729
7.	Jammu & Kashmir	0.831	18.	Sikkim	0.057
8.	Karnataka	4.901	19.	Tamil Nadu	6.449
9.	Kerala	3.783	20.	Tripura	0.172
10.	Madhya Pradesh	6.019	21.	Uttar Pradesh	13.184
11.	Maharashtra	17.082	22.	West Bengal	8.254

Source: *Report of the Seventh Finance Commission*, 1978, p. 62.

Table 21.2: Distribution of Additional Duties of Excise on Textiles and Tobacco among the States Recommended by the Seventh Finance Commission

(percent)

S. No.	State	Textiles	Tobacco
1.	Andhra Pradesh	8.020	8.018
2.	Assam	2.298	2.297
3.	Bihar	7.221	7.219
4.	Gujarat	6.015	6.013
5.	Haryana	2.790	2.789
6.	Himachal Pradesh	0.734	0.734
7.	Jammu & Kashmir	0.744	0.744
8.	Karnataka	6.083	6.081
9.	Kerala	4.020	4.019
10.	Madhya Pradesh	6.422	6.419
11.	Maharashtra	13.510	13.506
12.	Manipur	0.185	0.185
13.	Meghalaya	0.171	0.171
14.	Nagaland	0.084	0.084
15.	Orissa	3.457	3.456
16.	Punjab	4.270	4.268
17.	Rajasthan	4.366	4.365
18.	Sikkim	-	0.034
19.	Tamil Nadu	7.710	7.707
20.	Tripura	0.257	0.256
21.	Uttar Pradesh	12.549	12.544
22.	West Bengal	9.094	9.091

Source: *Report of the Seventh Finance Commission*, 1978, p. 63.

21.3 Grant in Lieu of Tax on Railway Passenger Fares

The Commission recommended that the grant to be made available to the States in each of the five years commencing from 1979-80, in lieu of tax under the repealed Railway Passenger Fares Tax Act 1957 be distributed among the States as given in Table 21.3.

Table 21.3: Percentage Share of Each State in Grant in Lieu of Tax on Railway Passenger Fares

S. No.	State	Percent	S. No.	State	Percent
1.	Andhra Pradesh	6.99	12.	Manipur	---
2.	Assam	2.46	13.	Meghalaya	---
3.	Bihar	9.50	14.	Nagaland	0.26
4.	Gujarat	5.28	15.	Orissa	1.73
5.	Haryana	1.97	16.	Punjab	3.81
6.	Himachal Pradesh	0.13	17.	Rajasthan	5.48
7.	Jammu & Kashmir	0.74	18.	Sikkim	---
8.	Karnataka	3.21	19.	Tamil Nadu	6.85
9.	Kerala	2.61	20.	Tripura	0.04
10.	Madhya Pradesh	5.84	21.	Uttar Pradesh	18.58
11.	Maharashtra	15.87	22.	West Bengal	8.65

Source: *Report of the Seventh Finance Commission*, 1978, p. 69.

21.4 Devolution and Distribution of Income Tax

In respect of distribution of the net proceeds of income tax in each of the years 1979-80 to 1983-84, the Commission recommended as follows.

1. Out of the net proceeds in each financial year, a sum equal to 2.19 percent thereof be deemed to represent the proceeds attributable to Union territories.
2. 85 percent of the net proceeds, except the portion representing the proceeds attributable to Union territories, be assigned to the States.
3. Distribution among the States inter se of the share assigned to the States in respect of each financial year should be on the basis of prescribed percentages (Table 21.4).

Table 21.4: Percentage Shares of the States in the Net Proceeds of Income Tax Assigned to the States as Recommended by the Seventh Finance Commission

S. No.	State	Percentage with Sikkim	Percentage without Sikkim
1.	Andhra Pradesh	8.021	8.023
2.	Assam	2.521	2.522
3.	Bihar	9.536	9.540
4.	Gujarat	5.957	5.959
5.	Haryana	1.819	1.819
6.	Himachal Pradesh	0.595	0.595
7.	Jammu & Kashmir	0.818	0.818

contd...

8.	Karnataka	5.440	5.442
9.	Kerala	3.948	3.950
10.	Madhya Pradesh	7.354	7.356
11.	Maharashtra	10.949	10.953
12.	Manipur	1.188	0.188
13.	Meghalaya	0.178	0.178
14.	Nagaland	0.085	0.085
15.	Orissa	3.738	3.739
16.	Punjab	2.713	2.714
17.	Rajasthan	4.362	4.364
18.	Sikkim	0.035	-
19.	Tamil Nadu	8.048	8.050
20.	Tripura	0.258	0.258
21.	Uttar Pradesh	15.422	15.429
22.	West Bengal	8.015	8.018
	All States	**100.000**	**100.000**

Source: *Report of the Seventh Finance Commission*, 1978, p. 83.

21.5 Devolution and Distribution of Union Excise Duties

VII-FC made the following recommendations regarding the sharing of Union excise duties during each of the years 1979-80 to 1983-84.

1. The entire net proceeds of the Union excise duty on generation of electricity should be paid out of the Consolidated Fund of India to each State in an amount equal to the collection in or attributable to that State.
2. Out of the balance of the net proceeds of the Union excise duties levied and collected on all other articles excluding cesses levied under special Acts and earmarked for special purposes, 40 percent should be paid out of the Consolidated Fund of India to the States and distributed among the States on the basis of the percentages indicated (Table 21.5).

21.6 Upgradation of Standards of Administration

For an assessment of the existing standards and of the gaps between the backward and the more advanced States, VII-FC decided to confine itself to the sectors and services which were more important elements in the basic administrative infrastructure of government. The following services and sectors were focussed upon by it.

1. Administration of taxes.
2. Treasury and Accounts administration.
3. Judicial administration.
4. General administration, consisting of revenue, district as well as tribal administration, and the Secretariat services.
5. Police.
6. Jails.

For the upgradation of judicial administration in the various States during 1979-80 to 1983-

84, the total provisions made by VII-FC added up to ₹ 2,399.45 lakh as shown in Table 21.6.

Table 21.5: Distribution of States' Share of Excise Duties among the States Recommended by the Seventh Finance Commission

(percentages)

S. No.	State	Excluding Sikkim	Including Sikkim
1.	Andhra Pradesh	7.698	7.691
2.	Assam	2.793	2.793
3.	Bihar	13.025	13.021
4.	Gujarat	4.103	4.101
5.	Haryana	1.177	1.177
6.	Himachal Pradesh	0.521	0.521
7.	Jammu & Kashmir	0.839	0.839
8.	Karnataka	4.877	4.876
9.	Kerala	4.036	4.035
10.	Madhya Pradesh	8.727	8.725
11.	Maharashtra	6.633	6.632
12.	Manipur	0.218	0.218
13.	Meghalaya	0.200	0.200
14.	Nagaland	0.097	0.097
15.	Orissa	4.682	4.682
16.	Punjab	1.226	1.226
17.	Rajasthan	4.813	4.813
18.	Sikkim	-	0.028
19.	Tamil Nadu	7.641	7.637
20.	Tripura	0.373	0.373
21.	Uttar Pradesh	18.293	18.290
22.	West Bengal	8.028	8.025

Source: *Report of the Seventh Finance Commission*, 1978, p. 88.

Table 21.6: Provisions for Upgradation of Judicial Administration in Various States Recommended by the Seventh Finance Commission

S. No.	State	Revenue (₹ Lakh)	Capital (₹ Lakh)
1.	Andhra Pradesh	54.77	29.20
2.	Assam	108.96	60.10
3.	Bihar	373.43	208.30
4.	Himachal Pradesh	5.02	2.80

contd...

5.	Jammu & Kashmir	5.02	2.80
6.	Kerala	8.56	4.10
7.	Madhya Pradesh	22.88	12.95
8.	Manipur	17.57	9.80
9.	Nagaland	-	70.00
10.	Orissa	68.64	35.25
11.	Rajasthan	136.41	73.05
12.	Tamil Nadu	10.04	5.60
13.	Tripura	42.51	21.35
14.	Uttar Pradesh	374.58	217.20
15.	West Bengal	262.26	156.30
	Total	**1,490.65**	**908.80**

Source: *Report of the Seventh Finance Commission*, 1978, pp. 96-97.

Endnotes

1. *The duty was abolished with effect from March 16, 1985.*
2. *Report of the Seventh Finance Commission*, 1978, pp. 121-122.

22

Eighth Finance Commission (VIII-FC): 1984-85 to 1988-89

Highlights of the Report	
Chairman	Shri Y.B. Chavan
Members	Justice Sabyasachi Mukherje Dr. C.H. Hanumantha Rao Shri. A.R. Shirali Shri G.C. Baveja, Secretary
Year and month of establishment	June 1982
Year and month of reporting	April 1984
Period of award	1984-85 to 1988-89
Main Recommendations	
1. States' share in income tax fixed at (percent): 85 2. Bases of distribution of States' share in income tax inter se (percent): Population: 22.5; Contribution: 10; Other factors: 67.5 3. States' share in Union excise duties fixed at (percent): 45 4. Bases of distribution of States' share in Union excise duties inter se (percent): Population: 25; Other factors: 75	

VIII-FC was constituted by the President by his Order dated the June 20, 1982. The Commission was asked to make recommendations as to the following matters.

1. Distribution between the Union and the States of the net proceeds of taxes which are to be, or may be, divided between them and allocation between the States of the respective shares of such proceeds.
2. Principles which should govern the grants-in-aid of the revenues of the States out of the Consolidated Fund of India and the sums to be paid to the States which are in need of assistance by way of grants-in-aid of their revenues under Article 275 of the Constitution for purposes other than those specified in the provisos to clause (1) of that article.

In making its recommendations on the various matters aforesaid, VIII-FC was required to adopt the population figures of 1971 in all cases where population was regarded as a factor for determination of devolution of taxes and duties and grants-in-aid.

22.1 Approach of the Commission on Financial Transfers

In the context of its duty of recommending the division of shareable taxes between the Centre and the States, and the making of grants-in-aid to the States in need of assistance, the Commission observed, "The crux of the problem is that the resources are limited, and the needs of the States are enormous. It is to their credit that they are impatient to achieve further development as fast as possible. The degrees of development vary. Some States are relatively more advanced while others are lagging behind. Naturally, this leads to many competing claims, and the Finance Commission is compelled to adopt some approach in fixing priorities. At the same time, it has to have regard to the needs of the Centre which has many responsibilities. The overriding consideration which has guided this Commission, is the national interest taken as a whole. Ultimately, the solutions we have chosen have been judged on this touchstone.

We have carefully considered the memoranda sent to us by the States, and the points made by the Chief Ministers and their colleagues during our discussions with them. They are unanimous in their demand for a larger share in the total Central revenues. There are divergent views as to how this should be done. The common thread, in all that they urged, was the desire for accelerated economic development, and the need for proper maintenance of assets already created. The extent of the share demanded by the States from the Centre's revenue varies from 40 percent to 75 percent.

In this connection, the demands on the Centre's resources, also, need to be remembered. The expenditure on defence, subsidies on food and fertilizers, and interest payments is, in the present circumstances, inescapable. These items alone absorb nearly half the Centre's revenues. Out of what remains with the Centre, about 37 percent is at present being transferred to the States, largely on the recommendations of the Finance Commission and the Planning Commission.

While we have the greatest sympathy for the needs of the States, the parameters within which we have to function are, thus, obvious. Within the scope which was available to us, we have tried to do our best". [1]

22.2 Reassessment of the Revenue and Expenditure Forecasts

In order to assess the revenue resources of States on a comparable and uniform basis, State Governments were requested to send their forecasts of revenue receipts and revenue expenditure in the proformae prescribed by it. The forecasts of revenue receipts were required to be based on the levels of taxation likely to prevail at the end of 1983-84. The forecasts of expenditure were similarly to be based on the normal level of standing charges on non-Plan account as at the end of 1983-84, i.e. after excluding all provisions for any fresh expenditure during the forecast period.

VIII-FC engaged the services of National Institute of Public Finance and Policy (NIPFP), New Delhi to help it in the matter of forecasting of receipts and expenditure of the State Governments. The NIPFP submitted reports on the following subjects which pertained to the State forecasts: (a) Revenue and Expenditure Projections: Evaluation and Methodology. (b) Relative Taxable Capacity and Tax Effort of Indian States.

Similarly, VIII-FC requested the Ministry of Finance, Government of India to send to it forecasts of the Central Government's receipts and expenditure on revenue account and capital account for the five years ending with the financial year 1988-89. The inputs received from various quarters were carefully examined and reassessed.

22.3 Devolution and Distribution of Income Tax

It recommended that the States' share in the net proceeds of income tax be maintained at 85 percent of the divisible pool during each of the years covered by its recommendations, i.e. 1984-85 to 1988-89.

As regards the criteria to be adopted for making the allocation, VIII-FC was in favour of more progressive criteria for allocating income tax than was the case with previous Commissions. In order to achieve this result, it suggested that 90 percent of the States' share of income tax remaining after distributing 10 percent on the basis of contribution, should be allocated amongst the States on the very same principles as those it applied for allocating the predominant part of their share of excise duties. In other words, the balance of 90 percent of the States' share of income tax, which remained after distributing 10 percent on the basis of contribution, was allocated among the States by giving a weightage of 25 percent to population, 25 percent to the inverse of per capita income multiplied by population, and 50 percent to the distance of per capita income. On the basis of these recommendations, the composite percentage shares of each State were determined.

As income tax had not yet been extended to Sikkim, it worked out the State-wise composite shares in income tax amongst the States including Sikkim as well as without Sikkim on the consideration that in case income tax was extended to that State, the basis of its distribution amongst the States might not pose any problem.

In short, it recommended the following steps for the distribution of the net proceeds of income tax in each of the years 1984-85 to 1988-89.

1. Out of the net proceeds in each financial year, a sum equal to 1.792 percent thereof be deemed to represent the proceeds attributable to Union territories.
2. 85 percent of net income tax proceeds, except the portion representing the proceeds attributable to Union territories and Union emoluments, be assigned to the States.
3. Distribution amongst the States inter se of the share assigned to the States in respect of each financial year should be on the basis of the prescribed percentages (Table 22.1).

Table 22.1: Percentage Shares of the States in the Net Proceeds of Income Tax Assigned to the States as Recommended by the Eighth Finance Commission

S. No.	State	Percentage with Sikkim	Percentage without Sikkim
1.	Andhra Pradesh	8.187	8.190
2.	Assam	2.789	2.789
3.	Bihar	12.080	12.085
4.	Gujarat	4.409	4.410
5.	Haryana	1.074	1.074
6.	Himachal Pradesh	0.555	0.555
7.	Jammu & Kashmir	0.838	0.838

contd...

8.	Karnataka	4.979	4.981
9.	Kerala	3.760	3.761
10.	Madhya Pradesh	8.378	8.382
11.	Maharashtra	8.392	8.396
12.	Manipur	0.220	0.220
13.	Meghalaya	0.184	0.184
14.	Nagaland	0.088	0.088
15.	Orissa	4.202	4.203
16.	Punjab	1.744	1.744
17.	Rajasthan	4.545	4.547
18.	Sikkim	0.035	-
19.	Tamil Nadu	7.565	7.567
20.	Tripura	0.269	0.269
21.	Uttar Pradesh	17.907	17.914
22.	West Bengal	7.800	7.803
	Total	**100.000**	**100.000**

Source: *Report of the Eighth Finance Commission*, 1984, p. 45.

22.4 Devolution and Distribution of Union Excise Duties

VIII-FC was of the opinion that the transfer of resources to the States should leave as many of them as possible with surpluses on revenue account so that they were able to implementation Five Year Plans. At the same time, it had also to keep in view the amount of surplus with the Centre as reassessed by it. Taking into account these considerations, it came to the conclusion that the share of the States in the net proceeds of excise duties, other than the duty on electricity, should be increased from 40 percent fixed by VII-FC to 45 percent. It further recommended that this be distributed amongst the States on the following basis.

1. 40 percent of the net proceeds of shareable excise duties excluding that on electricity, be distributed during each year of the forecast period among all States in the following manner:

- One-fourth of this amount (i.e. 25 percent) should be distributed among the States on the basis of the 1971 population.
- Another one-fourth should be distributed to States on the basis of inverse of per capita income.
- The remaining 50 percent should be distributed on the basis of the distance of per capita income.

2. The remaining 5 percent of the net proceeds of excise duties excluding that on electricity, be set aside and distributed to those States which have deficits after taking into account their shares from the devolution of all taxes and duties, including their shares of excise duties, under clause (a) above and grants in lieu of the repealed tax on railway passenger fares, but excluding their shares of estates duty and grants

on account of wealth tax on agricultural property. This distribution should be based on the proportion of the deficit of each State to the total of the deficits of all States as estimated by us, worked out separately for each year of the forecast.

The percentage share of each State in 40 percent of the net proceeds of shareable excise duties excluding that on electricity were worked out as shown in Table 22.2.

Table 22.2: Distribution of States' Share of Excise Duties (40 Percent of the Net Proceeds of Excise Duties for the years 1984-85 to 1988-89) among the States as Recommended by the Eighth Finance Commission

S. No.	State	Percent	S. No.	State	Percent
1.	Andhra Pradesh	8.587	12.	Manipur	0.233
2.	Assam	2.977	13.	Meghalaya	0.194
3.	Bihar	13.202	14.	Nagaland	0.096
4.	Gujarat	3.506	15.	Orissa	4.592
5.	Haryana	1.017	16.	Punjab	1.317
6.	Himachal Pradesh	0.589	17.	Rajasthan	4.695
7.	Jammu & Kashmir	0.856	18.	Sikkim	0.039
8.	Karnataka	5.077	19.	Tamil Nadu	7.317
9.	Kerala	3.800	20.	Tripura	0.292
10.	Madhya Pradesh	8.852	21.	Uttar Pradesh	19.097
11.	Maharashtra	6.216	22.	West Bengal	7.449
	Total				**100.000**

Source: *Report of the Eighth Finance Commission*, 1984, p. 54.

The percentage share of the deficit States in the 5 percent of the net proceeds of the shareable excise duties excluding that on electricity were also worked out by the Commission for each of the 5 years commencing from April 1, 1984 and these percentages are shown in Table 22.3.

22.5 Additional Duties of Excise

Having considered all pros and cons, the Commission recommended the distribution of the net proceeds of the additional excise duties on textiles, sugar and tobacco on the following basis.

1. A sum equal to 2.391 percent of such net proceeds be retained by the Central Governments as attributable to the Union territories.
2. The balance should be distributed amongst the States in accordance with the percentages mentioned (Table 22.4).

22.6 Grants-in-aid of Revenues

Under the substantive part of clause (1) of Article 275 of the Constitution, the Commission recommended for various States grants to cover the deficits on revenue account in the respective years as indicated in Table 22.5.

Table 22.3: Distribution of the Shares of Deficit States in 5 percent of Excise Duties as Recommended by the Eighth Finance Commission

S. No.	State	1984-85	1985-86	1986-87	1987-88	1988-89
1.	Assam	12.728	12.578	12.713	13.418	12.023
2.	Himachal Pradesh	10.340	11.528	12.914	14.098	16.475
3.	J&K	15.475	16.661	17.818	18.560	20.254
4.	Manipur	6.969	7.742	8.722	9.545	11.217
5.	Meghalaya	5.575	6.180	6.944	7.570	8.863
6.	Nagaland	8.837	9.944	11.240	12.371	14.482
7.	Orissa	9.214	8.154	5.457	3.109	0.598
8.	Rajasthan	1.940	-	-	-	-
9.	Sikkim	1.659	1.836	2.051	2.232	2.593
10.	Tripura	8.200	9.104	10.207	11.162	12.956
11.	West Bengal	19.081	16.273	11.934	7.935	0.539
	Total	**100.000**	**100.000**	**100.000**	**100.000**	**100.000**

Source: *Report of the Eighth Finance Commission*, 1984, p. 54.

Table 22.4: Distribution of Additional Duties of Excise among the States as Recommended by the Eighth Finance Commission

S. No.	State	Percent	S. No.	State	Percent
1.	Andhra Pradesh	7.504	12.	Manipur	0.178
2.	Assam	2.566	13.	Meghalaya	0.183
3.	Bihar	8.627	14.	Nagaland	0.098
4.	Gujarat	5.941	15.	Orissa	3.653
5.	Haryana	2.488	16.	Punjab	3.675
6.	Himachal Pradesh	0.663	17.	Rajasthan	4.827
7.	Jammu & Kashmir	0.853	18.	Sikkim	0.039
8.	Karnataka	5.561	19.	Tamil Nadu	7.549
9.	Kerala	3.963	20.	Tripura	0.287
10.	Madhya Pradesh	6.942	21.	Uttar Pradesh	14.318
11.	Maharashtra	11.461	22.	West Bengal	8.624
	Total				**100.000**

Source: *Report of the Eighth Finance Commission*, 1984, p. 128.

22.7 General Observations

The Commission reiterated the suggestion made by the First Finance Commission that there should be a permanent secretariat which should continue to function during the interregnum between one Commission and the next. Such a secretariat should be headed by a senior officer and function as a Division in the Ministry of Finance during the period intervening between two Finance Commissions. The Division which the Commission proposed should have the following functions.

1. To watch the implementation of the recommendations of the Finance Commission.
2. To watch closely and analyse the trends in the non-Plan receipts and expenditure of the State Governments and identify the reasons for variation between actuals and estimates made by the Finance Commission.
3. To monitor and evaluate the utilization of upgradation grants.
4. To preserve the records of the previous Commissions, and take such necessary action to obtain further information as might be of use to the future Commissions.
5. To continuously collect and keep up-to-date information on all aspects of State finances, including the financial working of the State enterprises.
6. To conduct studies and publish papers and data having a bearing on States' finances.

Table 22.5: Grants-in-aid of Revenues of the States as Recommended by the Eighth Finance Commission

(₹ crore)

S. No.	State	Total 1984-89	1984-85	1985-86	1986-87	1987-88	1988-89
1.	Assam	274.33	78.58	66.92	55.08	47.37	26.38
2.	Himachal	223.04	57.65	53.91	47.35	40.76	23.37
3.	J&K	329.18	89.22	81.14	68.79	57.34	32.69
4.	Manipur	146.95	38.14	35.51	31.25	26.87	15.18
5.	Meghalaya	119.15	30.92	28.96	25.30	21.75	12.12
6.	Nagaland	190.52	48.76	45.96	40.65	35.19	19.96
7.	Orissa	207.60	67.55	54.94	37.78	27.42	19.91
8.	Rajasthan	42.63	34.25	8.38	-	-	-
9.	Sikkim	36.16	9.38	8.71	7.66	6.59	3.82
10.	Tripura	187.05	47.83	44.71	39.57	34.41	20.53
11.	West Bengal	443.61	142.11	113.31	82.59	63.00	42.60
	Total	2200.22	644.39	542.25	436.02	360.70	216.86

Source: *Report of the Eighth Finance Commission*, 1984, p. 126.

Endnote

1. *Report of the Eighth Finance Commission*, 1984, p. 7.

23

Ninth Finance Commission (IX-FC): 1989-90 to 1994-95

Highlights of the Report	
Chairman	Shri N.K.P. Salve
Members	Shri V.P. Menon Justice R. Kaushalendra Rao Dr. B.K. Madan Shri M.V. Rangachari, Member-Secretary
Year and month of establishment	June 1987
Year and month of reporting	July 1988 and December 1989
Period of award	1989-90 and 1990-91 to 1994-95
Main Recommendations (for the period 1990-91 to 1994-95)	
1. States' share in income tax fixed at (percent): 85 2. Bases of distribution of States' share in income tax inter se (percent): Population: 22.5; Contribution: 10; Other factors: 67.5 3. States' share in Union excise duties fixed at (percent): 45 4. Bases of distribution of States' share in Union excise duties inter se (percent): Population: 29.94; Other factors: 70.06	

IX-FC was constituted by an Order of the President dated June 17, 1987. It was asked to make recommendations as to the following matters.

1. the distribution between the Union and the States of the net proceeds of taxes which are to be, or may be, divided between them and the allocation between the States of the respective shares of such proceeds;
2. the principles which should govern the grants-in-aid of the revenues of the States out of the Consolidated Fund of India and the sums to be paid to the States which are in need of assistance by way of grants-in-aid of their revenues under Article 275 of the Constitution for purposes other than those specified in the provisos to clause (1) of that article.

In making its recommendations, IX-FC was required to: (i) adopt a normative approach in assessing the receipts and expenditures on the revenue account of the States and the Centre and, in doing so, keep in view the special problems of each State, if any, and the special requirement of the Centre such as defence, security, debt servicing and other committed expenditure or liabilities, (ii) have due regard to the need for providing adequate incentives for better resource mobilisation and financial discipline as well as closer linking of expenditure and revenue-raising decisions, (iii) take into account the need for speed, efficiency and effectiveness of Government functioning and of delivery systems for Government programmes and (iv) keep in view the objective of not only balancing the receipts and expenditure on revenue account of both the States and the Centre, but also generating surpluses for capital investment.

With a view to making the recommendations of the Finance Commissions co-terminus with the Five Year Plans, IX-FC was asked to make two reports, the first covering one year period (1989-90), and the second covering five years period (1990-91 to 1994-95).

It presented its first report for the year 1989-90 to the President on July 29, 1988. The second report for the five year period 1990-91 to 1994-95 was submitted in December 1989. The report of IX-FC was not unanimous as one of its members Justice A.S. Qureshi disagreed with certain recommendations. His note of dissent formed part of the report.

23.1 First Report (for the year 1989-90)

23.1.1 Sharing of Income Tax: Recommendations of IX-FC in this regard for the year 1989-90 were as follows.

1. Out of the net proceeds, a sum equal to 1.044 percent thereof be deemed to represent the proceeds attributable to Union Territories.
2. Share of net income tax proceeds, except the portion representing the proceeds attributable to Union Territories and Union emoluments, to be assigned to the States be 85 percent.
3. Distribution amongst the States *inter se* of the share assigned to the States in respect of the financial year 1989-90 was on the basis of percentages specified by it.

23.1.2 Sharing of Union Excise Duties: IX-FC made the following recommendations in this regard.

1. It continued the then existing arrangement under which 45 percent of the net proceeds of shareable excise duties were distributed among States for the year 1989-90.
2. 40 percent of the net proceeds of shareable excise duties be distributed amongst all the States on the basis of percentages prescribed by it.
4. The remaining 5 percent of the net proceeds of shareable excise duties was distributed amongst the deficit States on the basis of the percentages specified by it.

23.1.3 Additional Duties of Excise in Lieu of Sales Tax: The Commission recommended that the net proceeds of the additional duties of excise on textiles, sugar and tobacco be determined on the following basis.

1. A sum equal to 2.023 percent of such net proceeds be retained by the Central Government as attributable to the Union Territories.
2. The balance should be distributed amongst the States in accordance with the percentages indicated by it.

23.1.4 Grant in Lieu of Tax on Railway Passenger Fares: In keeping with the spirit of the Constitutional provisions applicable to the repealed tax on railway passenger fares, IX-FC did not consider it possible to allot a share of the grant in lieu thereof to a State wherein there was no railway line nor any out agency and in which no railway ticket was purchased. Similarly, taking into account the financial difficulties of the railways and its unique role in the economic life of the nation from which all the States benefit, it retained the quantum of grant at the then existing level of ₹ 95 crore. The distribution of this grant among the States was on the basis of percentages specified by it.

23.2 Second Report (for the years 1990-91 to 1994-95)

The Commission made recommendations regarding the distribution between the Union and the States of the net proceeds of income tax and Union excise duties and the allocation among the States of their respective shares of such proceeds. It also made recommendations on two additional issues: (a) the principles on which the shares of the net proceeds of additional duties of excise in lieu of sales tax should be distributed among the States and their *inter se* shares therefrom and (b) the principles which should govern the distribution among the States of grants to be made available to them in lieu of the repealed Railway Passenger Fares Tax Act, 1957, and a few related issues.

23.2.1 Sharing of Income Tax: With the enactment of the Finance Act, 1989, the extension of the Income Tax Act, 1961, to Sikkim from the assessment year 1990-91 onwards was formalised. Therefore, the State-wise shares of income tax that the Commission prescribed included the share of Sikkim also.

It may be recalled that in its first report, the Commission had retained the States' share at 85 percent of the divisible pool. Almost all State Governments had asked for the enlargement of the States' share beyond the level of 85 percent. However, the Commission did not consider it necessary to increase the States' share beyond 85 percent.

As regards the criteria to be adopted for the distribution of income tax among the States, the Commission had assigned a weight of 10 percent to *contribution* factor in its first report which was retained in the second report. After considering other factors, the Commission finally recommend that the shareable proceeds of income tax be distributed among the States in the following manner.

1. 10 percent on the basis of *contribution* as measured by the assessment of income tax for the years 1985-86 to 1987-88.
2. 45 percent on the basis of *distance* of the per capita income of a State from that of the State with the highest per capita income multiplied by the 1971 population of the State concerned.
3. 22.5 percent on the basis of the population of the State in 1971.
4. 11.25 percent on the basis of composite index of backwardness compiled by the Commission.
5. 11.25 percent on the basis of the inverse of per capita income multiplied by the population of the State in 1971.

In short, the Commission made the following recommendations as regards the sharing of income tax between the Centre and the States and the States' share amongst the States for the period 1990-91 to 1994-95.

1. Out of the net distributable proceeds of income tax, a sum equal to 1.437 percent be deemed to represent the proceeds attributable to Union Territories.

2. Share of net income tax proceeds assigned to the States be 85 percent.
3. Distribution among the States of the share assigned to each of them in each financial year should be on the basis of the percentages shown (Table 23.1).

Table 23.1: Percentage Shares of the States in the Net Proceeds of Income Tax Assigned to the States as Recommended by the Ninth Finance Commission for the Period 1990-91 to 1994-95

S. No.	State	Percent	S. No.	State	Percent
1.	Andhra Pradesh	8.208	14.	Manipur	0.171
2.	Arunachal Pradesh	0.073	15.	Meghalaya	0.208
3.	Assam	2.631	16.	Mizoram	0.073
4.	Bihar	12.418	17.	Nagaland	0.096
5	Goa	0.110	18.	Orissa	4.326
6.	Gujarat	4.550	19.	Punjab	1.706
7.	Haryana	1.244	20.	Rajasthan	4.836
8.	Himachal Pradesh	0.595	21.	Sikkim	0.030
9.	Jammu & Kashmir	0.695	22.	Tamil Nadu	7.931
10	Karnataka	4.928	23.	Tripura	0.303
11.	Kerala	3.729	24.	Uttar Pradesh	16.787
12.	Madhya Pradesh	8.185	25.	West Bengal	7.976
13.	Maharashtra	8.191			
	Total				**100.000**

Source: *Second Report of the Ninth Finance Commission*, December 1989, p. 19.

23.2.2 Distribution of Additional Excise Duties in Lieu of Sales Tax: The Commission had expressed the view in its first report that since the additional duties of excise were levied in lieu of sales tax which itself was a tax on consumption, the shares of various States should correspond to their shares in the consumption of these commodities (textiles, sugar and tobacco).

In the absence of reliable data of State-wise consumption of these commodities, it had to rely on proxies, namely SDP and population of the respective States. It assigned equal weights to SDP and population in determining the shares of the individual States in the net proceeds of additional duties of excise. The share of the Union Territories was fixed at 1.903 percent. The balance should be distributed among the States in each year in accordance with the percentage shares prescribed by the Commission (Table 23.2).

23.2.3 Grant in Lieu of Tax on Railway Passenger Fares: This tax was first imposed in 1957 and was repealed in 1961. In fact, the tax was merged with the basic fare and the grant was introduced only to compensate the States for the consequential loss of revenue. The tax was revived in 1971 and again repealed in 1973. The Seventh Commission adopted the formula of distribution of the grant in proportion to the non-suburban passenger earnings from traffic originating in each State. The Eighth

Commission endorsed this practice. That Commission found it only logical that the taxable event being the payment of fare, the States should get the grant on the basis of the fare, paid within their boundaries. The route or the length of the journey was not material. The Commission under study agreed with the logic adopted by the Seventh and the Eighth Commissions. However, it recommended an increase in the size of the grant from the then existing level of ₹ 95 crore to ₹ 150 crore annually for the period 1990-91 to 1994-95. Shares of the States in each year were prescribed as shown in Table 23.3.

Table 23.2: Distribution of Additional Duties of Excise among the States as Recommended by the Ninth Finance Commission for the Period 1990-91 to 1994-95

S. No.	State	Percent	S. No.	State	Percent
1.	Andhra Pradesh	7.680	14.	Manipur	0.213
2.	Arunachal Pradesh	0.107	15.	Meghalaya	0.190
3.	Assam	2.743	16.	Mizoram	0.068
4.	Bihar	8.317	17.	Nagaland	0.120
5	Goa	0.228	18.	Orissa	3.486
6.	Gujarat	5.905	19.	Punjab	3.533
7.	Haryana	2.317	20.	Rajasthan	4.689
8.	Himachal Pradesh	0.621	21.	Sikkim	0.052
9.	Jammu & Kashmir	0.928	22.	Tamil Nadu	7.064
10	Karnataka	5.865	23.	Tripura	0.278
11.	Kerala	3.723	24.	Uttar Pradesh	14.657
12.	Madhya Pradesh	7.164	25.	West Bengal	8.165
13.	Maharashtra	11.886			
	Total				**100.000**

Source: *Second Report of the Ninth Finance Commission*, December 1989, p. 20.

23.2.4 Union Excise Duties: In its first report, the Commission had recommended that 40 percent of the net proceeds of excise duties should be distributed among all the States to take care of the revenue needs of the States in general. Another 5 percent was earmarked to help the deficit States so that their non-Plan revenue deficits could be reduced. Making a departure from this approach, it recommended distribution of the entire amount of 45 percent as consolidated amount without dividing it into two components of 40 percent and 5 percent. The Commission also revised the formula of devolution adopted in its first report. Accordingly, it recommended that the distribution among the States during 1990-91 to 1994-95 of 45 percent of the net proceeds of Union excise duties be done in the following manner:

1. 25 percent on the basis of 1971 population.
2. 12.5 percent on the basis of Income Adjusted Total Population (IATP). [1]
3. 12.5 percent on the basis of the index of backwardness.

4. 33.5 percent on the basis of *distance* of per capita income (New Series) of a State during the triennium 1982-83 to 1984-85 from that of the State having the highest per capita income, i.e. Punjab, multiplied by its 1971 population.
5. The remaining 16.5 percent be distributed among the States with deficits, after taking into account their shares from the income tax, excise duties, additional excise duties in lieu of sales tax and the grant in lieu of the repealed tax on railway passenger fares. Distribution should take place on the basis of the proportion of deficit of each State to the total of all States' deficits worked out by the Commission.

Table 23.3: Percentage Share of Each State in Grant in Lieu of Tax on Railway Passenger Fares for the Period 1990-91 to 1994-95

S. No.	State	Percent	S. No.	State	Percent
1.	Andhra Pradesh	7.484	14.	Manipur	0.013
2.	Arunachal Pradesh	0.008	15.	Meghalaya	0.040
3.	Assam	1.509	16.	Mizoram	---
4.	Bihar	8.266	17.	Nagaland	0.165
5	Goa	0.133	18.	Orissa	1.614
6.	Gujarat	5.717	19.	Punjab	3.110
7.	Haryana	1.637	20.	Rajasthan	4.579
8.	Himachal Pradesh	0.098	21.	Sikkim	0.004
9.	Jammu & Kashmir	0.520	22.	Tamil Nadu	6.893
10	Karnataka	3.271	23.	Tripura	0.042
11.	Kerala	3.562	24.	Uttar Pradesh	15.437
12.	Madhya Pradesh	6.061	25.	West Bengal	7.203
13.	Maharashtra	22.634			
	Total				**100.000**

Source: *Second Report of the Ninth Finance Commission*, December 1989, p. 21.

The percentage share of each State as worked out by the Commission for each of the year during 1990-91 to 1994-95 is given in Table 23.4.

Table 23.4: Distribution of States' Share of Excise Duties among the States as Recommended by the Ninth Finance Commission for the Period 1990-91 to 1994-95

S. No.	State	Percent	S. No.	State	Percent
1.	Andhra Pradesh	7.170	14.	Manipur	1.174
2.	Arunachal Pradesh	0.897	15.	Meghalaya	0.891
3.	Assam	3.810	16.	Mizoram	1.109

contd...

4.	Bihar	11.028	17.	Nagaland	1.348
5	Goa	0.523	18.	Orissa	5.358
6.	Gujarat	3.183	19.	Punjab	1.362
7.	Haryana	1.099	20.	Rajasthan	5.524
8.	Himachal Pradesh	1.943	21.	Sikkim	0.260
9.	Jammu & Kashmir	3.548	22.	Tamil Nadu	6.379
10	Karnataka	4.104	23.	Tripura	1.556
11.	Kerala	3.087	24.	Uttar Pradesh	15.638
12.	Madhya Pradesh	7.224	25.	West Bengal	6.600
13.	Maharashtra	5.185			
	Total				**100.000**

Source: *Second Report of the Ninth Finance Commission*, December 1989, p. 22.

23.2.5 Grants-in-aid of Revenues: To cover the net five-year (1990-91 to 1994-95) deficits on non-Plan revenue account and part of the deficits on plan revenue account, IX-FC recommended grants-in-aid of the revenues of various States under the substantive part of Clause (1) of Article 275 of the Constitution.

Endnote

1. For calculating IATP, the 1971 population of the States was to be weighted with the inverse of the average per capita income as per the New Series for the triennium 1982-83 to 1984-85. The share of a State was to be determined by the percentage of the Income Adjusted Total Population of that State to the aggregate of the income adjusted total population of all States.

24

Tenth Finance Commission (X-FC): 1995-96 to 1999-2000

Highlights of the Report	
Chairman	Shri K.C. Pant
Members	Dr. Debi Prosad Pal Shri B.P.R. Vithal Dr. C. Rangarajan Shri M.C. Gupta
Year and month of establishment	June 1992
Year and month of reporting	November 1994
Period of award	1995-96 to 1999-2000
Main Recommendations	
1. States' share in income tax fixed at (percent): 77.5 2. Bases of distribution of States' share in income tax inter se (percent): Population: 20; Contribution: Nil; Other factors: 80 3. States' share in Union excise duties fixed at (percent): 47.5 4. Bases of distribution of States' share in Union excise duties inter se (percent): Population: 20; Other factors: 80	

X-FC was constituted by the Order of the President dated June 15, 1992. It was asked to make recommendations relating to the following matters.

1. Distribution between the Union and the States of the net proceeds of taxes which are to be, or may be divided between them and the allocation between the States of the respective shares of such proceeds.
2. Principles which should govern the grants-in-aid of the revenues of the States out of the Consolidated Fund of India and the sums to be paid to the States which are in need of assistance by way of grants-in-aid of their revenues under Article 275 of the Constitution for purposes other than those specified in the provisos to clause (1) of that article.

X-FC was also asked to suggest changes, if any, in the principles governing the distribution of: (a) the net proceeds in any financial year of the additional excise duties leviable under the Additional Duties of Excise (Goods of Special Importance) Act, 1957, in replacement of the sales tax levied formerly by the State Governments and (b) the grants to be made available to the States in lieu of the tax under the repealed Railway Passenger Fares Act, 1957.

Furthermore, in making its recommendations on the various maters aforesaid, it was required to adopt the population figures of 1971 in all cases where population was regarded as a factor for determination of devolution of taxes and duties and grants-in-aid.

It is noteworthy that the Government dropped the *normative approach* (which was in the guidelines of IX-FC) from the terms of reference of X-FC. It was replaced by the *gap-filling approach.*

24.1 Devolution and Distribution of Income Tax

X-FC recommended that the share attributable to the Union Territories in the net distributable proceeds of income tax for each of the financial years during 1995-96 to 1999-2000 should be 0.927 percent.

Having considered this matter at length, it came to the conclusion that the following two considerations should guide its recommendations in this regard: (a) that the authority that levies and administers the tax should have a significant and tangible interest in its yield and (b) that any change in the share on this account should not materially affect the level of overall devolution to the States. In other words, any downward revision in the share of States in the net proceeds of income tax should be mirrored in a revenue equivalent increase in their share in the net proceeds of Union excise duties. Accordingly, it recommended that the share of States in the net proceeds of income tax be fixed at 77.5 percent.

It based its criteria for determining the *inter se* shares of the States in the shareable proceeds of income tax on the following indices.

1. 20 percent on the basis of population of 1971.
2. 60 percent on the basis of distance of per capita income.
3. 5 percent on the basis of *area adjusted.*
4. 5 percent on the basis of index of infrastructure.
5. 10 percent on the basis of tax efforts.

Thus, it recommended as follows for each financial year in the period 1995-96 to 1999-2000.

(a) Out of the net distributable proceeds of income tax, a sum equal to 0.927 percent be deemed to represent the proceeds attributable to Union Territories.
(b) The share of the net proceeds of income tax assigned to the States be 77.5 percent.
(c) The distribution among States of the share assigned to them in each financial year be on the basis of the percentages shown (Table 24.1).

24.2 Devolution and Distribution of Union Excise Duties

Taking into account the views of the Central and the State Governments in the matter, and having recommended a decrease in the States' share in the net proceeds of income tax, X-FC recommended that the share of States in the net proceeds of Union excise duties be raised to 47.5 percent.

It used the same set of criteria (i.e. as for income tax) for distribution of 40 percent of the net proceeds of Union excise duties. Accordingly it recommended that 40 percent of the net proceeds of Union excise duties during each financial year in the period 1995-96 to 1999-2000, should be distributed as per the share indicated (Table 24.2).

Table 24.1: Percentage Shares of the States in the Net Proceeds of Income Tax Assigned to the States as Recommended by the Tenth Finance Commission

S. No.	State	Percent	S. No.	State	Percent
1.	Andhra Pradesh	8.465	14.	Manipur	0.282
2.	Arunachal Pradesh	0.170	15.	Meghalaya	0.283
3.	Assam	2.784	16.	Mizoram	0.149
4.	Bihar	12.861	17.	Nagaland	0.181
5	Goa	0.180	18.	Orissa	4.495
6.	Gujarat	4.046	19.	Punjab	1.461
7.	Haryana	1.238	20.	Rajasthan	5.551
8.	Himachal Pradesh	0.704	21.	Sikkim	0.126
9.	Jammu & Kashmir	1.097	22.	Tamil Nadu	6.637
10	Karnataka	5.339	23.	Tripura	0.378
11.	Kerala	3.875	24.	Uttar Pradesh	17.811
12.	Madhya Pradesh	8.290	25.	West Bengal	7.471
13.	Maharashtra	6.126			
	Total				**100.000**

Source: *Report of the Tenth Finance Commission*, 1994, p. 25.

Table 24.2: Distribution of States' Share of Excise Duties among the States as Recommended by the Tenth Finance Commission

S. No.	State	Percent	S. No.	State	Percent
1.	Andhra Pradesh	8.465	14.	Manipur	0.282
2.	Arunachal Pradesh	0.170	15.	Meghalaya	0.283
3.	Assam	2.784	16.	Mizoram	0.149
4.	Bihar	12.861	17.	Nagaland	0.181
5	Goa	0.180	18.	Orissa	4.495
6.	Gujarat	4.046	19.	Punjab	1.461
7.	Haryana	1.238	20.	Rajasthan	5.551
8.	Himachal Pradesh	0.704	21.	Sikkim	0.126
9.	Jammu & Kashmir	1.097	22.	Tamil Nadu	6.637
10	Karnataka	5.339	23.	Tripura	0.378
11.	Kerala	3.875	24.	Uttar Pradesh	17.811
12.	Madhya Pradesh	8.290	25.	West Bengal	7.471
13.	Maharashtra	6.126			
	Total				**100.000**

Source: *Report of the Tenth Finance Commission*, 1994, p. 25.

It further recommended that the remaining 7.5 percent of the net proceeds of Union excise duties be distributed among the States in accordance with the shares specified by it for each financial year in the period 1995-96 to 1999-2000 (Table 24.3).

Table 24.3: Distribution of the Remaining 7.5 Percent of the Net Proceeds of Excise Duties among the States as Recommended by the Tenth Finance Commission

(percent)

S. No.	State	1995-96	1996-97	1997-98	1998-99	1999-00
1.	Andhra Pradesh	12.069	7.988	0.000	0.000	0.000
2.	Arunachal Pradesh	3.410	4.300	5.871	6.224	6.667
3.	Assam	8.543	9.836	11.849	10.748	9.290
4.	Bihar	6.434	2.965	0.000	0.000	0.000
5	Goa	0.973	1.058	1.161	0.917	0.604
6.	Himachal Pradesh	8.816	10.744	14.057	14.230	14.338
7.	Jammu & Kashmir	13.366	16.491	21.985	22.741	23.700
8.	Manipur	3.930	4.891	6.602	6.917	7.348
9.	Meghalaya	3.590	4.403	5.815	5.994	6.130
10	Mizoram	3.676	4.628	6.278	6.784	7.074
11.	Nagaland	5.818	7.417	10.247	11.072	12.025
12.	Orissa	4.815	5.248	4.934	2.773	0.680
13.	Rajasthan	0.835	0.000	0.000	0.000	0.000
14.	Sikkim	1.199	1.473	1.938	1.982	2.055
15.	Tripura	5.465	6.807	9.263	9.618	10.089
16.	Uttar Pradesh	17.061	11.751	0.000	0.000	0.000
	Total	100.00	100.00	100.00	100.00	100.00

Source: *Report of the Tenth Finance Commission*, 1994, p. 25.

24.3 Distribution of Additional Duties of Excise

In this regard the Commission observed, "In evolving our approach for the distribution of the States' shares, we have kept in view the basis adopted by the earlier Commissions, the views of the State Governments and the availability of reliable data for the proxies which would represent a fair approximation to the consumption of the three articles. The commodities on which additional excise duties are levied are articles of mass consumption and accordingly, in our view, population should have a substantial weight in the formula. We also agree with the views of the earlier Commissions that the level of State income has a significant bearing on the consumption of sugar, textiles and tobacco and should be a factor in distribution.

Since sales tax is a levy on consumption, some of the past Commissions have accepted proportion of sales tax revenues as capturing the consumption levels of the three commodities. Some of the States are of the same view. The other point of view is that since sales tax is levied on a host of commodities ranging from luxuries to raw materials, the proceeds of this tax do not represent the consumption levels of these three alone. Nevertheless, there is a relationship between consumption, as represented by sales tax, and consumption of these commodities. Accordingly, we feel some weight can be given to sales tax". [1]

Hence, it worked out the shares of the States by assigning a weight of 50 percent to population according to the 1991 census, 40 percent to the average of state domestic product for the three latest years 1987-88 to 1989-90 for which the requisite data was available and 10 percent to the average collection of State sales tax (excluding inter-State sales tax) for the three years 1990-91 to 1992-93, these being the latest three years for which final accounts were available. It agreed with the view of the IX-FC that distribution of additional excise duty was not in the nature of devolution for which the population figures of 1971 census should be used as per its terms of reference. Hence, it used the latest census figures of 1991. As regards the share of the Union territories, it agreed that their share be determined on the same basis as that of all the States. Accordingly, it fixed the share of Union territories at 2.203 percent to be retained by the Central Government. The balance was distributed among the States as shown in Table 24.4.

Table 24.4: Distribution of Additional Duties of Excise among the States as Recommended by the Tenth Finance Commission

S. No.	State	Percent	S. No.	State	Percent
1.	Andhra Pradesh	7.820	14.	Manipur	0.197
2.	Arunachal Pradesh	0.104	15.	Meghalaya	0.188
3.	Assam	2.483	16.	Mizoram	0.079
4.	Bihar	7.944	17.	Nagaland	0.137
5	Goa	0.232	18.	Orissa	3.345
6.	Gujarat	5.995	19.	Punjab	3.422
7.	Haryana	2.366	20.	Rajasthan	4.873
8.	Himachal Pradesh	0.595	21.	Sikkim	0.053
9.	Jammu & Kashmir	0.856	22.	Tamil Nadu	7.669
10	Karnataka	5.744	23.	Tripura	0.286
11.	Kerala	3.740	24.	Uttar Pradesh	14.573
12.	Madhya Pradesh	7.236	25.	West Bengal	8.036
13.	Maharashtra	12.027			
	Total				**100.000**

Source: *Report of the Tenth Finance Commission*, 1994, p. 28.

24.4 Grants in Lieu of Tax on Railway Passenger Fares

X-FC agreed with the views expressed by most States that of VIII-FC that the grants should be equal to 10.7 percent of the non-suburban railway passenger earnings. State-wise figures of non-suburban passenger earnings were made available to it by the

Ministry of Railways for the Year 1992-93. The total non-suburban passenger earnings for that year were ₹ 3,540.82 crore. Hence, it recommended that 10.7 percent of this i.e. ₹ 380.00 crore be paid to the States annually during the period covered by its award.

Turning to the principles of distribution, it was in agreement with VII-FC, VIII-FC and IX-FC which recommended distribution of the grant in proportion to the non-suburban passenger earnings from traffic originating in each State. The taxable event being the payment of fare, a State should get a grant in relation to the fare paid within its boundary.

In short, X-FC made the following recommendations in the matter.

1. The quantum of the grant in lieu of the railway passenger fares tax for 1995-96 to 1999-2000 should be ₹ 380 crore annually.
2. Share of the States be allocated in the same proportion as the average of the non-suburban passenger earnings in each State during the years 1988-89 to 1992-93 bears to the average of the aggregate non-suburban earnings in all States in those years. On this basis the shares of the States were calculated as shown in Table 24.5.

Table 24.5: Percentage Share of Each State in Grant in Lieu of Tax on Railway Passenger Fares

S. No.	State	Percent	S. No.	State	Percent
1.	Andhra Pradesh	8.345	14.	Manipur	0.018
2.	Arunachal Pradesh	0.005	15.	Meghalaya	0.034
3.	Assam	1.368	16.	Mizoram	0.001
4.	Bihar	9.326	17.	Nagaland	0.145
5	Goa	0.194	18.	Orissa	1.715
6.	Gujarat	6.901	19.	Punjab	3.280
7.	Haryana	1.917	20.	Rajasthan	4.445
8.	Himachal Pradesh	0.108	21.	Sikkim	0.010
9.	Jammu & Kashmir	0.728	22.	Tamil Nadu	6.458
10	Karnataka	3.388	23.	Tripura	0.039
11.	Kerala	3.495	24.	Uttar Pradesh	15.568
12.	Madhya Pradesh	6.882	25.	West Bengal	8.082
13.	Maharashtra	17.548			
	Total				**100.000**

Source: *Report of the Tenth Finance Commission*, 1994, p. 30.

Endnote

1. *Report of the Tenth Finance Commission*, 1994, p. 28.

25

Eleventh Finance Commission (XI-FC): 2000-01 to 2004-05

Highlights of the Report	
Chairman	Shri A.M. Khusro
Members	Shri N.C. Jain Shri J.C. Jetly Dr. Amaresh Bagchi Shri T.N. Srivastava
Year and month of establishment	July 1998
Year and month of reporting	July 2000
Period of award	2000-01 to 2004-05
Main Recommendations	
1. States' share in net proceeds of all Central taxes fixed at 28 percent. 2. 1.5 percent of the net proceeds of all Central taxes recommended for distribution amongst such States which do not levy sales tax on sugar, tobacco and textiles. 3. Total share of States in the net proceeds of all Union taxes: 28+1.5=29.5 4. Bases of distribution of States' share inter se (percent): Population: 10; Income (distance method): 62.5; Area: 7.5; Index of infrastructure: 7.5; Tax effort: 5.0; Fiscal discipline: 7.5	

XI-FC was constituted by an order of the President dated July 3, 1998. The Commission was asked to make recommendations as to the following matters.

1. Distribution between the Union and the States of the net proceeds of taxes which are to be, or may be, divided between them and the allocation between the States of the respective shares of such proceeds.
2. Principles which should govern the grants-in-aid of the revenues of the States out of the Consolidated Fund of India and the sums to be paid to the States which are in need of assistance by way of grants-in-aid of their revenues under Article 275 of the Constitution for purposes other than those specified in the provisos to clause (1) of that article.
3. Measures needed to augment the Consolidated Fund of a State to supplement the resources of the Panchayats in the State on the basis of the recommendations made by the Finance Commission of the State.
4. Measures needed to augment the Consolidated Fund of a State to supplement the resources of the Municipalities in the State on the basis of the recommendations made by the Finance Commission of the State.

25.1 States Share in All Central Taxes and Duties

The Constitution (Eightieth Amendment) Act, 2000 altered the pattern of sharing of Central taxes between the Centre and the States in a fundamental way. Prior to this amendment, taxes on income other than agriculture income and Union duties of excise were shared with States under Articles 270 and 272 respectively. The Eightieth Amendment Act substituted a new Article for Article 270 and omitted the old Article 272. The new Article 270 provided as follows: "All taxes and duties referred to in the Union List, except the duties and taxes referred to in Articles 268 and 269, respectively, surcharge on taxes and duties referred to in Article 271 and any cess levied for specific purposes under any law made by Parliament shall be levied and collected by the Government of India and shall be distributed between the Union and the States".

Thus, XI-FC was required to determine, first, the aggregate share of the States in all Union taxes and duties. This task required a comprehensive view of: (a) expenditure needs of the Centre, (b) aggregate resources of the Centre, (c) aggregate requirements of States on revenue account and (d) resources of the States from their own sources.

On the basis of the analysis and assessment of the budgetary requirements of the Centre and the States, the Commission fixed the share of States at 28 percent of the net proceeds of shareable Central taxes/duties for distribution amongst all such States where the Central tax/duty was leviable for each of the five years starting from April 1, 2000. In addition, 1.5 percent of the net proceeds of shareable Central taxes/duties in a year was recommended for distribution amongst such States which did not levy sales tax on sugar, tobacco and textiles during that year, thus totalling 28 + 1.5 = 29.5 percent of the net proceeds of all Union taxes and duties. The distribution of this 1.5 percent among the States was to be done in the same manner as the distribution of 28 percent of the net proceeds. It was further recommended that if any State levies and collects sales tax on sugar, textile and tobacco, it would not be entitled to any share from this 1.5 percent.

As regards States' views on the new scheme of devolution, the Commission observed, "In their memoranda, States are in unison in asking for the changeover to the alternative scheme of devolution and for giving up the present system of tax sharing of revenues from specified taxes, viz. income tax and Union excise duties. Many have, however, asked for a higher share in the pool of Central taxes as compared to the 29 percent share that was recommended by the Tenth Finance Commission". [1]

25.2 Distribution of the Share of States Inter Se

While States were almost unanimous in demanding an increase in the share of Union taxes, there were naturally wide divergences in their approach to the principles for determination of relative shares of the States in the divisible pool. Each State suggested a formula which it considered would benefit it the most, the richer States emphasising the *collection factor* and the poorer States the *backwardness factor*. The various criteria, often conflicting, suggested by the States to XI-FC, included population, consumption, collection of revenue, economic backwardness, relative financial weakness, sales tax collections, and percentage of scheduled castes and scheduled tribes. Not surprisingly, relatively industrialised States like Gujarat, and Maharashtra argued in favour of collection factor because bulk of the tax revenue originated there. Poorer States like Uttar Pradesh, Orissa, and Bihar wanted significant weightage for backwardness criterion while Madhya Pradesh and Rajasthan preferred high weightage for geographical area. It has rightly been said that fiscal federalism in India is a tug-of-war not only between the Centre and the States but also among the States themselves.

After examining claims and counter-claims of the States, XI-FC recommended percentage share of each State (in the share of all States) and indicated the criteria adopted in arriving at those percentage shares.

It asserted that the basic emphasis in its approach was to evolve a suitable structure of incentives in all mechanism of fiscal transfers. It may be recalled that X-FC had made a beginning in this direction by utilising an index of tax effort made by the States. Carrying forward the scheme of incentives, XI-FC observed, "we feel that given the present fiscal situation of the States and the need for restructuring, as also the reference in our TOR for better fiscal management, further incentives need to be provided for fiscal discipline, and that this may be integrated in the principles of devolution. Accordingly, we are suggesting the use of an index of fiscal discipline". [2] Keeping all these requirements in mind, it suggested six criteria with relative weights for determining the *inter se* shares of the States (Table 25.1). There were three main considerations before the Commission in the selection of criteria: (a) resource deficiency of States, (b) higher cost of providing services and (c) fiscal discipline.

Table 25.1: Criteria and Relative Weights for Determining Inter Se Shares of States

S. No.	Criteria	Relative weight (percent)
1.	Population	10.0
2.	Income (distance method)	62.5
3.	Area	7.5
4.	Index of infrastructure	7.5
5.	Tax effort	5.0
6.	Fiscal discipline	7.5

Source: *Report of the Eleventh Finance Commission*, June 2000, p. 58.

Based on the criteria and their relative weights as given in Table 25.1, the percentage shares of different States in the net proceeds of all shareable Union taxes and duties (except the expenditure tax and service tax) [3] were worked out in each of the financial years from 2000-01 to 2004-05. These percentage shares are shown in Table 25.2.

Expenditure tax and service tax were not at that time leviable in the State of Jammu and Kashmir. Share in the net proceeds of these taxes was, therefore, not assignable to this State. The Commission recommended the share of each of the remaining 24 States in the net proceeds of expenditure tax and service tax as indicated in Table 25.3. The Commission clarified that if in any year, these taxes become leviable in the State of

Jammu and Kashmir, the share of each State including that of Jammu and Kashmir would be in accordance with the percentages given in Table 25.2.

Table 25.2: Inter se Shares of States in the Net Proceeds of All Shareable Union Taxes and Duties

S. No.	State	Percent	S. No.	State	Percent
1.	Andhra Pradesh	7.701	14.	Manipur	0.366
2.	Arunachal Pradesh	0.244	15.	Meghalaya	0.342
3.	Assam	3.285	16.	Mizoram	0.198
4.	Bihar	14.597	17.	Nagaland	0.220
5	Goa	0.206	18.	Orissa	5.056
6.	Gujarat	2.821	19.	Punjab	1.147
7.	Haryana	0.944	20.	Rajasthan	5.473
8.	Himachal Pradesh	0.683	21.	Sikkim	0.184
9.	Jammu & Kashmir	1.290	22.	Tamil Nadu	5.385
10	Karnataka	4.930	23.	Tripura	0.487
11.	Kerala	3.057	24.	Uttar Pradesh	19.798
12.	Madhya Pradesh	8.838	25.	West Bengal	8.116
13.	Maharashtra	4.632			
	Total				**100.000**

Source: *Report of the Eleventh Finance Commission*, June 2000, p. 59.

Table 25.3: Share of States, other than Jammu and Kashmir, in the Expenditure Tax and Service Tax

S. No.	State	Percent	S. No.	State	Percent
1.	Andhra Pradesh	7.802	14.	Manipur	0.371
2.	Arunachal Pradesh	0.247	15.	Meghalaya	0.346
3.	Assam	3.328	16.	Mizoram	0.201
4.	Bihar	14.788	17.	Nagaland	0.223
5	Goa	0.209	18.	Orissa	5.122
6.	Gujarat	2.858	19.	Punjab	1.162
7.	Haryana	0.956	20.	Rajasthan	5.544
8.	Himachal Pradesh	0.692	21.	Sikkim	0.186
9.	Jammu & Kashmir	0.000	22.	Tamil Nadu	5.455
10	Karnataka	4.994	23.	Tripura	0.493
11.	Kerala	3.097	24.	Uttar Pradesh	20.057
12.	Madhya Pradesh	8.954	25.	West Bengal	8.222
13.	Maharashtra	4.693			
	Total				**100.000**

Source: *Report of the Eleventh Finance Commission*, June 2000, p. 60.

Furthermore, the Commission made it clear that if in any year during 2000-2001 to 2004-05, a tax under Union was not leviable in a State, the share of that State in that tax should be put to zero and the entire proceeds should be distributed among the remaining States by proportionately adjusting their share.

25.3 Grants-in-aid of Revenues of States

Even after the transfer to the States of a share of divisible taxes, the resources of some of the States may remain inadequate to meet their needs. Therefore, the Constitution provides for grants-in-aid by the Centre to such States as are in need of assistance. Two types of grants are provided by the Centre to the States: the first under Article 275 which are routed through the Finance Commission, and the second under Article 282 which have traditionally been determined by the Planning Commission.

XI-FC recommended grants-in-aid to be given under Article 275(1) equal to the amount of deficits assessed for each year during the period 2000-01 to 2004-05. Grants-in-aid amounting to ₹ 35,359 crore were recommended to such States, The amount of the grant for each State, having non-Plan deficits is indicated in Table 25.4.

Table 25.4: Grants-in-aid to Cover Non-Plan Gap on Revenue Account as Recommended by the Eleventh Finance Commission

(₹ crore)

S. No.	State	2000-01	2001-02	2002-03	2003-04	2004-05	Total
1.	Arunachal	245	247	246	242	249	1,228
2.	Assam	111	-	-	-	-	111
3.	Himachal	1,049	1,002	947	839	712	4,549
4.	J&K	2,111	2,241	2239	2,291	2,328	11,211
5	Manipur	355	355	352	345	339	1,745
6.	Meghalaya	338	330	326	301	277	1,572
7.	Mizoram	323	330	335	351	338	1,676
8.	Nagaland	644	674	720	734	764	3,536
9.	Orissa	358	36	279	-	-	674
10	Punjab	284	-	-	-	-	284
11.	Rajasthan	955	289	-	-	-	1,245
12.	Sikkim	170	171	170	166	164	841
13.	Tripura	493	493	495	476	456	2,414
14.	Uttar Pradesh	1,027	-	-	-	-	1,027
15.	West Bengal	1,690	1,034	522	-	-	3,246
	Total	**10,153**	**7,203**	**6,631**	**5,745**	**5,627**	**35,359**

Source: *Report of the Eleventh Finance Commission*, June 2000, p. 97.

25.4 Ceiling on Total Revenue Account Transfers

While working out the total quantum of share in Central taxes/duties and grants-in-aid to States, the Commission considered the trends in total transfers from the Centre to the States on revenue account. It recommended that tax devolution and Plan/Non-Plan grants from the Centre to the States should not exceed 37.5 percent of total Centre's revenues (both tax and non-tax). The rationale of the ceiling was explained by the Commission as follows, "in deciding the level of revenue transfers, all transfers have to be taken in their totality and their components like tax devolution, grants-in-aid and grants in other forms like Plan grants, should be decided in the light of the overall ceiling. Accordingly, after working out the likely profile of the revenue and expenditure of the Centre for the five years 2000-05, we have set a notional limit on the overall revenue transfers, taking into account the legitimate needs of the Centre to meet its revenue expenditure liabilities. In setting this ceiling, we have taken note of the level of transfers that have taken place as a proportion of Centre's revenues in recent years and postulated a proportion of 37.5 percent in order that there is no disruption in government finances at the two levels. This will serve to raise the volume of resource flow to the States over what has been prevailing of late but not beyond what can be accommodated within the Centre's resource profile, and the contemplated deficit levels". [4]

While accepting this ceiling on total revenue account transfers from the Centre to the States, the Government clarified that the acceptance of this recommendation did not imply the establishment of a principle of mandatory sharing of a fixed percentage of Centre's revenue receipts with the States.

The sharing of the proceeds from almost all Central taxes (global sharing) was welcomed universally. The earlier arrangement of sharing some of the taxes (itemised sharing) was criticised on the ground that Central Government paid more attention to the administration of non-shareable taxes and was lax in making the shareable taxes buoyant. In the new scheme, no tax, as such, is shareable. A percentage of the total tax proceeds of the Centre is assigned to the States. The total amount assigned has no identifiable parts to it. With the new scheme of tax devolution (effective April 1, 1996), the Central Government can pursue its tax reforms without the need to consider whether a tax is shareable with the States or not.

Endnotes

1. *Report of the Eleventh Finance Commission*, June 2000, p. 54.
2. *Ibid.*, p. 58.
3. Expenditure tax and service tax were not leviable in the State of Jammu & Kashmir. Hence, share in the net proceeds of these taxes was not assignable to this State. The share of each of the remaining States in the net proceeds of expenditure tax and service tax was worked out separately.
4. *Report of the Eleventh Finance Commission*, op. cit, p. 15.

26

Twelfth Finance Commission (XII-FC): 2005-06 to 2009-10

Highlights of the Report	
Chairman	Dr. C. Rangarajan
Members	Shri T.R. Prasad Professor D.K. Srivastava Shri Som Pal (Part-Time)
Year and month of establishment	November 2002
Year and month of reporting	December 2004
Period of award	2005-06 to 2009-10
Main Recommendations	
1. States' share in net proceeds of all Central taxes fixed at 30.5 percent. 2. Additional excise duties in lieu of sales tax treated as a part of the general pool of central taxes. 3. Bases of distribution of States' share inter se (percent): Population: 25; Income distance: 50; Area: 10; Tax effort: 7.5; Fiscal discipline: 7.5.	

XII-FC was constituted by an order of the President dated November 1, 2002. The Commission was asked to make recommendations as to the following matters.

1. Distribution between the Union and the States of the net proceeds of taxes which are to be, or may be, divided between them and the allocation between the States of the respective shares of such proceeds.
2. Principles which should govern the grants-in-aid of the revenues of the States out of the Consolidated Fund of India and the sums to be paid to the States which are in need of assistance by way of grants-in-aid of their revenues under Article 275 of the Constitution for purposes other than those specified in the provisions to clause (1) of that article.
3. Measures needed to augment the Consolidated Fund of a State to supplement the resources of the panchayats and municipalities in the State on the basis of the recommendations made by the Finance Commission of the State.

XII-FC was required to review the state of the finances of the Union and the States and suggest a plan by which the governments, collectively and severally, may bring about a restructuring of the public finances restoring budgetary balance, achieving macro-economic stability and debt reduction along with equitable growth.

In making its recommendations on various matters, it was required to take the base of population figures as of 1971, in all such cases where population was a factor for determination of devolution of taxes and duties and grants-in-aid.

26.1 Sharing of Union Tax Revenues

It may be recalled that prior to the enactment of the Constitution (Eightieth Amendment) Act, 2000, the sharing of the Union tax revenues with the states was in accordance with the provisions of Articles 270 and 272, as these stood then. While Article 270 provided for the compulsory sharing of the net proceeds of the income tax (excluding corporation tax), Article 272 permitted for sharing of the net proceeds of Union duties of excise (excluding duties of excise on medicinal and toilet preparations), if Parliament by law so provided. Consequently, the principles adopted for revenue sharing differed between the two taxes significantly.

The Eightieth Amendment of the Constitution altered the pattern of sharing of Union taxes in a fundamental way. Under this amendment, Article 272 was dropped and Article 270 was substantially changed. The new Article 270 provided for sharing of all the taxes and duties referred to in the Union list, except the taxes and duties referred to in Articles 268 and 269 respectively, surcharges on taxes and duties referred to in Article 271 and any cess levied for specific purposes. The basis for this change was the alternative scheme of devolution recommended by X-FC. There was considerable merit in the change, as it gave greater freedom and flexibility to the Centre in pursuing the tax reforms in an integrated manner and enabled the States to share the aggregate buoyancy of central taxes. XI-FC was the first to take these changes into account, while recommending the share of the states in the divisible pool.

Another Constitutional amendment that was of relevance to Centre-State fiscal relations was the Eighty-eighth Amendment, enacted in January 2004 through the Constitution (Eighty-eighth Amendment) Act, 2003. This was relating to service tax. This amendment provided for a specific entry in the Constitution to authorise levy of service tax. The Central Government had been imposing and collecting this tax as a residual item under Entry 97 in the Union List and the net proceeds thereof were distributed between the Centre and the States as per Article 270 of the Constitution on the recommendations of the Finance Commission.

26.2 Vertical Sharing

XI-FC recommended that the share of the States be fixed at 28 percent of the net proceeds of all taxes and duties. It further noted that as a consequence of the amendment, which *inter alia* deleted Article 272, additional excise duties levied under the Additional Excise Duties (Goods of Special Importance) Act, 1957, had become part of the revenue receipts of the Central Government and were shareable with the States. It was felt that there was a need for a review of the earlier arrangement and pending such a review, it recommended that 1.5 percent of all shareable Union taxes and duties be allocated to the States separately and its *inter se* distribution among the States may be done in the same manner as the distribution of 28 percent of the net proceeds. This brought the total tax devolution recommended by XI-FC to 29.5 percent of the net proceeds of all shareable Central taxes and duties.

Many States had asked XII-FC for increase in the share of States in the shareable pool from 29.5 percent to 33 percent. Some States suggested a figure of 50 percent. After considering various aspects of the issue, it recommended that the share of the states in the net proceeds of shareable Central taxes be raised from 29.5 percent to 30.5 percent. For this purpose, additional excise duties *in lieu* of sales tax on textiles, tobacco and sugar were treated as part of the general pool of Central taxes. Further, the indicative amount of overall transfers to States in Central gross revenue receipts, which was fixed at 37.5 percent by XI-FC, was fixed at 38 percent.

26.3 Horizontal Sharing

As regards the determination of the *inter se* shares of the states, the criteria and the weights assigned are shown in Table 26.1.

Table 26.1: Criteria and Weights Assigned for Inter Se Determination of Shares of States

Criteria	Weight (percent)
Population	25.0
Income distance	50.0
Area	10.0
Tax effort	7.5
Fiscal discipline	7.5

Source: *Report of the Twelfth Finance Commission*, November 2004, p. 133.

XII-FC tried to evolve a formula which could balance equity with fiscal efficiency. Table 26.2 records the shares of the States recommended by it in the net proceeds of all the shareable Union taxes (excluding service tax, as it was not leviable in Jammu and Kashmir) in each of the five financial years during the period 2005-06 to 2009-10.

Since service tax was not leviable in the state of Jammu and Kashmir, and its proceeds were, therefore, not assignable to this state, XII-FC worked out the share of each of the remaining 27 states in the net proceeds of service tax (Table 26.3). It further recommended that if in any year, this tax became leviable in Jammu and Kashmir, the share of each state including that of Jammu and Kashmir would be in accordance with the percentages given in Table 26.2.

Similarly, if in any year during the period 2005-06 to 2009-10, a tax under Union was not leviable in a state, the share of that state in that tax should be put to zero and the entire proceeds should be distributed among the remaining states by proportionately adjusting their share.

In short, the recommendations of the Commission regarding sharing of Union tax revenue were as follows.

1. The share of States in the net proceeds of shareable Central taxes was fixed at 30.5 percent, treating additional excise duties in lieu of sales tax as part of the general pool of Central taxes. Share of States to come down to 29.5 percent, when States are

allowed to levy sales tax on sugar, textiles and tobacco.

2. In case of any legislation enacted in respect of service tax, after the notification of the eighty-eighth amendment to the Constitution, revenue accruing to a State should not be less than the share that would accrue to it, had the entire service tax proceeds been part of the shareable pool.
3. The indicative amount of overall transfers to States was fixed at 38 percent of the Centre's gross revenue receipts.

Table 26.2: Inter se Shares of States in the Net Proceeds of All Shareable Union Taxes and Duties

S. No.	State	Percent	S. No.	State	Percent
1.	Andhra Pradesh	7.356	15.	Maharashtra	4.997
2.	Arunachal Pradesh	0.288	16.	Manipur	0.362
3.	Assam	3.235	17.	Meghalaya	0.371
4.	Bihar	11.028	18.	Mizoram	0.239
5	Chhattisgarh	2.654	19.	Nagaland	0.263
6	Goa	0.259	20.	Orissa	5.161
7.	Gujarat	3.569	21.	Punjab	1.299
8.	Haryana	1.075	22.	Rajasthan	5.609
9.	Himachal Pradesh	0.522	23.	Sikkim	0.227
10.	Jammu & Kashmir	1.297	24.	Tamil Nadu	5.305
11.	Jharkhand	3.361	25.	Tripura	0.428
12	Karnataka	4.459	26.	Uttar Pradesh	19.264
13.	Kerala	2.665	27.	Uttranchal	0.939
14.	Madhya Pradesh	6.711	28.	West Bengal	7.057
	Total				**100.000**

Source: *Report of the Twelfth Finance Commission*, November 2004, p. 133.

26.4 Grants-in-aid to States

XII-FC disfavoured the then existing system of imposing a 70:30 ratio between loans and grants for extending plan assistance to non-special category states (10:90 in the case of special category states). Instead, it recommended that the centre should confine itself to extending plan grants to the states, and leave it to the states to decide how much they wish to borrow and from whom.

It recommended a total non-plan revenue deficit grant of ₹ 56,855.87 crore during the award period for 15 States. Eight States were recommended for grants amounting to ₹ 10,171.65 crore over the award period for the education sector, with a minimum of ₹ 20 crore in a year for any eligible state. Seven States were recommended for grants amounting to ₹ 5,887.08 crore over the award period for the health sector, with a minimum of ₹ 10 crore a year for any eligible State. Grants for the education and health sectors were additionality, over and above the normal expenditure to be incurred by the States in these sectors.

Table 26.3: Shares of the States (excluding Jammu and Kashmir) in the Net Proceeds of Service Tax

S. No.	State	Percent	S. No.	State	Percent
1.	Andhra Pradesh	7.453	15.	Manipur	0.367
2.	Arunachal Pradesh	0.292	16.	Meghalaya	0.376
3.	Assam	3.277	17.	Mizoram	0.242
4.	Bihar	11.173	18.	Nagaland	0.266
5	Chhattisgarh	2.689	19.	Orissa	5.229
6	Goa	0.262	20.	Punjab	1.316
7.	Gujarat	3.616	21.	Rajasthan	5.683
8.	Haryana	1.089	22.	Sikkim	0.230
9.	Himachal Pradesh	0.529	23.	Tamil Nadu	5.374
10.	Jharkhand	3.405	24.	Tripura	0.433
11	Karnataka	4.518	25.	Uttar Pradesh	19.517
12.	Kerala	2.700	26.	Uttranchal	0.952
13.	Madhya Pradesh	6.799	27.	West Bengal	7.150
14.	Maharashtra	5.063			
	Total				**100.000**

Source: *Report of the Twelfth Finance Commission*, November 2004, p. 133.

A grant of ₹ 15,000 crore over the award period was recommended for maintenance of roads and bridges. This amount was in addition to the normal expenditure which the States would be incurring on maintenance of roads and bridges. This amount was to be provided in equal instalments over the last four years (i.e. 2006-07 to 2009-10) of the award period, so that the States got a year for making preparations to absorb these funds. An amount of ₹ 5,000 crore was recommended as grants for maintenance of public buildings.

A grant of ₹ 1,000 crore spread over the award period was recommended for maintenance of forests. This was additionality over and above what the States would be spending through their forest departments. A grant of ₹ 625 crore spread over the award period was recommended for heritage conservation. This grant was to be used for preservation and protection of historical monuments, archaeological sites, public libraries, museums and archives, and also for improving the tourist infrastructure to facilitate visits to these sites. An amount of ₹ 7,100 crore was recommended as grant for state specific needs.

26.5 Restructuring Public Finances

The Commission made the following recommendations in this regard.

1. Centre and States should improve the combined tax-GDP ratio to 17.6 percent by 2009-10.
2. Combined debt-GDP ratio, with external debt measured at historical exchange rates, should be brought down to 75 percent by 2009-10.

3. Fiscal deficit to GDP targets for the Centre and States should be fixed at 3 percent.
4. Revenue deficit of the Centre and States should be brought down to zero by 2008-09.
5. Interest payments relative to revenue receipts should be brought down to 28 percent and 15 percent in the case of the Centre and States respectively.
6. States to follow a recruitment policy in a manner so that the total salary bill, relative to revenue expenditure, net of interest payments, does not exceed 35 percent.
7. Each State should enact a fiscal responsibility legislation providing for elimination of revenue deficit by 2008-09 and reducing fiscal deficit to 3 percent of State Domestic Product.
8. The system of on-lending should be brought to an end over time. The long-term goal should be to bring down debt-GDP ratio to 28 percent each for the Centre and the States.

27

Thirteenth Finance Commission (XIII-FC): 2010-11 to 2014-15

Highlights of the Report	
Chairman	Dr. Vijay L. Kelkar
Members	Dr. Indira Rajaraman Dr. Abusaleh Shariff Professor Atul Sarma Shri B.K. Chaturvedi (Part-Time) Shri Sumit Bose (Secretary)
Year and month of establishment	November 2007
Year and month of reporting	December 2009
Period of award	2010-11 to 2014-15
Main Recommendations	
1. States' share in net proceeds of all Central taxes fixed at 32.0 percent. 2. Bases of distribution of States' share inter se (percent): Population: 25; Area: 10; Fiscal capacity distance: 47.5; Fiscal discipline: 17.5 3. Indicative ceiling on overall transfers to States on revenue account set at 39.5 percent of gross revenue receipts of the Centre.	

XIII-FC was constituted in pursuance of the provisions of Article 280 of the Constitution of India by the President vide a Notification dated November 13, 2007. It was asked to make recommendations covering a period of 5 years commencing on April 1, 2010.

It was asked to make recommendations as to the following matters:

1. The distribution between the Union and the States of the net proceeds of taxes which are to be, or may be, divided between them under Chapter I Part XII of the Constitution and the allocation between the States of the respective shares of such proceeds;
2. The principles which should govern the grants-in-aid of the revenues of the States out of the Consolidated Fund of India and the sums to be paid to the States which are in need of assistance by way of grants-in-aid of their revenues under Article 275 of the Constitution for purposes other than those specified in the provisos to clause (1) of that article; and
3. The measures needed to augment the Consolidated Fund of a State to supplement the resources of the Panchayats and Municipalities in the State on the basis of the recommendations made by the Finance Commission of the State.

In making its recommendations on various matters, it was asked to take the base of population figures as of 1971, in all such cases where population was a factor for determination of devolution of taxes and duties and grants-in-aid.

27.1 Sharing of Union Tax Revenues

The share of States in net proceeds of shareable Central taxes was increased from 30.5 percent to 32 percent in each of the financial years from 2010-11 to 2014-15. Under the Additional Duties of Excise (Goods of Special Importance) Act, 1957, all goods were exempted from payment of duty from March 1, 2006. Following this, the Centre had adjusted the basic duties of excise on sugar and tobacco products. In view of these developments, the States' share in the net proceeds of shareable Central taxes remained unchanged at 32 percent.

The indicative ceiling on overall transfers to States on the revenue account was set at 39.5 percent of gross revenue receipts of the Centre.

27.2 Criteria and Weights for Determining Inter Se Shares of States

The criteria for determining the inter se shares of states in tax devolution, along with the weights assigned to them, are shown in Table 27.1.

Table 27.1: Criteria and Weights for Tax Devolution

(percent)

Criterion	Weight
1. Population (1971)	25.0
2. Area	10.0
3. Fiscal capacity distance	47.5
4. Fiscal discipline	17.5

Source: *Report of the Thirteenth Finance Commission*, December 2009, p. 122.

The inter se shares of States in the net proceeds of Central taxes (excluding service tax) as recommended by XIII-FC in each of the 5 years 2010-15 are shown in Table 27.2.

Since service tax was not levied in the state of Jammu and Kashmir, therefore net proceeds of service tax were not assignable to this state. The shares of the remaining 27 States in the proceeds of service tax are shown in Table 27.3.

27.3 Grants-in-aid to States

27.3.1 Non-plan Revenue Deficit (NPRD) and Performance Incentive: Total non-plan revenue grant of ₹ 51,800 crore was recommended over the award period for eight states. A performance grant of ₹ 1,500 crore was recommended for three Special Category States who had graduated from a NPRD situation.

27.3.2 Elementary Education: A grant of ₹ 24,068 crore was recommended for elementary education over the award period. The education grant was additionality to the normal expenditure of the States for elementary education. The expenditure (plan + non-plan) under elementary education, exclusive of grants recommended, was expected to grow by at least 8 percent annually during 2010-15.

Table 27.2: Distribution of States' Share in the Net Proceeds of Central Taxes (Excluding Service Tax) among the States as Recommended by the Thirteenth Finance Commission

S. No.	State	Percent	S. No.	State	Percent
1.	Andhra Pradesh	6.937	15.	Maharashtra	5.199
2.	Arunachal Pradesh	0.328	16.	Manipur	0.451
3.	Assam	3.628	17.	Meghalaya	0.408
4.	Bihar	10.917	18.	Mizoram	0.269
5	Chhattisgarh	2.470	19.	Nagaland	0.314
6	Goa	0.266	20.	Orissa	4.779
7.	Gujarat	3.041	21.	Punjab	1.389
8.	Haryana	1.048	22.	Rajasthan	5.853
9.	Himachal Pradesh	0.781	23.	Sikkim	0.239
10.	Jammu & Kashmir	1.551	24.	Tamil Nadu	4.969
11.	Jharkhand	2.802	25.	Tripura	0.511
12	Karnataka	4.328	26.	Uttar Pradesh	19.677
13.	Kerala	2.341	27.	Uttranchal	1.120
14.	Madhya Pradesh	7.120	28.	West Bengal	7.264
	Total				**100.000**

Source: *Report of the Thirteenth Finance Commission*, December 2009, p. 122.

Table 27.3: Share of States (other than Jammu and Kashmir) in the Service Tax

S. No.	State	Percent	S. No.	State	Percent
1.	Andhra Pradesh	7.047	15.	Maharashtra	5.281
2.	Arunachal Pradesh	0.332	16.	Manipur	0.458
3.	Assam	3.685	17.	Meghalaya	0.415
4.	Bihar	11.089	18.	Mizoram	0.273
5	Chhattisgarh	2.509	19.	Nagaland	0.318
6	Goa	0.270	20.	Orissa	4.855
7.	Gujarat	3.089	21.	Punjab	1.411
8.	Haryana	1.064	22.	Rajasthan	5.945
9.	Himachal Pradesh	0.793	23.	Sikkim	0.243
10.	Jammu & Kashmir	Nil	24.	Tamil Nadu	5.047
11.	Jharkhand	2.846	25.	Tripura	0.519
12	Karnataka	4.397	26.	Uttar Pradesh	19.987
13.	Kerala	2.378	27.	Uttranchal	1.138
14.	Madhya Pradesh	7.232	28.	West Bengal	7.379
	Total				**100.000**

Source: *Report of the Thirteenth Finance Commission*, December 2009, p. 123.

27.3.3 Environment: An amount of ₹ 5,000 crore was recommended as forest grant for the award period. Grants for the first 2 years were untied but priority was given to the preparation of working plans. Release of grants for the last 3 years was linked to progress in the number of approved working plans.

27.3.4 Improving Outcomes: States were incentivised to enrol such of their residents who participate in welfare schemes within the Unique Identification (UID) programme. A grant of ₹ 2,989 crore was recommended to be given to State Governments in this regard.

States were incentivised to reduce their Infant Mortality Rates (IMR) based upon their performance beyond December 31, 2009. A grant of ₹ 5,000 crore was recommended for this purpose.

A grant of ₹ 5,000 crore was recommended to support improvement in a number of facets in the administration of justice. These included operation of morning/evening courts, promotion of alternate dispute resolution (ADR) mechanisms, enhancing support to Lok Adalats, as well as legal aid and training.

A grant of ₹ 20 crore was recommended for promotion of innovation by setting up a Centre for Innovation in Public Systems (CIPS) to identify, document and promote innovations in public services across states. The second grant of ₹ 1 crore per district was for the creation of a District Innovation Fund (DIF) aimed at increasing the efficiency of the capital assets already created.

To enhance the quality of statistical systems, a grant of ₹ 616 crore was recommended for State Governments at the rate of ₹ 1 crore for every district to fill in statistical infrastructure gaps in areas not addressed by the India Statistical Project (ISP).

A grant of ₹ 10 crore was provided to each General Category State and ₹ 5 crore to each Special Category State to set up an employees' and pensioners' data base.

27.3.5 Maintenance of Roads and Bridges: An amount of ₹ 19,930 crore was recommended as grant for maintenance of roads and bridges for 4 years (2011-12 to 2014-15) of the award period. The maintenance grants for roads and bridges were additionality to the normal maintenance expenditure to be incurred by the States. Release of this grant and expenditure was subject to certain conditions.

27.3.6 State-specific Needs: A total grant of ₹ 27,945 crore was recommended for state-specific needs.

In addition to certain other stipulations, state-specific grants were subject to the following conditions:

1. No funds from any of the state-specific grants were to be used for land acquisition by the States. Wherever land was required for a project/construction, such land was to be made available by the State Government.
2. The phasing of the state-specific grants was only indicative. States could communicate their required phasing to the Central Government. The grant could be released in a maximum of 2 instalments per year.
3. Accounts were to be maintained and utilisation certificates (UCs)/statements of expenditure (SOEs) provided as per General Finance Rules (GFR), 2005.

27.3.7 Monitoring: The High Level Monitoring Committee headed by Chief Secretary to review the utilisation of grants and to take corrective measures, set up as per the recommendation of XII-FC, was continued.

The total grants-in-aid recommended for the States over the award period are shown in Table 27.4.

Table 27.4: Grants-in-aid to States

(₹ crore)

S. No.	Purpose	Amount
1.	Local bodies	87,519
2.	Disaster relief (including for capacity building)	26,373
3.	Post-devolution non-plan revenue deficit	51,800
4.	Performance incentive	1,500
5.	Elementary education	24,068
6.	Environment	15,000
7.	Improving outcomes	14,446
8.	Maintenance of roads and bridges	19,930
9.	State-specific	27,945
10.	Implementation of model GST	50,000
	Total	**3,18,581**

Source: *Report of the Thirteenth Finance Commission*, December 2009, p. 10.

27.4 Disaster Relief

Recommendations in this regard were as under:

1. National Calamity Contingency Fund (NCCF) should be merged into the National Disaster Response Fund (NDRF) and the Calamity Relief Fund (CRF) into the State Disaster Response Funds (SDRFs) of the respective States. Contribution to the SDRFs should be shared between the Centre and States in the ratio of 75:25 for General Category States and 90:10 for Special Category States.
2. Balances as on March 31, 2010 under State CRFs and the NCCF should be transferred to the respective SDRFs and NDRF.
3. Budgetary provisions for the NDRF need to be linked to expenditure of the previous year from the fund. With cesses being subsumed on introduction of the GST, alternative sources of financing need to be identified.
4. The total size of the SDRF was worked out as ₹ 33,581 crore, to be shared in the ratio given above, with an additional grant of ₹ 525 crore for capacity building.
5. Assistance of ₹ 250 crore to be given to the National Disaster Response Force to maintain an inventory of items required for immediate relief.
6. Provisions relating to the District Disaster Response Fund (DDRF) in the Disaster Management Act may be reviewed and setting up of these funds left to the discretion of the individual states.
7. Mitigation and reconstruction activities should be kept out of the schemes funded through Finance Commission grants and met out of overall development plan funds

of the Centre and the States.

8. The list of disasters to be covered under the scheme financed through FC grants should remain as it currently exists. However, man-made disasters of high-intensity may be considered for NDRF funding, once norms have been stipulated and the requisite additional allocations made to the NDRF.
9. The administrative mechanism for disaster relief to be as prescribed under the Disaster Management, i.e. the National Disaster Management Authority (NDMA)/National Executive Council (NEC) at the Centre and the State Disaster Management Agency (SDMA)/State Executive Council (SEC) at the state level. Financial matters to be dealt with by the Ministry of Finance as per the existing practice.
10. Prescribed accounting norms should be adhered to for the continuance of central assistance to the SDRFs.

28

Fourteenth Finance Commission (XIV-FC): 2015-16 to 2019-20

Highlights of the Report	
Chairman	Dr. Y.V. Reddy
Members	Ms. Sushma Nath Dr. M. Govinda Rao Dr. Sudipto Mundle. Professor Abhijit Sen (part-time)
Year and month of establishment	January 2013
Year and month of reporting	February 2015
Period of award	2015-16 to 2019-20
Main Recommendations	
1. States' share in net proceeds of all Central taxes fixed at 42.0 percent. 2. Bases of distribution of States' share inter se (percent): Population (1971): 17.5; Population (2011): 10; Fiscal capacity/income distance: 50; Area: 15; Forest cover: 7.5. 3. An aggregate corpus of ₹ 61,219 crore for State Disaster Response Fund (SDRF) for all the States for the award period. 4. Creation of an autonomous and independent GST Compensation Fund through legislative actions.	

XIV-FC was appointed on January 2, 2013. It submitted its report, covering the five-year period from April 1, 2015, in February 2015.

In addition to its primary objectives—making recommendations regarding the sharing of taxes between the Centre and the States from the divisible pool and formulating a formula for the distribution of the states' share in divisible pool among the states—the terms of reference for the commission sought suggestions regarding the principles which should govern the quantum and distribution of grants-in-aid (non-plan grants to states), the measures, if needed, to augment State government finances to supplement the resources of local governments and to review the state of the finances, deficit and debt conditions at different levels of government.

28.1 Sharing of Union Tax Revenues

XIV-FC radically enhanced the share of the states in the central divisible pool from the existing 32 percent to 42 percent which was the biggest ever increase in vertical tax devolution. The previous two Finance Commissions, viz. XII-FC (period 2005-06 to 2009-10) and XIII-FC (period 2010-11 to 2014-15) had recommended a share for states at 30.5 percent (increase of 1 percent) and 32 percent (increase of 1.5 percent), respectively in the central divisible pool.

It also recommended that a commensurate reduction in Central Assistance to State Plans, which flowed through Centrally-sponsored Schemes and Block Grants. These recommendations reflected the demand from the States for an increase in flows in the form of tax devolution and a reduction in Centrally-sponsored Schemes, in terms of both numbers and outlays.

28.2 Criteria and Weights for Determining Inter se Shares of States

XIV-FC formulated a new horizontal formula (Table 28.1) for the distribution of the states' share in divisible pool among the states. There were changes both in the variables included/excluded as well as the weights assigned to them. Relative to the XIII-FC, XIV-FC incorporated two new variables: 2011 population and forest cover; and excluded the fiscal discipline variable.

Further, 11 States were identified for revenue deficit grant of ₹ 1,94,821 crore.

Table 28.1: Horizontal Devolution Formulas of XIII-FC and XIV-FC

Variable	Weights accorded	
	XIII-FC	XIV-FC
Population (1971)	25	17.5
Population (2011)	0	10
Fiscal capacity/income distance	47.5	50
Area	10	15
Forest cover	0	7.5
Fiscal discipline	17.5	0
Total	100	100

Sources: *Reports of Thirteenth and Fourteenth Finance Commissions.*

Inter se shares of States in the net proceeds of Central taxes (excluding service tax) as recommended by FC-XIV in each of the 5 years period of its award are shown in Table 28.2.

All the States stood to gain from XIV-FC transfers in absolute terms. The biggest gainers in absolute terms under General Category States (GCS) were Uttar Pradesh, West Bengal and Madhya Pradesh while for Special Category States (SCS) they were Jammu and Kashmir, Himachal Pradesh and Assam. The major gainers in per capita terms were Kerala, Chhattisgarh and Madhya Pradesh for GCS and Arunachal Pradesh, Mizoram and Sikkim for SCS.

Among the GCS, XIV-FC transfers had more favourable impact on the states which were relatively less developed. It indicated that the transfers were progressive, i.e. states with lower per capita net state domestic product (NSDP) received, on average, much larger transfers per capita. In other words, XIV-FC recommendations went in the direction of equalizing the income and fiscal disparities between the major states.

Table 28.2: Distribution of States' Share in the Net Proceeds of Central Taxes (Excluding Service Tax) among the States as Recommended by the XIV-FC

S. No.	State	Percent	S. No.	State	Percent
1.	Andhra Pradesh	4.305	16.	Manipur	0.617
2.	Arunachal Pradesh	1.370	17.	Meghalaya	0.642
3.	Assam	3.311	18.	Mizoram	0.460
4.	Bihar	9.665	19.	Nagaland	0.498
5	Chhattisgarh	3.080	20.	Odisha	4.642
6	Goa	0.378	21.	Punjab	1.577
7.	Gujarat	3.084	22.	Rajasthan	5.495
8.	Haryana	1.084	23.	Sikkim	0.367
9.	Himachal Pradesh	0.713	24.	Tamil Nadu	4.023
10.	Jammu & Kashmir	1.854	25.	Telangana	2.437
11.	Jharkhand	3.139	26.	Tripura	0.642
12	Karnataka	4.713	27.	Uttar Pradesh	17.959
13.	Kerala	2.500	28.	Uttranchal	1.052
14.	Madhya Pradesh	7.548	29.	West Bengal	7.324
15.	Maharashtra	5.521			
	Total				**100.000**

Source: *Report of the Fourteenth Finance Commission*, 2015, p.95.

Shares of States in the proceeds of service tax are shown in Table 28.3.

Table 28.3: Share of States (other than Jammu and Kashmir) in Service Tax

S. No.	State	Percent	S. No.	State	Percent
1.	Andhra Pradesh	4.398	15.	Manipur	0.623
2.	Arunachal Pradesh	1.431	16.	Meghalaya	0.650
3.	Assam	3.371	17.	Mizoram	0.464
4.	Bihar	9.787	18.	Nagaland	0.503
5	Chhattisgarh	3.166	19.	Odisha	4.744
6	Goa	0.379	20.	Punjab	1.589
7.	Gujarat	3.172	21.	Rajasthan	5.647
8.	Haryana	1.091	22.	Sikkim	0.369
9.	Himachal Pradesh	0.722	23.	Tamil Nadu	4.104
10.	Jharkhand	3.198	24.	Telangana	2.499
11	Karnataka	4.822	25.	Tripura	0.648
12.	Kerala	2.526	26.	Uttar Pradesh	18.205
13.	Madhya Pradesh	7.727	27.	Uttranchal	1.068
14.	Maharashtra	5.674	28.	West Bengal	7.423
	Total				**100.000**

Source: *Report of the Fourteenth Finance Commission*, 2015, p.96.

An interesting finding related to the decomposition of the resource transfers through tax devolution due to the increase in the divisible pool per se and due to the change in the horizontal devolution formula itself. The significant impact due to increase in the divisible pool was on states like Uttar Pradesh, Bihar, Madhya Pradesh, West Bengal and Andhra Pradesh (United) while states like Arunachal Pradesh, Chhattisgarh, Madhya Pradesh, Karnataka and Jharkhand were the major gainers due to a change in the horizontal devolution formula which gave greater weight to a state's forest cover.

The spirit behind XIV-FC recommendations was to increase the automatic transfers to the states to give them more fiscal autonomy and this was ensured by increasing the share of states from 32 to 42 percent of divisible pool. However, to protect the fiscal space of the Centre, commensurate reductions in the Central Assistance to States (CAS)—known as *plan transfers*—were suggested.

XIV-FC made far-reaching changes in tax devolution that moved the country toward greater fiscal federalism, conferring more fiscal autonomy on the states.

28.3 Grants to Local Bodies

Focus on local bodies has been an ongoing concern of successive Finance Commissions. XIV-FC recommended that grants to local bodies should be only for basic services and functions assigned to them under relevant legislation. It worked out the total grant to local bodies at ₹ 2.87 lakh crore for five years.

After studying the structure and functioning of local bodies, XIV-FC made the following main recommendations:

1. Local bodies should be required to spend the grants only on the basic services within the functions assigned to them under relevant legislations.
2. Grants should go to gram panchayats, which are directly responsible for the delivery of basic services, without any share for other levels. State Governments are expected to take care of the needs of the other levels. The earmarked basic grants for gram panchayats would be distributed among them, using the formula prescribed by the respective State Finance Commissions (SFCs) for the distribution of resources. Similarly, the basic grant for urban local bodies would be divided into tier-wise shares and distributed across each tier, namely the municipal corporations, municipalities (tier II urban local bodies) and the nagar panchayats (tier III local bodies) using the formula given by the respective SFCs. The State Governments should apply the distribution formula of the most recent SFC, whose recommendations have been accepted.
3. Stern action should be ensured if irregularities in the application of funds are noticed or pointed out.
4. State Governments should strengthen State Finance Commissions (SFCs). This would involve timely constitution, proper administrative support and adequate resources for smooth functioning and timely placement of the SFC report before State legislature, with action taken notes.
5. Vacant land tax by peri-urban panchayats be considered. In addition, a part of land conversion charges can be shared by State Governments with municipalities/ panchayats.

6. States should review the position and prepare a clear framework of rules for the levy of betterment tax.
7. States may like to consider steps to empower local bodies to impose advertisement tax and improve own revenues from this source.
8. States should review the structure of entertainment tax and take action to increase its scope to cover more and newer forms of entertainment.
9. State Governments should take action to assign productive local assets to the panchayats, put in place enabling rules for collection and institute systems so that they can obtain the best returns while leasing or renting common resources.
10. Urban local bodies should rationalise their service charges in a way that they are able to at least recover the operation and maintenance costs from the beneficiaries.

28.4 Financing of Disaster Relief

The financing of disaster relief has been an important aspect of federal fiscal relations. Successive Finance Commissions since the II-FC have provided *margin money* for such contingencies. From the time of the VI-FC, the terms of reference (ToR) have specifically entrusted each Commission with the task of considering the arrangements between the Union Government and State Governments relating to financing disaster management and making recommendations on the subject. When earlier Commissions examined the issues, there was no specific law relating to disaster management. By the time the XIII-FC was constituted, Parliament had enacted the Disaster Management Act, 2005.

The Disaster Management Act provides for the effective management of disasters and all related matters, including the mechanisms for funding disaster relief and response. The Act defines disaster in very broad terms to include both natural and man-made disasters. It envisages the constitution of two types of funds, one for disaster response and the other for mitigation. These are to be set up at the national, state and district levels.

Thus, for disaster response, the Act envisages a National Disaster Response Fund (NDRF), a State Disaster Response Fund (SDRF) in each State and, within the States, a District Disaster Response Fund (DDRF) in each district.

Similarly, the Act envisages a National Disaster Mitigation Fund (NDMF), State Disaster Mitigation Funds (SDMF) and District Disaster Mitigation Funds (DDMF) for disaster mitigation.

So far, at the national level, only the NDRF has been constituted. All State Governments have constituted an SDRF, but only a few have constituted an SDMF. Very few State Governments have constituted District Disaster Response Funds (DDRFs). During a disaster, relief activities at the district level are generally carried out through transfers from the SDRF.

28.4.1 Existing Arrangements for Disaster Management: The primary responsibility for undertaking rescue, relief and rehabilitation measures during a disaster lies with the State Governments. The Union Government supplements their efforts through logistic and financial support during severe natural disasters. Based on the recommendations of the XIII-FC, the National Calamity Contingency Fund (NCCF) was merged with the newly constituted NDRF. Similarly, at the state level, the Calamity Relief Fund (CRF) was merged with the SDRF. Financing of the SDRF is based on the recommendations of the Finance Commissions, which determine the annual size of the Funds as well as the respective contributions of the Union and State Governments.

The NDRF is financed through the levy of a cess on certain items, chargeable to excise and customs duty, and approved annually through the Finance Bill. The requirement for funds beyond what is available under the NDRF is met through general budgetary resources. The Union Government has issued guidelines on the items and norms of assistance, the natural calamities eligible for funding, accounting norms and audit arrangements, procedures for the release of funds and the respective share of each State as well as its contribution under the award of the XIII-FC towards the SDRF.

The notified calamities based on the recommendations of successive Finance Commissions include cyclones, droughts, earthquakes, fires, floods, tsunamis, hailstorms, landslides, avalanches, cloud bursts and pest attacks. The Union Government has recently added cold waves and frost to that list. The norms under each type of disaster were last revised in November 2013.

The National Policy on Disaster Management (NPDM) issued under the Disaster Management Act envisages building a safe and disaster-resilient India by developing a holistic, proactive, multiple disaster-oriented and technology-driven strategy through a culture of prevention, mitigation, preparedness and response. Under the provisions of the Act, the National Disaster Management Authority (NDMA) has been set up and the National Disaster Response Force raised.

At the state level, the institutional mechanisms of State Disaster Management Authorities (SDMA) and the District Disaster Management Authorities (DDMAs) have been put in place. Existing institutions have been strengthened to give priority to, and enhance their capacities for, rescue, relief, rehabilitation and mitigation. Some States have raised a State Disaster Response Force along the lines of the National Disaster Response Force. States have also focussed on training and generating awareness to help cope with disasters.

28.4.2 Recommendations of XIV-FC: These were as follows:

1. The financing of the NDRF has so far been almost wholly through the levy of cess on selected items, but if the cesses are discontinued or when they are subsumed under the GST in future, the Union Government should consider ensuring an assured source of funding for the NDRF.
2. While making appropriations into the NDRF, the past trends of outflows from it should be taken into account by the Union Government to ensure adequacy of the Fund in order to assure timely availability and release of funds to the States.
3. Recognising that contributions from the public and institutions could be another source of financing the NDRF, a decision on granting tax exemption to private contributions to the NDRF be expedited and that the Union Government consider invoking the use of Schedule VII of the Companies (Corporate Social Responsibility Policy) Rules 2014 as an enabling provision for financing the NDRF.

4. A review of the current arrangements for the reimbursement of expenditure incurred by the defence forces on disaster relief should be undertaken.
5. Considering the usefulness of a scientifically validated risk vulnerability indicator to measure the type, frequency and intensity of disasters, and in view of the very wide responsibility cast on governments at different levels by the statute, the Union Government should expedite the development and scientific validation of the Hazard Vulnerability Risk Profiles of States.
6. While calculating the requirement for funds from the NDRF during severe calamities, the existing practice of adjusting the contribution made by the Union Government to the SDRF should continue.
7. All States should contribute 10 percent to SDRF during the award period, with the remaining 90 percent coming from the Union Government.

XIV-FC adopted the practice of the previous Commissions and used past expenditure on disaster relief for the period 2006-07 to 2012-13 to determine the SDRF corpus for each State. Further, it followed the methodology of the XIII-FC to arrive at an aggregate corpus for all States of ₹ 61,219 crore for the award period.

XIV-FC was in agreement with the views of the XIII-FC that the decision of constituting DDRFs should best be left to the wisdom of the State Governments, and hence, separate grants for the financing of DDRFs were not recommended.

Considering the need for flexibility in regard to state-specific disasters, XIV-FC recommended that up to 10 percent of the funds available under the SDRF can be used by State Governments for natural disasters that they consider to be *disasters* within the local context in the State and which are not included in the notified list of disasters of the Ministry of Home Affairs.

29

Fifteenth Finance Commission (XV-FC): 2020-21 to 2025-26

Highlights of the Report	
Chairman	Shri N.K. Singh
Members	Shri Shaktikanta Das Dr. Anoop Singh Dr. Ashok Lahiri (Part Time) Dr. Ramesh Chand (Part Time) Shri Arvind Mehta (Secretary)
Year and month of establishment	November 2017
Year and month of reporting	December 2019 and November 2020
Period of award	2020-21 and 2021-22 to 2025-26
Main Recommendations (for the period 2021-22 to 2025-26)	
1. States' share in net proceeds of all Central taxes was fixed at 41 percent. This was less than the 42 percent share recommended by XIV-FC for the period 2015-16 to 2019-20. The adjustment of 1 percent was to provide, for the newly formed union territories of Jammu and Kashmir, and Ladakh, from the resources of the centre. 2. Bases of distribution of States' share inter se (percent): Population (2011 Census): 15; income distance: 45; geographical area: 15; forest and ecology: 10; demographic performance: 12.5; tax effort: 2.5. 3. Various amounts of revenue deficit grants, sector-specific grants, state-specific grants and grants to local bodies were recommended. 4. The existing cost-sharing patterns between the centre and states for disaster management funds retained. The cost-sharing pattern between centre and states is: (a) 90:10 for north-eastern and Himalayan states, and (b) 75:25 for all other states. 5. Centre should bring down fiscal deficit to 4 percent of GDP by 2025-26. For states, fiscal deficit limit (as percent of GSDP) was suggested as follows: (a) 4 percent in 2021-22, (b) 3.5 percent in 2022-23, and (c) 3 percent during 2023-26.	

In pursuance of clause (1) of Article 280 of the Constitution, read with the provisions of the Finance Commission (Miscellaneous Provisions) Act, 1951, the President constituted XV-FC on November 27, 2017.

XV-FC was asked to make recommendations on the following matters:

1. The distribution between the Union and the States of the net proceeds of taxes which are to be, or may be, divided between them under Chapter I, Part XII of the Constitution and the allocation between the States of the respective shares of such proceeds.

2. The principles which should govern the grants-in-aid of the revenues of the States out of the Consolidated Fund of India and the sums to be paid to the States by way of grants-in-aid of their revenues under Article 275 of the Constitution for purposes other than those specified in the provisos to clause (1) of that article.
3. The measures needed to augment the Consolidated Fund of a State to supplement the resources of the Panchayats and Municipalities in the State on the basis of the recommendations made by the Finance Commission of the State.

It was asked to use the population data of 2011 while making its recommendations.

XV-FC job was harder because of the rollout of goods and service tax (GST) regime from July 1, 2017, as it had taken certain powers concerning taxation away from the Union and the States, and given them to the newly formed GST Council. Further, even after the passage of the Fiscal Responsibility and Budget Management Act, 2003, some states still incurred revenue deficits.

Politicians, retired civil servants, judges and economists from South Indian states opposed, in the terms of reference of the Commission, the use of data of 2011 census, instead of the data of 1971 census, as previous commissions had done. They believed that this would dilute the share of South India in the pool of Union tax revenue, because of its shrinking population *vis-à-vis* the north since 1971.

29.1 Extension of the Tenure of XV-FC

The Union Cabinet on November 27, 2019 extended the tenure as well as the award period of XV-FC by one year. It was asked to submit its first report for 2020-21 and the second report for 2021-22 to 2025-26. Thus, the award period of XV-FC is 6 years instead of the usual 5 years. This was the second instance of the constitutionally-mandated body giving recommendations for finances of Central and State Governments for more than 5 years. IX-FC (Chairman: N.K.P. Salve) was the first to do so in order to synchronize the recommendations of the Finance Commission with the duration of the Five Year Plans.

The main reason for the extension was the bifurcation of the state of Jammu and Kashmir into two Union Territories, namely Jammu and Kashmir, and Ladakh. To accommodate these new realities, XV-FC needed more time.

29.2 First Report of XV-FC for 2020-21

The report for 2020-21 was tabled in Parliament on February 1, 2020.

29.2.1 Vertical Distribution: It may be recalled that XIV-FC had recommended a 42 percent share for states in the divisible pool of taxes. This was applicable to 29 states [including Jammu and Kashmir (J&K)] existing at that time. The share of J&K was close to 0.85 percent out of 42 percent. The number of states was reduced to 28 because of the reorganization of J&K into two Union Territories (UTs). Taking out this share and rounding if off to 1 percent, XV-FC allocated 41 percent of the divisible pool to 28 states. In effect, the share of states remained unchanged, barring the marginal advantage to Centre due to rounding off. According to XV-FC, the rounding off was necessary to meet special needs of the two newly constituted UTs, viz. J&K and Ladakh.

29.2.2 Horizontal Distribution: For horizontal distribution, XV-FC introduced tax effort as a criterion and gave it a weight of 2.5 percent. It reduced the weight of the income distance criterion from 50 percent to 45 percent and introduced a criterion of demographic change, giving it a weight of 12.5 percent. The demographic change is a performance-based criterion where data for the state-wise total fertility rate was used.

The revamped formula resulted in significant gains for Maharashtra, Rajasthan, Arunachal Pradesh and Bihar. The southern states of Karnataka, Kerala, Telangana and Andhra Pradesh were the biggest losers.

Unlike its predecessor, XV-FC used the 2011 census as the sole criterion for population but reduced the weight for population to 15 percent from the earlier 27.5 percent. While retaining the 15 percent assigned to geographical area, it enhanced the focus on forests and ecology from 7.5 percent to 10 percent.

Through the new mix of parameters, XV-FC sought to address concerns that some of the states that had managed to control the pace of population expansion were being penalized for this achievement. Criteria and weights for horizontal distribution of states' share inter se are given in Table 29.1.

Table 29.1: Criteria and Weights for Horizontal Distribution of States' Share among Themselves

Criterion	Weight (percent)	
	FC-XIV	First report of FC-XV
Population	27.5*	15**
Income distance	50	45
Geographical area	15	15
Forest and ecology	7.5	10
Demographic performance		12.5
Tax effort		2.5
	100	100

*17.5 percent according to 1971 census and 10 percent according to 2011 census.
** 2011 census.
Source: *First Report of the Fifteenth Finance Commission (for 2020-21).*

29.3 Second Report of XV-FC for 2021-22 to 2025-26

The second (final) report was tabled in Parliament on February 1, 2021. Key recommendations in the report included the following:

29.3.1 Share of States in Central Taxes (Vertical Sharing): The share of states in the central taxes for the 2021-22 to 2025-26 was recommended to be 41 percent, same as that for 2020- 21. This was less than the 42 percent share recommended by XIV-FC for the period 2015-16 to 2019-20. The adjustment of 1 percent was to provide for the newly formed union territories of Jammu and Kashmir, and Ladakh from the resources of the centre. In this context, Finance Minister Nirmala Sitharaman in her budget speech to the Parliament on February 1, 2021 remarked, "On 9th December 2020, the 15th Finance Commission submitted its final report, covering the period 2021-2026 to the Rashtrapati ji. The Government has laid the Commission's report, along with the explanatory memorandum in the Parliament retaining the vertical shares of the states at 41 percent. We recognise our commitment to fiscal federalism and propose therefore to adhere to this recommendation. Jammu and Kashmir in the 14th Finance Commission was entitled to get devolution being a State. Now, the funds to the UTs of Jammu and Kashmir and Ladakh would be provided by the Centre". [1]

29.3.2 Determination of States' Share Inter Se (Horizontal Sharing): Table 29.2 shows the criteria used by XV-FC to determine each state's share in central taxes, and the weight assigned to each criterion. The criteria for distribution of central taxes among states for 2021-22 to 2025-26 were same as that for 2020-21. However, the reference period for computing income distance and tax efforts were different (2015-16 to 2017-18 for 2020-21 and 2016-17 to 2018-19 for 2021-22 to 2025-26), hence, the individual share of states may still change.

Table 29.2: Criteria and Weights for Horizontal Distribution of States' Share among Themselves (2021-22 to 2025-26)

Criterion	Weight (percent)
Population (2011 Census)	15
Income distance*	45
Geographical area	15
Forest and ecology	10
Demographic performance	12.5
Tax effort*	2.5
	100

*Reference period 2016-17 to 2018-19.
Source: *Second Report of the Fifteenth Finance Commission (for 2021-22 to 2025-26).*

A. Income Distance: Income distance is the distance of a state's income from the state with the highest income. Income of a state was computed as average per capita GSDP during the three-year period between 2016-17 and 2018-19. A state with lower per capita income will have a higher share to maintain equity among states.

B. Forest and Ecology: This criterion was arrived at by calculating the share of the dense forest of each state in the total dense forest of all the states.

C. Demographic Performance: The Terms of Reference of XV-FC required it to use the population data of 2011 while making recommendations. Accordingly, it used 2011 population data for its recommendations. The demographic performance criterion was used to reward efforts made by states in controlling their population. States with a lower fertility ratio were scored higher on this criterion.

D. Tax and Fiscal Efforts: This criterion was used to reward states with higher tax collection efficiency. It was measured as the ratio of the average per capita own tax revenue and the average per capita state GDP during the three years between 2016-17 and 2018-19.

29.3.3 Grants: Over the period 2021-22 to 2025-26, the following grants are to be provided from the centre's resources:

A. Revenue Deficit Grants: 17 states will receive grants worth ₹ 2.9 lakh crore to eliminate revenue deficit.

B. Sector-specific Grants: Sector-specific grants of ₹ 1.3 lakh crore will be given to states for the following 8 sectors:

1. Health.
2. School education.
3. Higher Education.
4. Implementation of agricultural reforms.
5. Maintenance of Pradhan Mantri Gram Sadak Yojana (PMGSY) roads.
6. Judiciary.
7. Statistics.
8. Aspirational districts and blocks.

A portion of these grants will be performance-linked.

C. State-specific Grants: State-specific grants of ₹ 49,599 crore were recommended. These will be given in the following areas:

1. Social needs.
2. Administrative governance and infrastructure.
3. Water and sanitation.
4. Preservation of culture and historical monuments.
5. High-cost physical infrastructure.
6. Tourism.

XV-FC recommended a high-level committee at state-level to review and monitor utilisation of state-specific and sector-specific grants.

D. Grants to Local Bodies: The total grants to local bodies will be ₹ 4.36 lakh crore (a portion of grants to be performance-linked) including: (a) ₹ 2.4 lakh crore for rural local bodies, (b) ₹ 1.2 lakh crore for urban local bodies, and (c) ₹ 70,051 crore for health grants through local governments.

The grants to local bodies will be made available to all three tiers of Panchayat, viz. village, block, and district. The health grants will be provided for: (a) conversion of rural sub-centres and primary healthcare centres (PHCs) to health and wellness centres (HWCs), (b) support for diagnostic infrastructure for primary healthcare activities, and (c) support for urban HWCs, sub-centres, PHCs, and public health units at the block level.

Grants to local bodies (other than health grants) will be distributed among states based on population and area, with 90 percent and 10 percent weightage, respectively. It prescribed certain conditions for availing these grants (except health grants). The entry level criteria include: (a) publishing provisional and audited accounts in the public domain and (b) fixation of minimum floor rates for property taxes by states and improvement in the collection of property taxes (an additional requirement after 2021-22 for urban bodies). No grants will be released to local bodies of a state after March 2024 if the state does not constitute State Finance Commission and act upon its recommendations by then.

29.3.4 Disaster Risk Management: XV-FC recommended retaining the existing cost-sharing patterns between the centre and states for disaster management funds. The cost-sharing pattern between centre and states is: (a) 90:10 for north-eastern and Himalayan states, and (b) 75:25 for all other states. State disaster management funds will have a corpus of ₹ 1.6 lakh crore (centre's share is ₹ 1.2 lakh crore).

29.3.5 Fiscal Roadmap:

A. Fiscal Deficit: XV-FC suggested that the centre bring down fiscal deficit to 4 percent of GDP by 2025-26. For states, it recommended the fiscal deficit limit (as percent of GSDP) of: (a) 4 percent in 2021-22, (b) 3.5 percent in 2022-23, and (c) 3 percent during 2023-24 to 2025-26. It recommended forming a high-powered inter-governmental group to: (a) review the Fiscal Responsibility and Budget Management Act (FRBM), and (b) recommend a new FRBM framework for centre as well as states, and oversee its implementation.

B. Revenue Mobilisation: Income and asset-based taxation should be strengthened. To reduce excessive dependence on income tax on salaried incomes, the coverage of provisions related to tax deduction and collection at source (TDS/TCS) should be expanded. Stamp duty and registration fees at the state level have large untapped potential. Computerised property records should be integrated with the registration of transactions, and the market value of properties should be captured. State governments should streamline the methodology of property valuation.

C. GST: The inverted duty structure between intermediate inputs and final outputs present in GST needs to be resolved. Revenue neutrality of GST rate should be restored which has been compromised by multiple rate structure and several downward adjustments. Rate structure should be rationalised by merging the rates of 12 percent and 18 percent. States need to step up field efforts for expanding the GST base and for ensuring compliance.

D. Financial Management Practices: A comprehensive framework for public financial management should be developed. An independent Fiscal Council should be established with powers to assess records from the centre as well as states. The Council will only have an advisory role. A time-bound plan for phased adoption of standard-based accounting and financial reporting for both centre and states should be prepared while eventual adoption of accrual-based accounting is being considered. The centre as well as states should not resort to off-budget financing or any other non-transparent means of financing for any expenditure. A standardised framework for reporting of contingent liabilities should be devised. Both centre and states should strive to improve the accuracy and consistency of macroeconomic and fiscal forecasting.

29.3.6 Other Recommendations:

A. Health: States should increase spending on health to more than 8 percent of their budget by 2022. Primary healthcare expenditure should be two-thirds of the total health expenditure by 2022. Centrally-sponsored schemes (CSS) in health should be flexible enough to allow states to adapt and innovate. Focus of CSS in health should be shifted from inputs to outcome. All India Medical and Health Service should be established.

B. Funding of Defence and Internal Security: A dedicated non-lapsable fund called the Modernisation Fund for Defence and Internal Security (MFDIS) should be constituted to primarily bridge the gap between budgetary requirements and allocation for capital outlay in defence and internal security. The fund should have an estimated corpus of ₹ 2.4 lakh crore over the five years (2021-22 to 2025-26). Of this, ₹ 1.5 lakh crore should be transferred from the Consolidated Fund of India. Rest of the amount should be generated from measures such as disinvestment of defence public sector enterprises, and monetisation of defence lands.

C. Centrally-sponsored Schemes (CSS): A threshold should be fixed for annual allocation to CSS below which the funding for a CSS should be stopped (to phase out CSS which has outlived its utility or has insignificant outlay). Third-party evaluation of all CSS should be completed within a stipulated timeframe. Funding pattern should be fixed upfront in a transparent manner and be kept stable.

Endnote

1. Government of India, Ministry of Finance, Budget Papers (2021-22), *Speech of the Finance Minister*, para 146.

Select Bibliography

Bibliography

A. Premchand (1989), "Government Budgeting and Expenditure Controls: Theory and Practice", fourth edition, International Monetary Fund, Washington D.C.

A. Shah (2007), "Budgeting and Budgetary Institutions", World Bank Publications, Washington D.C.

A.J. Makin and R. Arora (2012), "Fiscal Sustainability in India at State Level", *Public Finance and Management*, Volume 12, Number 4, October.

A.R. Prest (1970), "Public Finance in Theory and Practice", London: Weidenfeld and Nicolson.

Administrative Reforms Commission (1968), "Report of the Study Team on Centre-State Relationships", Volume I.

Alan Peacock and Francesco Forte (eds.) (1981), "The Political Economy of Taxation", Oxford: Basil Blackwell.

Alberto Alesina and R. Perotti (1995), "The Political Economy of Budget Deficits", IMF Staff Papers.

Alejandro Foxley, Eduardo Aninat and J.P. Arellano (1979), "Redistributive Effects of Government Programmes: The Chilean Case", Pergamon Press.

Amaresh Bagchi, et al. (1994), "Reform of Domestic Trade Taxes in India: Issues and Options", National Institute of Public Finance and Policy, New Delhi.

Aronson, Richard (1985), "Public Finance", New York: McGraw-Hill Book Company.

Arvind Panagariya, Pinaki Chakraborty and M. Govinda Rao (2015), "Growth and Development of States in India", New York: Oxford University Press.

B. Vithal and M. Shastry (2001), "Fiscal Federalism in India", London: Oxford University Press.

Burkhead, Jesse (1956), "Government Budgeting", New York: John Wiley and Sons.

C. Rangarajan and D.K. Srivastava (2011), "Federalism and Fiscal Transfers in India", New Delhi: Oxford University Press.

C.V. Brown and P.M. Jackson (1983), "Public Sector Economics", Oxford: Martin Robertson and Co. Ltd.

E. Ahmad and N. Stern (1991), "Theory and Practice of Tax Reforms in Developing Countries", Cambridge University Press.

E.V. Leemput and E.A. Wiencek (2017), "The Effect of the GST on Indian Growth", International Finance Discussion Paper, March.

Empowered Committee of State Finance Ministers (2008), "A Model and Roadmap for Goods and Services Tax in India", New Delhi.

Government of India, *Budget Papers* (various years).

——*Economic Survey* (various issues).

——*Reports of Finance Commissions.*

——*Five Year Plans.*

——*Constitution of India.*

——*Report of the Commission on Centre-State Relations* (Chairman: R.S. Sarkaria), 1988, Part I.

Harvey Rosen and Ted Gayer (2009), *Public Finance,* McGraw-Hill.

J. Hindriks and G. Myles (2006), "Intermediate Public Economics", MIT Press.

James Danziger (1978), "Making Budgets", London: Sage Publications.

John Cullis and Philip Jones (1998), "Public Finance and Public Choice", Oxford University Press.

John Wojthley and William Ludwin (1979), "Zero-Base Budgeting in State and Local Government", New York: Praeger Publishers.

Joseph E. Stiglitz (2000), "Economics of Public Sector", W.W. Norton and Company.

Kavita Rao (2014), "Revenue Implications of GST and Estimation of Revenue Neutral Rate: Estimates for 2011-12", National Institute of Public Finance and Policy, New Delhi.

M. Rakshit (2006), "Budgetary Rules and Plan Financing", *Economic and Political Weekly*, Volume 41, pp. 43-44.

M.G. Rao and N. Singh (2005), "The Political Economy of Federalism in India", New Delhi: Oxford University Press.

M.M. Sury (1992), "Centre-State Financial Relations in India: 1870-1990", *Journal of the Indian School of Political Economy*, Volume 4, No. 1, January-March.

Mark Krasnick (1986), "Fiscal Federalism", Toronto: University of Toronto Press.

Michael Keen (2015), "Targeting an Indirect Tax Design: Inequality and Fiscal Policy", International Monetary Fund.

Pinaki Chakraborty and Manish Gupta (2016), "Evolving Centre-State Financial Relations", *Economic and Political Weekly*, Volume L1, Number 16.

Richard Aronson (1985), "Public Finance", New York: McGraw-Hill Book Company.

Richard Musgrave and Peggy Musgrave (1989), "Public Finance in Theory and Practice", New York: McGraw-Hill Book Company.

Robert Lee and Ronald Johnson (1970), "Public Budgeting Systems", Baltimore: University Park Press.

S.L. Shakdher (1979), "The Budget and the Parliament", New Delhi: National Publishing House.

Simon James and Christopher Nobes (1978), "The Economics of Taxation", Oxford: Philip Allen.

Reserve Bank of India, *Report on Currency and Finance* (various years).

——*Handbook of Statistics on Indian Economy* (various years).

——*Bulletins*

——*Occasional Papers*

World Bank (2015), "Fiscal Policy for Equitable Growth", India Development Report.

Index

Index